FUSION ECONOMICS

This page intentionally left blank

FUSION ECONOMICS

HOW PRAGMATISM IS CHANGING THE WORLD

LAURENCE J. BRAHM

FUSION ECONOMICS
Copyright © Laurence J. Brahm, 2014.

Softcover reprint of the hardcover 1st edition 2014 978-1-137-44417-2

All rights reserved.

Muhammed Yunus epigraph © The Nobel Foundation (2006). Source www.nobelprize.org.

First published in 2014 by
PALGRAVE MACMILLAN®
in the United States—a division of St. Martin's Press LLC,
175 Fifth Avenue, New York, NY 10010.

Where this book is distributed in the UK, Europe and the rest of the world, this is by Palgrave Macmillan, a division of Macmillan Publishers Limited, registered in England, company number 785998, of Houndmills, Basingstoke, Hampshire RG21 6XS.

Palgrave Macmillan is the global academic imprint of the above companies and has companies and representatives throughout the world.

Palgrave® and Macmillan® are registered trademarks in the United States, the United Kingdom, Europe and other countries.

ISBN 978-1-349-49556-6   ISBN 978-1-137-44418-9 (eBook)
DOI 10.1057/9781137444189

Library of Congress Cataloging-in-Publication Data

Brahm, Laurence J.
    Fusion economics : how pragmatism is changing the world / Laurence Brahm.
        pages cm

    1. Marketing—Planning. 2. International business enterprises—Developing countries. 3. Social entrepreneurship—Developing countries. 4. International finance. 5. BRIC countries—Foreign economic relations. I. Title.

HF5415.13.B6753 2014
338.6'42091724—dc23   2014013538

A catalogue record of the book is available from the British Library.

Design by Newgen Knowledge Works (P) Ltd., Chennai, India.

First edition: October 2014

10 9 8 7 6 5 4 3 2 1

You can't evict an idea whose time has come.

—Occupy Wall Street protesters

Peace is threatened by unjust economic, social and political order, absence of human rights. Poverty is the absence of all human rights. The frustrations, hostility and anger generated by abject poverty cannot sustain peace in any society. For building stable peace we must find ways to provide opportunities for people to live decent lives.

—Muhammed Yunus Nobel Laureate

CONTENTS

PREFACE Voice of the Voiceless: *Fed Up with Television Talking Heads? Listen to People in the Street* ix

Acknowledgments xv

INTRODUCTION The Washington Consensus Is Dead! 1

Part I **Fusion Economics:** *Burying Ideology, Dumping Theory, and Adopting Pragmatism* **17**

CHAPTER 1 Reengineering China: *Ending Ideology and Getting Pragmatic* 19

CHAPTER 2 Voodoo Economics: *Oust Outside Theory and Adopt Local Solutions* 29

CHAPTER 3 Red Guards with Credit Cards: *Merge Planning and Market the Fusion Way* 43

Part II **Pragmatic Idealism:** *Compassionate Capital, Stakeholder Value, and Social Enterprise* **57**

CHAPTER 4 The Tao of Shangri-la: *Learning Social Enterprise from Nomads and Monks* 59

CHAPTER 5 The Positive Energy Bank: *Quantum Economics Taught by Lamas and Bodhisattvas* 69

| CHAPTER 6 | Creating Shambhala: *Building a Social Enterprise on Top of the World* | 77 |

Part III   **Diversified Localization:** *Empowering People Brings Sustainable Security*   **91**

CHAPTER 7	The Disempowerment Factor: *Stop Terrorism at Its Root*	93
CHAPTER 8	The Himalayan Consensus: *Happiness, Micro-Finance, and Community Development*	105
CHAPTER 9	The African Consensus: *Community Empowerment to Prevent Violence*	119

Part IV   **The New Earth Consensus:** *Community Consciousness and Planetary Survival*   **135**

CHAPTER 10	Occupy Your Mind: *The Peaceful Revolution Comes to America*	137
CHAPTER 11	"Re-Pioneering" America: *Revitalizing Communities and Environmental Economics*	151
CHAPTER 12	The World Is Not Flat: *Back to Basics, Local Diversity, and Community Capital Regeneration*	171
CHAPTER 13	From Russia with Fusion Economics: *The National Response, The BRICS, and the Changing World Order*	189
CHAPTER 14	We Want a Future: *To Save Our Planet, We Need New Leaders*	203
CHAPTER 15	Environmental Economics: *Cutting Semantics, Creating Genuine Green Growth for Survival*	211
CONCLUSION	The Post Occupy World: *Imagine an Economy Without Greed*	225

Notes   235

Index   247

PREFACE

VOICE OF THE VOICELESS:
Fed Up with Television Talking Heads? Listen to People in the Street

WE SHALL OCCUPY

I am standing in Zuccotti Park, embedded with Occupy Wall Street protesters. Rings of police surround the park. Media trucks are parked on one side. Surveillance equipment is rigged on the other. And between them, a vast cross-section of America is out on the street.

One protester holds aloft a piece of cardboard inscribed with crayon. It reads: "Arab Spring, European Summer, American Autumn." The protests that began in North Africa, followed by the Middle East and then Europe, had spread to New York. Frustration with incompetent government, politics of oligarchy, and economic squandering on self-interest at the expense of the general public was shared across continents.

In 2011, protesters globally had joined hands to express outrage at an unjust order. Greed-based economics and the irrational use of capital had widened income gaps, increased unemployment, and neglected infrastructure, while waging useless ideologically driven wars that have only bankrupted the countries starting them. For some reason, this had gone on for years, more or less unquestioned by corporate- and lobbyist-sponsored media.

A revolution sparked by the middle class was underway. The gap between rich and poor were widening, while the global middle-class was being pinched into extinction, essentially joining ranks with the poor.

Suddenly, elite New York University and New School students facing decades of debt repayments in exchange for their education, saw no future. Inspired by the protesters in Tahrir Square who epitomized the Arab Spring, and Catalonia Square, where the European *Indignant* and tent movement began, they joined hands with the homeless in New York and on September 17 occupied Wall Street. Within a few weeks, the Occupy movement spread across America, in turn inspiring the world.

I returned to New York City to join Occupy Wall Street, after having spent three decades in Asia, working as a corporate lawyer and development economist fixing broken economies, and later as social entrepreneur building new ones from the grass roots. Arriving in my hometown, I sensed that frustration with the system had reached a boiling point. People on the right and the left had lost jobs. They all knew what was wrong, but did not know how to fix it. They called for a new economic paradigm, but did not know how to get there.

And many office floors above the street, almost as if flying over the protesters in an airplane, glued to their Bloomberg screens, nobody could hear the cries below, much less bother to listen. Assuredly they knew that Mayor Michael Bloomberg would soon use brutal police force to clear the protesters from his streets.

IT'S TIME FOR A PEACEFUL REVOLUTION

This book is not about the Occupy movement. It is about a global movement of which Occupy has been a part in the sequence of events leading to change. Change is already happening. It is broader in scope than just protest, already spanning continents and about to propel an economic tectonic shift.

It is about a change in values and business dynamics: a move away from greed and profitability for individualist egoism, toward greater community and global sustainability. The problem is that our greed-based neo-liberal system is all about me, me, me- for the short term. That is why it is not sustainable.

The actors who are propelling this change are not politicians making speeches or central bankers conjuring up fiscal alchemy. Real change now comes from two seemingly opposite camps. On one end of the spectrum are NGO leaders and community activists who are turning into social entrepreneurs in order to support their programs and vision for social betterment. On the other end are multinational corporations figuring out how to become socially responsible, driven by the demand of clients and customers who want change. They are voting with their purchasing power—"conscientious consumption".

These widely divergent forces are moving toward the middle, and they represent another dimension of this movement.

Remarkably, Coca-Cola's CEO Muhtar Kent came right out at the World Economic Forum in January 2013 and said capitalism needs to be transformed. "You can probably say capitalism is the worst model—except for all the others," Kent admitted. "We have to evolve it to make sure it is better socially connected to the people's wishes and needs and to create a better harmony in the world." Reflecting a shift in thinking, he suggested, "I think it's going to end up where we have that 'golden triangle' working better with government, business, and civil society."

Obviously, not everyone is thinking like Kent or voicing these ideas. There are people who do not want to see this change occur. Our governments have become dysfunctional, manipulated by wealthy market hard-liners, and no longer represent people's rights, dreams, and aspirations—hence the "1 percent versus 99 percent" slogan. That spells classic class struggle, the formula for revolution. Protests that erupted in 2011 opened the curtain on the decade of global revolt. However, protesters, inspired by Mahatma Gandhi, have done their best to remain generally peaceful despite being sprayed with mace in some cities and targeted with bullets in others.

The protests may be dispersed in America, for the moment. But rest assured, they are coming back! Our politicians are refusing to address the core problems. As elsewhere—in Turkey, Brazil, and Ukraine—they are coming to a neighborhood near you soon. That is because everyone knows deep down inside that something is wrong. Nobody believes those talking heads who assure us that everything is just fine. Our current economic system is rusted, corroded, corrupted, not working anymore, and certainly not transparent. It's time for more than change. We need a new system.

From Cairo to Barcelona, to Moscow, Athens, and New York, everyone is fed up with the greed conundrum, the widely accepted ethos that profit and self-interest are the end-all of economic efficiency and that conspicuous consumption is the measurement of one's worth and success.

And that is what the Peaceful Revolution is all about. It is not about violence or anger to vent frustration, but rather a conscious transformation away from our current system that has become environmentally unsustainable and economically inequitable, on a planet of diminishing resources, increased poverty gaps, and upheaving upward social pressures.

The *peaceful revolution* underway is not antibusiness. The issues should not be confused. The protesters are calling for those very values that underlie the way we do business to change. They are screaming outrage against the interests of a small global elite who have prevented the empowerment of people to run their own businesses.

The protesters who shook the world in 2011 were driven by an overriding grievance: our planet is not sustainable the way it is being run!

Let's cut through the confusion and attempt to sum up what demonstrators across the globe have been demanding. Let's write it on a single poster board that can be paraded before police barricades. If not sprayed with mace, it reads something like this:

1) *It's time for an economic middle way. We need pragmatic holistic economics, not theory. Put an end to the dogma of market fundamentalism.*
2) *Promote social enterprise, compassionate capital, conscientious consumption, and stakeholder value to protect our communities and environment.*
3) *Sustainable local economics is the best guarantee for water and food security and for the prevention of ethnic violence and terror, both in the developing and the industrialized world.*
4) *We must redesign our financial architecture to support green growth and conversion from fossil fuels to renewable energy as the next global economic driver. It is the biggest challenge our planet faces if we want to have a planet on which to live.*
5) *It is time for our global youth to be stakeholders in this process. It is their inherent right, because it is their future!*

Underlying these five parallel demands is a shift in the global political economic order. Countries that were underdeveloped just two decades ago are now among the fastest-growing economies and the most dynamic societies on our planet, changing the flow of capital. The BRICS (Brazil, Russia, India, China, South Africa) have become the world's economic drivers, and with the rising power of the G77, they are leading development with their own very different and fusion approach to economics. Some of the most dynamic economies on our planet are now in Africa, but the mainstream media won't tell you that. They espouse values of diversified localization rather than monolithic globalization. Their newfound strength and rejection of old models is affecting the global order as we have known and accepted it for decades.

Changes in the flow of capital currents bring a diversification of values. International economic, financial, and political policy changes will have to reflect this. People's demands in the street can also be seen and understood as a parallel force against the backdrop of this change.

The "megatrends" described above—social outrage and protest, convergence of social enterprise and corporate responsibility and a realignment of our financial architecture being driven by the "new south"—are occurring in tandem. They are interconnected aspects of our changing world order. It is multidimensional.

It is not happening at grandly staged meetings of presidents, prime ministers, sheiks, or finance ministers. Nor do the keys come from fancy development models cooked up at Ivy League Universities and Washington think tanks.

Rather, the way forward is being spawned from a vast network of people. Some are visionaries in government who are fighting their own bureaucracies. Others are NGO workers, social entrepreneurs, and activists. Many have no education at all. Few have a PhD in economics. They are individuals simply committed to helping people. They treasure our planet and its natural environment. Amazingly, they are driven by motivations other than greed. Joining the force are responsible businessmen, with power, wealth, and a pragmatic view of how our world works.

They seek realistic solutions to address conditions of impoverishment and environmental degradation. More often, they draw upon local wisdom rather than a distant model to find an answer.

Even though these people are very different, working for different causes in different places, they will all agree on one point: our current systems are unsustainable if run as they currently are.

These people are our new economic pioneers.

With this book I try to connect the dots between seemingly independent but converging efforts and show how change is occurring on multiple levels simultaneously. Driven by the same sets of concerns or frustrations, these various initiatives represent parallel responses to a global economic predicament. I believe that in the coming decade they will collectively be recognized as the new earth consensus. It may sound radical or "alternative" now. But it will become the new mainstream.

This book is not intended to be all inclusive. There are many people, movements, organizations, and businesses out there experimenting and creating a plethora of fresh and holistic approaches to solving our global economic mess and the distorted values underlying it. They need to be recognized as different facets of a new global consensus. But they cannot be covered in a single book. I would not even attempt to do that.

This book is written as a memoir to share my journey, to offer some practical alternatives to the business and development models that made a few people rich at the expense of everyone else. By telling my story and shedding light on the changes I witnessed, my wish is to inspire others to come forth with their own story too. Write, video, blog, tweet it—whatever. Let's shut up the academics and talking heads, and call for pragmatic solutions from the street (or jungle) that work and can actually accomplish something. Then let's force our politicians to react and do something constructive rather than get rich at everybody else's expense while making long-winded speeches that have nothing to do with us.

It's time to overthrow the market fundamentalism that turned economics into ideology. It's time for institutions and governments to think out of the box and bring common sense back into it all.

It's time for a peaceful revolution.

ACKNOWLEDGMENTS

I wish to thank my agent Sharon Galant, from Zeitgeist Media Group Literary Agency, for all of her time, patience, and perseverance from the inception of this book over coffee in a Brussels train station to seeing it through to completion. Without her guidance, *Fusion Economics* would have never been written. I am indebted to her dedication.

I wish to thank my executive editor, Laurie Harting, from Palgrave Macmillan for her belief in the ideas of *Fusion Economics* and her commitment to bringing it to publication. Her final edits underscore the Zen approach that saying less is more.

I met countless anonymous people on this journey: activists, protesters, grass-roots workers, and so forth who devote time and energy to making our world a better and fairer place. Each of these individuals has been part of making this book a reality. It is impossible to mention them all here. However, I wish to thank and acknowledge a number of people whose dialogues particularly helped crystallize the ideas presented in this book. I have done my very best to reflect their thoughts as accurately as they were expressed to me in many conversations over the years that are the story of *Fusion Economics*. For convenience, they are mentioned by their city, as reflected in this book: in Beijing, former premier Zhu Rongji, Zhu Yanlai, Li Jiange, Li Wei, Pan Jiying, Ai Jing, Li Lin, Sun Yiting, Seth Cooper, Chen Boping, Charles Gay, Noah Skocilich; in Ulan, Bator Surin Bardal; in Vientiene, Madame Pany Yathotou, Kham Leuang Sayalath, Sisavath Sisane, Samane Savannasao; in Hanoi, Ngyuen Doanh Hung; in Honolulu, Henk Rogers, Joshua Cooper, Henry Noa and Luka, Carol Fox, Spencer Kim, Dan Leaf; in Lhasa, Nanqin Rinpoche, Nyima Tsering,

Pembala, Beru Khyentse Rinpoche; in Maduo County, Jigme Jensen; in Thimphu, Prime Minister Lyonpo Jigmi Y. Thinley, Dasho Meghraj Gurung, Lungan Gyatso, Thshering Phuntsho; in Islamabad, Risa Mohammad Khan, Kamrin Lashari, Momin Agha, Donglin Li; in Kathmandu, Ian Baker, Pushpa Kamal Dahal "Prachanda," Bauburam Bhattarai; in Delhi, Arundahti Roy; in Dhaka, Muhammad Yunus, Ashfquar Rahman; in Colombo, President Mahinda Rajapaksa, Nihal Rodrigo, Athuraliya Rathana; in Dakar, Didier Awadi, Alioune Tine, Rokhaya, Mamadouba, Minane Diouf, Charles Owens; in Barcelona, Marti Olivella, Rahel Aschwanden, Acradia Oliveres, Sister Teresa; in Moscow, Boris Kagarlitsky, Ian Vodin, Barri Gills, Andrey Kolganov, Nikolaj Kolomejtsev; in Rio, Anita Nayan, Leida Rijnhout; in Stockholm, Robert Bergquist; in Santa Barbara, Reza Aslan; and in New York, all of those who Occupied Wall Street.

In particular, I wish to thank those individuals who made my 2011–2012 winter fellowship at the East-West Center in Honolulu possible as this was where the most intensive writing for this book took place: Scott Mcleod, Mangmang Brown, John Barkai, Shirley Daniel, Jim Kelly, Jerry Sumida, Jim Hirai, Puong Phung and Warren Luke.

Moreover, I wish to express particular thanks to Victor Hao Li, Caroline Puel, David Shambaugh, and John and Doris Naisbitt for encouraging me to finally sit down and write this book.

INTRODUCTION

THE WASHINGTON CONSENSUS IS DEAD!

WE NEED A NEW CONSENSUS

Bretton Woods, New Hampshire 1944: Delegates from 44 countries convened at a plush country club hotel. Their mission: to reshape the global financial system into a new order that functioned according to fixed rules. The architects: US president Franklin D Roosevelt and UK prime minister Winston Churchill. They fixed the rules.

Present at the discussions was British economist John Maynard Keynes. He foresaw and warned that this monetary system would be manipulated by these controlling nations. Keynes even tried to block their agenda by proposing a global central bank and a single global currency, insisting that neither be tied to either gold or politics.

As we know from history books, Keynes lost that argument.

Three institutions emerged from the meeting: the International Monetary Fund (IMF), the World Bank, and a precursor to the World Trade Organization (WTO). A set of fixed exchange rates were linked to the dollar, and the dollar was linked to gold.

Then in 1972, the US dollar was delinked from gold (upon the US federal government's discovering that the Treasury had inadequate reserves). Thereafter, no standard applied.

But that did not matter. The so-called system of Bretton Woods continued as envisioned, dominated by a couple of nations and those three institutions.

The Bretton Woods system gave the US currency the dominant position in the world economy. It allowed the US to print as much money as it wants while running a trade deficit and a national debt, without ever having to devalue.

We have all come to know and accept this arrangement haplessly. But now, it is about to change. A global tectonic shift is underway... on multiple levels.

THE ANATOMY OF GREED

The sound of polished shoes clicked across shiny red marble. C-Span cameras were rolling as a heavy colonial-era wooden door was slammed closed by an aide with a ricochet thud. Romanesque statues of America's Founding Fathers stared down from the grand rotunda of the US Capitol Building in Washington, DC. If their ghosts only knew how the American people had been ripped off by their leaders, they would return to the green in Lexington and fight.

It was October 28, 2008. Former US Federal Reserve chairman Alan Greenspan was hauled before Congress. He was commanded to testify on the causes of a global financial crisis spreading from Wall Street that was threatening to become the worst recession since the Great Depression of the 1920s. The banking morass was sinking the whole Western world into a financial black hole. Greenspan admitted, "I made a mistake in presuming that the self-interest of organizations, specifically banks and others, was such that they were best capable of protecting their own shareholders."[1]

He had overestimated the power of self-interest.

"The whole intellectual edifice," he testified, "collapsed in the summer of last year." Greenspan confessed he had "found a flaw" in the accepted thinking of the time.

He was responding to questions from Representative Henry Waxman, the liberal California Democrat of the House Oversight Committee. Waxman asked whether "the prevailing attitude in Washington" still made sense. He was questioning the basic assumption under America's fiscal and regulatory policy that holds "that the market always knows best."

It doesn't. Markets reflect the fragility of human psychology, which is always imperfect. Markets function efficiently when information is complete. Most of the time, it is not.

Five days later, Stephen Roach, then chairman of Morgan Stanley Asia, observed in the *Financial Times*, "Driven by its ideological convictions, the Fed flew blind on the derivatives front." He added, "This trust in ideology over objective metrics was a fatal mistake."[2]

It was all about greed and the assumption that greed, left to its own accord, would always naturally guide markets to reach a state of divine equilibrium. Everyone just accepted this. It was taught in our Econ 01 textbooks in school. Milton Friedman had pontificated on it for half a century. *The Wall Street Journal* wrote about it ad nauseam. So, of course, it must be true.

Shockingly, it took yet another four years of recession before the American people woke up and challenged this notion. In autumn 2011, Occupy movements across America condemned Wall Street and corporate "greed." But did they really understand what they were condemning? Everyone had internalized that something was seriously wrong. It became increasingly clear that leaders—both political and corporate—were not about to fix it. But what was that thing that had gone wrong? And how could we fix it?

The problem all along had been naked greed, the philosophy of self-interest, that driving force that is supposed to be behind capitalism.

Most economic historians credit Adam Smith as the founder of capitalism. America's greatness was built on the philosophy of capitalism. I remember attending my first economics class during high school in Connecticut. The teacher taught us the basic principles articulated by Smith, and communism as expressed by Karl Marx. The next day angry parents called the principal, infuriated that communism was being taught in our high school, which was located in a cozy exurb of New York. So Marx was toned down and then kicked out of the course content. That is because we as Americans are all capitalists—God forbid, we are not socialists!

We have all been taught how Smith argued that people do the right thing out of self-interest, and that greed as a personal driving motivation will always bring markets to equilibrium at all times. We have taken his gospel on its face, put him on a pedestal, and worshiped his idea as the underlying assumption of our economic model. Our entire financial edifice has been built upon this assumption.

The problem is, Adam Smith never said that.

If Smith were alive and knew what was being promoted in his name today, one thing he would certainly do is join the protestors at Occupy Wall Street.

Smith's classic *The Wealth of Nations*, published in 1776, is in fact a radical condemnation of state-supported business monopolies.

Smith did not advocate unrestrained greed at all! He envisioned free markets—primarily for farmers and artisans—so that they could get fair prices for their goods and be rewarded commensurately for their labor. In turn they would be able to provide for their families and support their local economy. In his treatise *The Wealth of Nations* he made it explicitly clear that the assumption underlying his economic model was that investors would root capital in their locality, so as to benefit the community in which they lived.

For Smith, diversified localization was the premise upon which his invisible hand could actually work.[3]

Smith was not talking about free trade and globalization. He was talking about fair trade and localized sustainable development, businesses being stakeholders in their communities—our modern day "stakeholder value"! Smith could have been born in Seattle. He would have hated Goldman Sachs, Morgan Stanley, Exxon-Mobil, and Donald Trump. He would have strongly detested government and corporations, viewing them as working together as coteries in collusion. His perception of government was that it was an instrument of elites, used to extract taxes to subsidize their business interests. His condemnation of market intervention was its use as a tool by elites who manipulated government to protect their monopolies. If *Mother Jones*, America's leading progressive magazine, were published in 1776, Smith would be the front cover "man of the year."

Smith's version of self-interest was about bucolic village markets, which were a far cry from federal stimulus packages being spent to support Wall Street bankers drawing multimillion dollar bonuses. He would have choked over bank efforts to fund political campaigns while laying off thousands of workers and gambling people's retirement funds on derivatives.

So how did we take this quantum leap from farmer and artisan labor rights to the globalization of unrestrained market deregulation?

ACADEMIC SHAMANISM AND VOODOO ECONOMICS

Let's fast-forward to 1989. At the Institute for International Economics, a pristine Washington DC think tank, an economist named John Williamson issued a formal academic formula. It consisted of ten policy measures.⁴ Cooked up in a clinically insular institution isolated from the cacophonous realities in the street, the formula—when analyzed over brown bag lunches—looked just perfect and was prescribed as a panacea for developing countries. It was a kind of voodoo economics.

The notion was that unrestrained greed could be applied universally through the simple unbridled liberalization of all markets at once. This framework distorted Adam Smith's thinking, and then took the distortion to the extreme.⁵

Ethnic, social, religious, demographic, or geographic complexities were ignored both at home and abroad. The theory was deliberately kept simple, so as to be uncontaminated by those factors.

Coming from a Washington think tank, this "neoliberal" framework received immediate and unquestioned buy-in from the World Bank, the IMF, and the US Treasury Department. Dubbed the "Washington Consensus," this model became their mantra. Unfettered greed had graduated from presumed economic assumption to a full-blown alchemic concoction to be dispensed by multilateral aid institutions everywhere.

Classic Adam Smith had been abstracted through artistic license into a kind of economic Andy Warhol. Williamson himself was later chagrined at how his framework became a banner for "market fundamentalism."

The framework was then taught in Ivy League schools, where it took the form of "shock therapy." This model was then applied with cookie-cutter uniformity to developing countries and transitional economies alike, regardless of geography, culture, or conditions. Shock therapy in the Soviet Union contributed to its collapse. In the post-Soviet nations of Eastern Europe, it left basket cases. Forced upon Indonesia and Thailand by the IMF during the 1997 Asian Financial Crisis, it created economic and social disaster, pushing people to extremities. Violence and even acts terrorism arose in both countries. The shock therapists left in their wake a trail of economic dislocation, cyclical poverty, and political unrest.

It was all driven by ideological conviction, not common sense.

In America, the "market fundamentalism" mantra sanctioned deregulation as well. In 2008, its effects would finally be felt at home. Capital markets trading debt-leveraged instruments became the source of wealth creation, which ultimately led to the subprime lending crisis that brought the house down.

Our entire financial architecture was built around capital markets as the source of wealth creation. Money issued against debt without limit created cheap capital without value. Leveraged financial instruments were traded into infinity.

Deregulation was the mantra, Adam Smith the excuse. Individuals and communities were left out of the equation, as were local culture and the environment.

But that was alright because from the late 1990s onward "globalization" was the sacrosanct word. Multinational corporations outsourced productivity. Huge amounts of capital were invested into China, a market tightly regulated, with many built-in protections. Was corporate management so naïve as to think they could penetrate and then dominate the China market? Of course not! Their real objective was to claim a stake over global markets before the international media, and then push stock prices up. Senior management could conveniently sell shares and retire. That was good for them. But it was not so good for the rest of us.

Old neighborhoods disappeared. A sense of individualism and community was lost. Plush shopping malls filled our landscape, with Mercedes and BMWs in the parking lots. In them, one could find the same brand shops: Starbucks, Abercrombie and Fitch, Brooks Brothers, Prada, and so on. We judged each other by how many of those things we could fit into our garages and how much we could buy at these malls and cram into our houses. Were we really happy collecting all that stuff?

It was all on credit.

When hedge funds hit Asia in 1997, markets there that were already teetering high crashed, and capital flowed the other way, flooding America. Our snotty institutional economists derided the "tiger economies." The IMF looked down its nose and said that Asia needed "structural re-adjustment." They said there was too much capital and speculation on real estate, and not enough "playing by the rules of the game."

But who set those rules?

Suddenly there were new rules. In 1999, the Glass-Steagall Act was repealed. Passed in 1933 in response to the Great Depression, it mandated separation of commercial and investment banking, thus protecting depositors from risky investments and speculation. It worked fine for 50 years and provided a wall that prevented investment banks from taking depositors' money and investing it into debt. During the 1980s, when Reagan market fundamentalism was at its height, the banking sector lobbied for its repeal. Democrats, embracing "neoliberalism," wholeheartedly obliged.

From that point on, it was neoliberalism on steroids.

Stock markets went berserk. All kinds of junk were listed. First America and then Europe were soon just trading debt. Productivity was outsourced to Asia and South America. The World Economic Forum met in Davos each year and pontificated on how wonderful it all was. Americans had high tech, and were going to take over the world with the Internet. Meanwhile, without any real productivity, the once vibrant manufacturing communities on both continents became ghost towns.

It would not be long before there was a backlash.

It began in Seattle during the Third Ministerial of the WTO in December 1999. The meeting and the world were shocked by the riots that tore up Seattle. Charlene Barshefsky, who was then US trade representative observed: "The process was a rather exclusionary one. All meetings were held between twenty and thirty key countries [during the Seattle summit] and that meant 100 countries were never in the room.... This led to an extraordinarily bad feeling that they were left out of the process and that the results...had been dictated to them by the twenty-five or thirty privileged countries in the room."[6]

From that point on, screaming protesters swarmed every World Bank, IMF, WTO, Group of 8—now Group of 7 (G7)—, and World Economic Forum meeting that followed for nearly a decade. They became known as the "antiglobalization movement." But they organized themselves with the very tools of globalization—the Internet and mobile phones. These movements were the precursor to Occupy. The post-Bretton Woods institutions that they were protesting against ignored cries from the street, as did the mainstream media, which dismissed these protest movements as fringe, not believing that the alternative could one day become the new mainstream.

They were not "alternative," however. They represented a new majority, the voice of the voiceless.

Mainstream media networks could not give them a voice because they were either owned or underwritten with advertising from those same corporate monopolies that the new, yet gagged, majority protested against.

Of course, with so much capital flooding America, who cared about communities, ethnicity, or the environment? When the cost of capital is cheap, people tend to do stupid things with their money. Investments became irrational. Speculation led to a dot.com boom that then went bust. We deluded ourselves into thinking that websites were productive businesses, and started to list this stuff on stock markets. We declared a "new economy" without assets or productivity, just good ideas. It was all about "burning money" to make more money. Economists forgot about basics like supply and demand. It was politically incorrect to say that websites are in endless supply. Americans were puffed up on what we thought was our technological superiority. But it was short-lived. Nobody thought that in China and India, kids could hack, copy, and create zillions of websites. California led our tech boom. Today the state is bankrupt with the highest unemployment rate in America.

America's leaders, assuming the world would embrace all this (without asking anyone), tried to transform the Middle East to look like America by exporting this model through war. A Roman Empire-style military spending spree right out of Caligula drained America's coffers by $3 trillion back in 2008 (it has now reached $6 trillion). Meanwhile, at home excess liquidity fueled a housing boom. They were stretching it. Enter subprime loans and then the crash of 2008.

Now, with 10 million unemployed ("hidden unemployment" estimates double this official figure), a trade deficit of over $40 billion, and national debt exceeding $17 trillion, Americans are left wondering: How did all that happen? How do we fix it?

DISMANTLE THE IVORY TOWERS, JUST LIKE THE BASTILLE

My answer is that we need a new consensus, not another theory. (The wars in Iraq and Afghanistan were premised on theories to fix a problem that was barely understood!) We have enough of those. This book does not espouse an economic theory.

Economics is not about theory. Economics is about the redistribution of resources to cope with realities of scarcity in the most efficient way. That calls for pragmatism. Economics is not about classroom formulas devised by academics who are out to win awards.

Economics cannot be understood by focusing on one single issue. It involves many inconsistent events that run parallel and intersect with each other. It requires understanding of cultural, religious, and social factors. Because economics is about human psychology and how people react to changes in their environment and the scarcity or oversupply of resources—whether food, water, oil, or capital—we cannot rely only on mathematical formulas to encompass that.

We need a fresh economic paradigm, a new way of approaching old problems, because the old ways simply don't work.

Why a paradigm?

A paradigm is not a theory or model because it is not written in stone. It is just a set of coordinates, a compass, if you will. It offers examples we can draw upon, or not, while navigating a path out of where we are to where we want to go. Leaders and policymakers have been too stuck on models, black-white, wrong or right, us against them, capitalism versus socialism, globalization versus localization, top-down versus bottom-up, without actually understanding how they can affect our life positively or negatively. We must explore how seemingly opposite viewpoints or negatively polarized states of mind can in fact work together to make something really positive happen, that is, if our leaders and policy makers can overcome their ideological prejudices.

An Asian American martial artist friend teaches his teenage students, "Life does not go in straight lines," and neither do capital flows, climate change, or ethnic, cultural, or regional emotions. They must be understood in their entirety as they relate to or conflict with each other. This is the economic law of the interconnectivity of everything. Martial arts classes should be a prerequisite to an economics degree.

Economics should be about finding a holistic yet rational middle way of balancing resources. We cannot get caught between the ideological excesses of fossilized political interests. Practical ways are needed to survive on a planet of diminishing resources, which are now being used inefficiently.

SEEK PRACTICAL ALTERNATIVES

People in the street may have clearer answers than the economists in multilateral institutions who advise them. They don't need models cooked up by outsiders in ivory tower university classrooms or sterile think tanks. Local wisdom knows best, whether one lives in a corrugated hut in Bangladesh, a working-class apartment in Athens, or a suburban ghetto in Detroit. Looking within one's own country, neighborhood, and culture is the first step to a suitable and sustainable answer.

One society's tolerance for a certain way of doing things may be very different from another's. Where China's economics is like a wok of stir-fry crackling in popping oil under a hot flame, India's is like a simmering curry. India cherishes the spice of its pluralist, open, and free society, rather than the melting wok of conformity that China insists upon. Instead of hypergrowth, India's economy boils at a mathematically calculated temperature. Some even predict, most remarkably, that India's economy will overtake China's in 15 or 20 years because the simmer in a clay pot remains steady and burns longer, while the wok overheats. Who knows? They may be right.

The whole point of the China-India example is that there is nothing wrong with experimenting and doing it your way, the local way. Look deep into your own roots, and tollerance. Find out what works comfortably for you. Then go do it.

The first experiment of "fusion economics" began three decades ago when China rejected unsolicited advice about neoliberalism and shock therapy from the World Bank, the IMF, and the US Treasury and instead adopted its own policies. The results are self-proving. Between the years 1981–2005, an estimated 600 million Chinese people moved out of sheer poverty. And for many Chinese today, climbing out of poverty remains their first priority. China's poverty rate dropped from 85 percent to 15 percent during the same period.

For decades, South and Central America scrupulously followed the Washington Consensus formulas. Now led by Brazil and Chile, many South American countries have been joining the new consensus. The results speak for themselves.

The main lesson here is that China proved to other developing nations that there is a viable alternative to the Washington Consensus and discredited market fundamentalism. It unabashedly combined tools of market and planning to get where it wanted to go. China adopted pragmatism and a back-to-basics economic view rooted in local reality. It did not care about theory. This approach inspired virtually every country in the developing world to think out of the box and seek alternatives.

Maybe Europe—faced with a major debt crisis and hugely unpopular austerity programs—will follow next in evolving its own model.

That is not to say there are not problems with China's way: environmental desecration, social dislocation, and outrageously bad business ethics and corruption. That is all true, and will be discussed later in this book. The point being made here is that China dumped ideological theory, and its national economy leaped ahead. And others want to do the same.

Today, China's newly rich and middle class are the consumers of our planet, displacing the Japanese in spending power. During the European debt crisis in 2011 and 2012, Italy and Greece offered their debt to China's sovereign wealth fund. Maybe China could buy the Colosseum or Acropolis? No debt, please, only bricks and mortar. Yes, the real stuff. And please, no websites. Keep them in California, and figure out what to do with that state before advising the world.

China got to where it is through pragmatism—picking and choosing the tools of both planning and market—something I dubbed "fusion economics." It did not get there through deregulation and certainly not shock therapy.

WHAT THE _____ IS FUSION ECONOMICS?

We have all heard of fusion cuisine. Picture the restaurant of Wolfgang Puck in San Francisco: a wide Chinese porcelain plate is served. In the center is a seared *ahi* (Hawaiian for tuna). Basically it is Japanese sashimi burned on the edges over a Northwest Pine grill. Chinese sesame seeds are flaked around it, and three elegant French asparagus stems rest on the side of the plate with a dash of Indian chutney on top. The whole thing comes with choice of chopsticks or a fork, and is presented as a piece of art.

In short, fusion cuisine is a juxtaposition of seemingly discordant ingredients that work. So is fusion economics. It is more sophisticated than McDonalds, Kentucky Fried Chicken, Starbucks, and Jamba Juice. It does not follow one single model, but rather integrates many different practices to create something new. It seeks to displace the old.

At the same time, fusion economics is not only about merging tools of market and planning, what some deride as state capitalism. I read and hear Western media talk about the Brazil, Russia, India, China, and South Africa (BRICS) as adopting "state capitalism."

This is utter nonsense. These five nations have completely different economic systems. In many ways they are only connected by the fact that they are not buying into the Washington Consensus unilateral model. They are each doing their own thing, and each is doing it very differently.

Probably what irks the establishment most is that the BRICS and Group of 77 (G77) are in fact all expressions of the same phenomenon, a new global realignment as power shifts from the once industrialized "North" to the "South." Adopting fusion economics, these nations have become the new source of industrial output, resources, and productivity. The G7 must work with these powers or be eclipsed by them. Their fast-emerging economies are dramatically shifting the way our planet functions, making it somewhat more balanced, with a new multilateral, more even playing field. They are seamlessly creating a new global financial order through action, not talk. New capital flows are determining this. They are going East not West.

Guidance and planning are only part of the equation. Top-down alone is not enough. Bottom-up is important too. China's experiments contributed to the evolution of fusion economics, but these experiments represent only one aspect, and not the whole.

Another force contributing in the evolution of fusion economics came from the other side of the economic spectrum. The grass-roots and nongovernmental organization (NGO) movements that are using business to support their programs, filling the elasticity of failed multilateral aid and dysfunctional government social services. Their efforts have given rise to a new notion, the social enterprise. At the same time, multinational corporations realize that if they don't get on the social responsibility bandwagon, people will boycott their products and services. So both are moving toward a new center.

In the end, economics is about the interconnectivity of all things. Fusion economics is more about yin and yang and finding a sustainable balance that embraces both.

It is time for an economic middle way. And we need fusion economics to get there, not as something new and trendy like Wolfgang Puck's cuisine, but rather as a back-to-basics approach that adopts economically pragmatic rationality in place of politically extremist ideology.

Remember, if we don't have a peaceful revolution, it will be a violent one.

A NEW GLOBAL CONSENSUS IS ON THE RISE

A new global consensus of fusion economics, compassionate capital, stakeholder value, and conscientious consumption are all fresh concepts presented in this book. They are based on fresh economic assumptions.

Business can provide employment, and if managed sensitively, it can eliminate poverty, transfer skills, and empower people. A social enterprise can achieve more than an aid program because it is self-perpetuating. If it is run with consciousness and a long-term vision, it can strengthen individual identity and community. These are not mutually exclusive. We have to think fusion (market and planning, top-down and bottom-up), not black versus white. Environmental protection and carbon reduction can also become an engine driving a new generation of technology, entrepreneurship, business, and growth.

In many ways, the new global consensus is already happening. New approaches (it's time to stop calling them "alternative") are replacing the old Bretton Woods edifice as it fossilizes and crumbles. This is occurring on many levels—local, national, and multilateral—in many places across the globe at once.

However, you won't hear about it on CNN, Fox News, or the *The Tonight Show* with Jimmy Fallon. It has formed under our noses as we watched television and played with Facebook and Twitter.

It is not what we have been taught to believe. It is not what the theorists claim will work, in their pristine think tanks and classrooms. The talking heads on the morning shows just don't speak like that.

So somebody has got to say it.

CONNECTING THE DOTS THROUGH EXPERIENCE

Fusion Economics: How Pragmatism Is Changing the World is told through my own reflections over three decades. There is a reason for telling it as a personal story. This book is not about theory, but actual experiences.

My journey is shared in four parts.

Part I, Fusion Economics, tells how China discarded ideology and rose from an economic backwater to a powerhouse by adopting pragmatism and mixing the tools of market and planning. The similar transition of other Southeast Asian countries further proves that alternatives exist to the models we have taken for granted. In fact, no one model is sacrosanct. There are many choices out there. Look inside, not outside. The answers are right there in your own neighborhood.

Part II, Pragmatic Idealism, explains the power of compassionate capital and stakeholder value through the creation of social enterprises. People are motivated by more than profit alone. We are entering a new era in which social entrepreneurs (needing finance) and multinational corporations (feeling the pressure to act socially responsible) are moving toward a new middle ground. It is equally satisfying to help your community and protect the environment. And business is economically the most efficient way to do that.

Part III, Diversified Localization, discusses how fusion economics fuses top-down with bottom-up. Empowering communities with economic means for their own sustainability and identity is the best framework for water-food security and the prevention of violence. This is as relevant in Detroit as it is in Dhaka and Dakar.

Part IV, New Earth Consensus, delves into the sources of global protest and provides answers to guide us toward a sustainable future. Maintaining peace is about the equitable allocation of resources on a planet in which resources are diminishing. Governments face the urgent task of massive grid transformation from fossil fuel to renewable energy. Environmental economics will generate new jobs, and emerging economies are changing the rules of the game.

THE ALTERNATIVE AS A NEW MAINSTREAM

This book is told from a personal journey, on multiple levels. Across villages and cities—whether in China, the Himalayas, Africa, or Europe and America—I found a whole generation of youth coming together with socially and environmentally conscious entrepreneurs as a silent majority, becoming not so silent. But by putting holistic values into action, they had already begun shaping a collective vision for our planet and our children's future.

The concepts of the Himalayan and the African Consensus are articulated here. They are gaining ground in many parts of our planet. Many of the BRICS initiatives are also seeking a multilateral rather than a bi- or trilateral world. The idea of regional consensuses fits the need for a new global financial architecture in the minds of many leaders of developing nations. Not one to replace the old structure, but rather an alternative financial architecture, emerging in parallel with the existing structure.

Occurring alongside these events is a fresh awakening among those nations that are already feeling the acute impact of climate change, the need to shift into a new epoch of environmental economics.

Experiences count—real, hard knocks, failures, and success. In sharing experiences answers arise, and from working together comes strength. Regardless of how different these parallel trends are across the world, many are seeking the same vision: a world economy without greed (realistically one that is not driven only by greed).

Together we have already formed a global movement, perhaps without even realizing it. The new earth consensus will become a new mainstream—regardless of whether the Washington think tanks or World Economic Forum like it or not.

And yes, it can be a peaceful revolution.

This page intentionally left blank

PART I

FUSION ECONOMICS:
Burying Ideology, Dumping Theory, and Adopting Pragmatism

Fire in the Lake is the Image of Revolution.
The image is a leopard being transformed into a tiger.
The symbol is to reform the old to the new.

—I Ching (*The Book of Changes*)

We need pragmatic holistic economics to replace theory and put an end to the dogma of market fundamentalism. It's time for an economic middle way.

There are two Chinese "takeaways" (a new kind of Group A and Group B). First, there is no one single model to be applied universally. Second, ideologically premised economics is impractical. The fortune cookie message is simple: end the socialist versus capitalist debate, dump the theory, and do what works.

The Chinese government lets the market run its course. When it runs out of control, they rein it in. If fiscal measures, taxes, and interest rates don't work, they slap on administrative measures, fees, and quotas. They don't care what you call it, as long as the methods used get a result.

Eyeing the China experiment, other countries across Asia began adopting their own version of this "fusion" economics, mixing tools of market and central planning, sometimes more, sometimes less. Vietnam, Laos, and Malaysia have been examples of mixed economies. Each did it their own way, based on their own local circumstances. They sought "sequenced," step-by-step reforms, and did not use "shock." Brazil, Russia, India, China, and South Africa (BRICS) and the Group of 77 (G77) take China's approach seriously. They borrow what is useful and discard what is not. They don't get hung up on ideology or theory.

China, despite all of its problems, demonstrated that an alternative is possible. It unabashedly both used the tools of market and planning and transformed its economy from scarcity to oversupply, from poverty to conspicuous consumption wealth. It also made a lot of mistakes.

Within two decades, China pulled more people out of poverty than any other country in history, and also became the world's worst polluter. Environmental degradation and the loss of culture and identity (the very roots of a people's soul) are examples of what can go wrong when there is overreliance on economic growth. Stuffing homes with brands did not bring happiness in China, as it did not bring happiness in America either. In both countries, conspicuous consumption has created greed conundrums and distorted values.

Excessiveness in any form, whether neoliberalism, socialism, or state capitalism, will ultimately work against itself. There is a negative karma effect in any form of extremism—economic or political.

We need an economic middle way, one that is more pragmatic and more holistic. Enter the Tao of fusion economics.

CHAPTER 1

REENGINEERING CHINA:
Ending Ideology and Getting Pragmatic

ECONOMIC DISTORTIONS AND DISTRUST

Beijing, 1981. In late spring 1981, I first arrived in Beijing. The airport felt like an oven, baking in stifling flat heat. Sweat poured. There was no conveyor belt for luggage. Scowling airport staff just threw luggage off a cart. They could not care less what was inside your bag. There was no concept of service. That was the work ethic after the Cultural Revolution. Nobody cared about anything.

I remember walking out of the cavernous Soviet-era airport that had art deco red stars on the ceiling, right into Beijing's broiling summer heat. I later learned there was no spring season in this city. Everyone in the crowd waiting outside wore either green army or blue worker pants. Men and women alike wore short-sleeve shirts so poor in quality they were see-through. I tried speaking some broken Mandarin to find my way. Nobody answered. They simply stared at me.

I felt like an alien who had dropped from space. It was like a science fiction movie, *Planet of the Apes* or something like that.

The old narrow road from Capital Airport into Beijing seemed long. There were poplar trees lining both sides. The bus broke down several times. Each time, everybody got out talking all at once and tried to fix it. China's economy was like that bus!

My first stop, like that of most foreigners in those days, was the Friendship Store, a five-story, cavernous department store reserved for foreigners. It was then the tallest building on Chang An Avenue. I bought a Coke. It was imported and cost one dollar. That would have been more than any Chinese could have ever conceived of spending on a drink. At that time, there was only one local soft drink, called *qishui'er*, meaning "gas water." It tasted like it sounded. It came in green and orange colors, with a spectrum of shades like teenage punk rockers might dye their hair. My Chinese teachers were distraught that I had paid one dollar for a Coke. It was totally decadent, and told me so to my face. In those days, ordinary Chinese citizens were not permitted to enter the Friendship Store. And, of course, nobody could afford an imported Coke.

On that stiflingly hot day, that simple act of buying a Coke brought into sharp focus the distortions and disconnected perceptions between the developed and the underdeveloped world. That one-dollar Coke juxtaposed all of the economic assumptions I had been brought up with.

Most Chinese did not have access to money, because in 1981 China hardly had any money in circulation. And even if someone had money, there were few commodities to buy. Aside from the Friendship Store, most state-run department stores had empty shelves, or just blue and green pants.

It was an economy of scarcity.

I was a fresh, idealistic university exchange student. The idea of improving China's economic condition started as a vision I had. It was the main thing that motivated me each day as I filled up a cheap white tin cup with sticky venomous Shanghai-produced instant coffee. Soon I learned to drink tea. Slinging a green army bag over my shoulder, I went off to Mandarin class each day, determined to learn this language, as the key to opening up the Pandora's box that was this nation's predicament.

China's economic backwardness struck me. Coming from America, then the most affluent society in the world, I had to get my mind around China's lack of everything. Was it possible to change this condition? Along the lake at Nankai University each afternoon, Chinese students gave me their Red Books as gifts. Was it to share Mao's thoughts? Actually, they wanted to get rid of the books.

Joking and smoking, these Chinese classmates in their burr haircuts were actually military officials and cadres undergoing training for future careers in international relations. Part of their training was befriending me, unbeknownst to me until years later. The friendships seemed so innocent, they practicing their English, I practicing Chinese.

Some of these friendships lasted through my life, becoming keys that opened doors into the labyrinth of China's corridors of power. These classmates would rise to positions of power. Some would keep rising and go very deep into the system. They became my guarantors in a political culture of tense security, suspicion, and schizophrenia. It was all about passing through doors and gates of trust in an atmosphere of complete distrust.

THE HONORABLE TEACHINGS OF MASTER VICTOR LI

When I was supporting myself through school as a tour guide, a couple from Honolulu on one of my tours told me about Victor Li, the president of the East-West Center in Hawaii. Li served as translator for the American Ping-Pong team that broke the diplomatic ice with China. The leading expert on Chinese law, he authored a book called *Law without Lawyers* (the title says it all). He was also professor at the University of Hawaii law school.

So in 1983, I showed up at a round table on Chinese law at the East-West Center, located amid the lush green University of Hawaii campus. Catching Victor Li over coffee, I offered myself as his research assistant. Taken off guard by my spoken Mandarin, he immediately agreed. I soon entered the University of Hawaii school of law, living in a local tenement behind Japanese mom-and-pop shops and an organic farm market, in a rundown strip called Puck's Alley.

Victor Li was soft-spoken, an almost introverted thinker who always seemed in balance with himself. Li taught how to look at any single issue—economy, law, politics, or business—from a multiple set of different ethnic, cultural, and geographic coordinates at once. This way of thinking was the crucible of fusion economics.

Under his guidance, I became a lawyer and economist, specializing in China. However, China business had little to do with law (remember Li's book title?).

One day, as I entered Li's office, he was rubbing his eyes with frustration. I started to brief him on a new law China had issued. He pointed at a map of the Asia-Pacific region. "I am no longer interested in China laws. I am already looking at this."

"At what?"

"At the Asia-Pacific region and how China will transform these countries and the alignment of power by its sheer economic weight over the next decade." Li was looking way ahead of the curve, seeing issues on the horizon that others in the 1980s could not even guess.

During Premier Zhao Ziyang's maiden visit to America in January 1984, his first stop was Honolulu, and it was Li who received him at the East-West Center. The Chinese totally bought into the symbolism of all this. Li subtly let me join his meeting with Zhao. I quietly stood in the back of the room taking notes. That moment was arguably the pinnacle of American-Chinese relations. Nobody imagined that these relations would sour in only five years. In the wake of Tiananmen on June 4, 1989, the US-China honeymoon ended abruptly. In many ways the relationship, despite its mutual dependence, never really recovered the spirit of trust and hope that characterized those earlier years.

When I returned to China after graduation, old classmates appeared when least expected. They invited me to attend meetings where economic questions were asked in a roundabout way.

For China's leaders, spouting socialist rhetoric was just a façade. They could hardly care less. The desire to get ahead put pragmatism first. China's policymakers were open to fresh perspectives, even though they stared at you through thick black horn-rimmed glasses and wore Mao suits in the winter to assure warmth from the political cold.

Within two decades, China would shift from a position of complete scarcity to one of oversupply of virtually every product and service. Three decades later, it would become the second-largest economy in the world, the most powerful economic force to be reckoned with next to the United States.

It was unimaginable that this would happen so quickly, or that I might play a part in this process. The thought was furthest from my mind on that dry hot day, drinking a Coke in the Friendship Store, its dreary staff staring from behind dusty counters stacked with grotesque jade carvings and box-like imported Japanese television sets.

THE RICKETY BICYCLE AND PRAGMATIC ECONOMICS

In 1979, a tiny experiment occurred in far-off Anhui Province. Against the backdrop of three decades of impoverishing communalization, 18 village families agreed by contract that they would pool resources. As simple as it sounds, it was a bold breakthrough against the harsh socialist policies of that time. The pact among these families was turn over to the state only their quota of crops harvested, sell the rest, and retain the proceeds. Wan Li, then provincial party secretary, supported their defiant move. It was later dubbed the "self-responsibility system."

This little experiment, allowing one small group the right to grow their own rice and cabbage, transformed China.

Wan Li was promoted to the top by Deng Xiaoping. Our paths would cross. In 1992, Wan Li at the height of his power was chairman of the National People's Congress, China's rubber stamp parliament. He controlled the stamp. He received me in the Great Hall of the People because I was advising Chinese enterprises in Hong Kong, where the arrival of red capital would change the corporate and capital market landscape.

Wan Li met me in one of those vast dreary rooms with overstuffed sofas and dusty red curtains. He had one burning question: how to transform China's debt-ridden rusty state-owned enterprises into global conglomerates that could compete with American corporations for international markets? Five years later, I would be on the ground in Anhui Province, where his own reforms first began, blueprinting the "corporatization" of China's state-owned enterprises.

A decade and a half later, the far-flung dream of an old revolutionary became a reality that would shake the economic order of our planet.

Following Wan Li's "self-responsibility" experiment in Anhui, Chinese in the street whispered the words "free market." But what did it really mean? A few bold peasants brought vegetables and peanuts folded in rough cloth—because they had no bags. Squatting on the curbside, they sold them for cash. Remarkably, they kept the money. People talked about it excitedly.

It was the beginning of the free market. But nobody dared to openly say "market economy." The free market was on the fringes of China's economy. It was something on the curbside.

When I was studying in Tianjin in 1981, there was a fledgling free market near the university gate. There were few other choices. People queued every day to buy food because there were no refrigerators. State-distributed food supplies were sparse and irregular; state store employees were dour and irascible. Each day people lined up at those state-run stores with tickets to exchange for staples. Even with money, you could not buy rice or dough without quota-rationed coupons.

However, across the street the free market farmers had all sorts of fruits and vegetables. There was variety. People could just see the difference right in front of them

When the student cafeteria served scraps of pork fat, we students were very happy, because there was no meat on the market. Together with a classmate, I found a small roasted baby chicken in the window of one of these state-run stores. We had not seen one before. Little did we realize that that little skinny chicken in and of itself, roasted and hanging upside down on a hook, indicated that economic reforms were already at work.

In China, every single item was used and reused. Coming from America, where so much of our resources—from energy to food—are wasted, I thought it was both shocking and an education!

Before coming to China, I had been studying at Duke University. At the Duke cafeteria, a Taiwanese student pointed to an American wolfing down a massive steak sandwich, "There is more meat between those two pieces of bread than my whole family of six would enjoy at dinner," she said. The juxtaposition in values cut into me like a knife. At Nankai University, when a pen ran dry, students found a way to put water in it and make more ink come out; every scrap of paper was written on until there was no white left. Nothing in this society was wasted.

I bought a bicycle in China. As the hot summer dragged on, it fell apart. Each day, a different piece had to be replaced. The quality of state-produced products was just that bad. Eventually, the bike I ended up with was different from the one I originally bought! Rattling along the muddy potholed streets of Tianjin, it was unimaginable that China would one day dominate global exports.

A forlorn innocence seemed to prevail throughout the entire society in China. Each night I wandered the streets performing simple magic tricks I had learned as a kid. It was a way to meet people and practice my spoken Chinese. Crowds gathered, laughed, and asked me to perform again, and again, and again. They never seemed to get tired of watching the same tricks.

Money had less meaning in that society—hardly any was in circulation, yet.

When I paid one *mao* (ten Chinese cents) more than the stated price for something, a vendor chased me all over the city to give back the change. He finally showed up at the door of my dormitory at Nankai University apologizing for the oversight.

But such innocence would not last long.

After classes were finished, it came time to leave Nankai University. When the school held a banquet for us foreign students, the teachers took home the leftovers in tiny metal boxes hidden in baggy green army bags, shouldered over their flimsy shirts that never seemed to fit. It was unthinkable that over the next three decades, China would grow out of those army bags and replace them with Prada and Louis Vuitton apparel, which Chinese now purchase en masse like no other nation on earth.

The thought did not even occur to me, as I sold my bike—on the freshly emerging black market.

OPEN A WINDOW FOR FRESH AIR, THEN SWAT THE FLIES AS THEY ENTER

Throughout the 1980s, China struggled to open its economy. An internal debate thrashed between Deng Xiaoping and rival leader Chen Yun, who proposed the "bird-cage theory" of economics. The market could flutter within the cage of state planning, like a parakeet, but not fly free. Deng's answer: open the cage. Deng challenged the other leaders: "If you open the window, a few flies will come in with the fresh air. So what? You can always swat them."

By 1987, there was a wind of change. Zhao Ziyang became secretary general of the Chinese Communist Party (CCP). At the CCP congress that year, Deng boldly declared China as "socialist"—not communist—and remarkably only "at the first stage of socialism," adding that this first stage would take "a relatively long period of time." It was another political maneuver, shifting the goal posts toward the market.[1]

Hong Kong's business elite sensed the dragon awakening. They could smell opportunity in the air. Some read political change and openness in the tea leaves. Nobody expected the tea to be spilled in just two years by a sequence of events at the politically sensitive and symbolic Tiananmen Square.

In 1988, a group of young Chinese economists who were influenced by the neoliberal school advised Zhao Ziyang to reform prices and not to bother controlling inflation. This was the standard "shock therapy" economics then promoted by American advisers to the Kremlin. Such advice helped collapse the Soviet economy.

China's leadership was very sensitive about inflation. Many elder leaders knew deep down inside that inflation—more so than fighting—had brought down the Nationalist Kuomintang government in 1949, forcing Chiang Kai-shek's escape to Taiwan. They remembered how people rolled wheelbarrows of cash notes to the market in exchange for vegetables and goods. These older leaders who surrounded Deng did not buy into the shock therapy model. It is possible that the fallout between Deng and Zhao began at this point.

Zhao Ziyang called a session of his economists. Younger ones enthused with shock therapy advocated immediately freeing price controls and removing all subsidies on grain and rice. More mature economists—Wu Jinglian and Ma Hong—warned of the need to control inflation first. Gradually liberalize price controls only after stabilizing inflation. Zhao Ziyang did not listen to them. He dabbled with shock therapy, liberalizing price controls. China got shocked.

In the spring of 1989, students protested in Tiananmen Square, angered over nepotism and corruption. Soon workers joined in, outraged by high inflation. Store shelves emptied as people scrambled to hoard goods. It was inflation that aligned China's burly urban workers behind the idealistic students! The leadership feared exactly this situation. Orders were given by Deng to clear Tiananmen Square, and the protests were brutally crushed by military hard-liners. It was heavy-handed fly swatting. Reforms stopped. Zhao Ziyang was put under house arrest.

The June 4, 1989, Tiananmen crackdown disturbed and bewildered a world once enchanted by China's opening. America's honeymoon with China seemed over. In the wake of June 4, 1989, both dissidents and businessmen fled from Beijing to Hong Kong. Pro-China Hong Kong businessmen-cum-politicians became disillusioned. Anxiety over Hong Kong's imminent handover to China surged among Hong Kong's population. Those who could not obtain foreign passports vented frustration, and a democracy movement imploded.

The repercussions from all of this set Deng's own reforms back.

Following June 4, 1989, multilateral institutions such as the World Bank, the International Monetary Fund, and the Asian Development Bank all put a moratorium on China. As a result, commercial banks stopped lending, and foreign investment ceased. For three years, China's top leadership stagnated on reform. The political mood reverted to inward looking and conservative.

In 1989, foreign investors had written off China. It was considered too politically unstable, and an investment risk.

Looking back, when I arrived in China in 1981 it was a broken economy in a state of scarcity. The main cause was nearly four decades of ideological argument over capitalism versus communism and what their economy should be.[2] This got China nowhere except into poverty.

It was not until 1992, when then the new vice premier, Zhu Rongji, called upon Wu Jinglian and Ma Hong (those same economists who opposed shock therapy) for advice in combating inflation and sequencing reforms, that China's leaders finally became pragmatic. They buried the ideological debate. It was the beginning of what I dubbed "China Inc": the CCP operating like a corporate board and running the economy like a company.[3]

In 1989, the law firm where I worked concluded there was no business future in China. Southeast Asia's economies were booming. There seemed other places worth putting one's money.

The partners talked about opening an office in Taiwan. As a compromise, I suggested opening an office in Vietnam or Lao, two other underdeveloped socialist countries about to open their markets. It sounded crazy. Then a twist of fate changed everything.

It would lead to the story of fusion economics.

This page intentionally left blank

CHAPTER 2

VOODOO ECONOMICS:
Oust Outside Theory and Adopt Local Solutions

LESS SHOCK, MORE THERAPY, PLEASE!

Vientiane, 1990. I was sitting in an office provided by Madame Pany Yathotou, then central bank governor of Laos. Outside the window: the street could have been a postcard from any bucolic French country town, except for the jungle overgrowth and restaurants with creaking ceiling fans serving sticky rice in small tightly woven baskets alongside croissants. Long boats navigated the Mekong River that sluggishly rolled past.

Madame Pany Yathotou was a quiet woman, who despite the challenges she faced, always smiled with a typical Lao softness. Regardless of how much the currency depreciated that week, she exuded an aura of calm. She wore long black traditional skirts, with red and gold patterns woven in waves down to her sandals. Her assistant was a beautiful Lao girl, who always giggled with one hand coyly over her face, no matter how serious our conversation about the financial or banking crisis was, or how high inflation had rocketed on the free market that day.

The Asian Development Bank (ADB) had appointed me as Madame Pany's adviser with a mandate to draft a blueprint for financial and banking reform in Laos, followed by legislation to implement it.

With China temporarily written off and investors' hope lost, all eyes turned to Southeast Asia. Indochina's reconstruction became the new focus.

Vietnam had adopted its own *Doi Moi*, "new thinking," open policy in 1986. Then Thai prime minister Chatichi Choonhaven called for "turning battlefields into markets." Laos followed. Their reforms were clearly modeled after China's 1979 Open Door policy. Certainly, the Vietnamese as a people seemed flexible, not as uptight as their northern neighbors. So there was reason for optimism that Vietnam might liberalize faster than China.

But multilateral assistance was restricted by the continuing US embargo against Vietnam (although the Vietnam War had ended a generation ago). There was no choice but to find the next socialist country waiting in line to be reformed. Imagine aid specialists sitting in Washington ticking off China, Vietnam, and Cambodia in that order.

Sure enough, next on the list was sleepy Laos. There was no US embargo against Laos. America even had an embassy there. Organizations like the World Bank and the International Monetary Fund (IMF) envisioned Laos as the new testing ground of neoliberal reform, a warm-up for the opening of Vietnam, and one day back to China.

The ADB took the lead. I was recruited because of my China experience. The mission: give Laos a blueprint for financial reform. That meant separating commercial banks from the central bank and kicking in foreign exchange controls to stabilize currency depreciation and slow inflation. And it meant devising corporate legislation so that business could legally exist.

Sitting in a room down the corridor from Madame Pany, ancient ceiling fans creaking above my head, I breathed deeply and thought about how to do all this at once. Clearly in conflict with the World Bank and IMF officers, I decided to take it one step at a time and sequence it.

SEEKING ALTERNATIVES THAT REALLY WORK

One hot afternoon, Madame Pany called a meeting. Her assistant came in with a tray on which precariously balanced ridiculously tall drinking glasses that probably should have been used for flower arrangements. But instead each was filled with Pepsi. Madame Pany explained that Pepsi had opened a joint venture bottling plant in Laos and that the central bank would start serving it as a national drink. She then asked about shock therapy.

Shock therapy, theorized by American academic economist Jeffrey Sachs, was the development mantra of the day. It preached the sudden privatization of state-owned enterprises, withdrawal of all subsidies and price controls, immediate free foreign exchange convertibility, and the opening of capital markets. In short, it consisted of "shocking" a planned economy into the market. This was, in effect, a sink or swim strategy.

The underlying assumption was that everyone embraces American-style capitalism, so the economy would swim, the supposition being that Adam Smith's invisible hand would drive everyone to make all the right decisions.

Such thinking was remarkably naïve, and clearly an example of theory brainstormed in the isolation of a classroom that was out of touch with the real world. But, because it was endorsed by Harvard University and Columbia University professors, it was considered at face value to be a panacea, and readily embraced by Washington-based multilateral aid and lending institutions. This version of neoliberal "market fundamentalism" was entirely theory based.

Many in the developing world deride it as "voodoo economics."

It was based more on wishful thinking than reality, and it was accompanied by arrogance. The type of attitude was "we know better than you.". It was assumed that the formula, "our formula," when applied everywhere, works "because it is our formula." This outlook permeated much of the discourse on development for nearly two decades. It infuriated recipients of aid, who had no choice but to go along with this belittling attitude in exchange for the soft loans that their countries required for development.

Predictably, in most countries where shock therapy was applied—such as the former Soviet states—the economy was shocked into crashing. Political and social crises ensued.

Madame Pany asked if there was any alternative.

There was another way. Gradually untie the knot of state controls in a logical sequence, to release a market economy. Aim for smooth transition—evolution not revolution. Use the tools of market and planning; they are not mutually exclusive. The gradualist approach can apply to economic, fiscal, and financial policy, as well as law.

I was staring at the tall glass of sticky sweet black soda, and felt a bit nauseous in the sweltering heat. Green tea would be more cooling. Then I bluntly suggested that Lao tea and rich coffee were better national drinks than Pepsi: "be proud of who you are; consider cultural psychology in deciding economic and financial policy; take in local practices when drafting legislation. Otherwise, whatever measures you take, they will be impractical to implement."

Madame Pany nodded in approval. She mandated: make it work!

Buddhist monasteries distributed rice to local farmers in exchange for part of their annual yield. This became the framework for credit cooperative legislation. Village heads use traditional approaches in settling family, property, and trade disputes. Drawing upon such local practice became the source from which to code procedures and processes for meditation and arbitration. I often thought about Victor Li's *Law without Lawyers.*

All of this flew in the face of shock therapy.

The World Bank's program for legal reform advocated introducing New York-style corporate law to the Lao people—shock the nation into modernity. But Lao was a small country with few laws and (lucky them) even fewer lawyers. I infuriated World Bank legal specialists by asking whether they intended to encourage private enterprise or discourage it.

When legislation is too complicated, who bothers reading it, or cares about following the procedures? (Most congressmen don't read the legislation they vote on. But their decisions affect people.)

Legislation as thick as the New York Yellow Pages only creates more bureaucracy. But professors and consultants sitting in think tanks draft first-class sophisticated laws that may be irrelevant to those people whom they are supposed to help.

The whole point: encourage people to start their own business in *their* community. When more gobbledygoop is required to register a legal private enterprise, people just won't bother. Instead, they will operate illegally. Black markets will emerge. That is exactly what happened in Russia after shock therapy collapsed the Soviet Union. Instead, try practical, easy-to-read understandable regulations. Then people will know what they are doing.

A real market economy should evolve on terms acceptable to the people themselves. Don't force something that is outside their reality, especially when it is just a theory.

In Lao, even the idea of a private enterprise was embryonic. Trying to understand their reality, I asked Madame Pany's office to arrange a visit to the enterprise registration department.

We located the department within the Ministry of Economy, Planning and Finance (first, they had to find out where it was!) in a dusty corner room on the first floor. A clerk was asleep at the single desk. He guarded two old metal cabinets of Vietnam War vintage, with a couple of files stuffed inside, keeping company with a lot of dust. That was the total sum of enterprise registrations.

In drafting a new corporate law, the prime objective was to define what existed. Laos had three types of enterprises: state owned, mixed state-private, and private. In the minds of many people, these differences were blurred. As far as they were concerned, these were all just "enterprises."

There was no such thing as a limited liability corporation or partnership. They had never even had to deal with this idea before. These structures therefore had to be created out of what already existed. But what was that? The first step was to define and spell out concepts, so that people could understand what they actually had, and what they could do with it. The next step: explain how to register and capitalize each kind of enterprise. What was limited liability? How could it protect investors? I put the whole thing down in just five pages. At this stage a full-blown law was unnecessary. The government could just issue an enterprise decree, and then add more regulations later, when needed.

Infuriated World Bank consultants ran to the Ministry of Justice and complained. I really did not know what was going on until one night someone knocked on my door. It was Kham Leuang Sayalath, ranking minister in the Council of Ministers Office, and the personal adviser of elusive Pathet Lao leader Kaysone (the Mao Zedong of Lao). He arrived at the guesthouse that stood along the sleepily drifting moonlit Mekong River, having been driven there by a tough general named Thong Phachuanh Sonnasina, who was introduced as the director of the cabinet. They rolled up to the guesthouse in a rattling 1970s vintage VW Bug.

Kham Leuang slapped my draft enterprise decree on the table of my dimly lit room. "I know you will meet the vice minister of justice tomorrow." He had a scratchy voice and made a lot of gestures when he spoke, very uncharacteristic for a Lao. I always suspected he might be part Vietnamese. "All these foreign lawyers are running around asking to 'change this sentence' or 'change that word.' Enough changes! Lao is a poor country. We need laws so we can finally develop. So just pass law, lots of law. Tomorrow when you see the vice minister, tell him I said, pass this decree!" He was visibly upset and frustrated with academics arguing about semantics. His point was that Lao needed to develop basic legislation for the banking and business sector. He needed clear, straightforward and very basic laws to begin building an economic system.

Then Kham Leuang left the room with the same haste he had entered, and the general drove him off into the mosquito-biting night in that rattling Bug.

THE NOMADS INVENTED MOVABLE ASSETS

Then one morning, without notice, I was summoned to the Mongolian embassy in Vientiane. As a country in the socialist camp, far-off Mongolia had intimate relations with Lao.

Surin Badral, Mongolia's ambassador to Lao, greeted me enthusiastically in the reception room of the embassy. We sat on sofas under an oil painting of Mongolian nomads riding horses. I recalled my love for horseback riding as a kid. He smiled and pointed to the picture, "One day I will take you there."

He was interested in the reforms taking place at the Lao central bank. He told me to expect a day when he would call and ask me to apply the same approach in Mongolia.

Seven years later, Badral was foreign affairs adviser to Mongolia's prime minister, Mendsaikhany Enkhsaikhan. Sure enough, the World Bank was recommending corporate legislation to push Mongolia's privatizations. The young prime minister wanted a second opinion. So I flew from Beijing to Mongolia on a moment's notice from Badral. Stepping into the chilly mid-summer air, the first thing I noticed was that people in Mongolia still live in yurts. Driving from the airport to the capital Ulan Bator, Badral pointed to wood and cement constructed homes, each with a yurt in its front yard. He explained, "Even when people are settled in a nice home, they still put a yurt in their yard. They sometimes prefer to sleep there."

Even inside the vast cavernous Soviet-style parliament building there was a yurt pitched in the central courtyard. "The prime minister prefers to hold meetings in here," Badral explained. "We are nomads. It is in our blood. You can never settle a nomad in one place. So when we cannot be on the back of a horse, we prefer to be inside a yurt. If we have to move, the yurt can always be thrown on the back of a horse. Then we just ride to the next place. You cannot do that with a house or a parliament building. So the yurt gives us a sense of security."

The point is that people in different cultures and places simply have their own views based on the economic relativity of their world. The whole idea of security being not in a house but in a yurt and with horses because they can be moved is a nomadic notion that completely contravenes how we are conditioned to think. But to them it is perfect logic.

That evening Badral gave me a Yellow Pages-size piece of legislation. "Is this the proposed corporate law?" I did not even have to ask. Flipping through the pages, I commented, "You know, I have read this once before." Then I had an idea. "Tomorrow, can you take me to Ulan Bator's department of enterprise registrations? I would like to see it myself."

Sure enough, it was a small room in an old Soviet-style building, with nostalgic wooden cabinets, filled with a few files of registered enterprises. One Mongolian official was asleep at a big wooden desk.

The next morning, the prime minister received me. Huge men right out of a history book on Ghenghis Khan guarded his office. After looking at me with hard eyes, they just let me into the prime minister's office with a hearty wave. There was no other security procedure.

The prime minister listened intently. We laid out the issues. Mongolia—the world's largest land-locked country—then had a population of 2.5 million. Half lived in Ulan Bator, and the rest were nomadic. Physical money hardly circulated in the nomadic regions, and the nomads could not have cared less. A complex corporate law would not encourage free enterprise. In fact, it would discourage it. Instead, a simple code would not only allow privatization of state-owned enterprises (the obvious World Bank policy objective) but also empower rural nomads to start their own herding companies or partnerships. I went further and suggested a valuation system for sheep and horses, allowing nomads to register these asset values. The prime minister seemed to like the idea. In many cases, sheep and horses were the nomad's only real assets.

Curious, I asked how the nomads care for so much livestock during the winter months, when the Mongolian steppes are steeped in snow. Stocking grain must be quite a chore.

"It is no problem at all," Badral explained. "They just release them."

"You mean release the animals?"

"Yes, let the horses run wild for the winter. They know instinctively how to survive. It is not our problem."

"But then the assets will be disposed of?" I was dumbstruck trying to figure out how to depreciate assets on the books of a nomadic enterprise.

"No problem," laughed Badral. "The nomads can go out and just round up the horses again in the spring. They are movable assets."

CONSTITUTIONAL REFORM, LAO STYLE

Back in Lao, I pedaled my bicycle to the National Assembly along the wide Champs Elysees-like boulevard running through Vientiane, and the imposing Lao-style Arc de Triomphe that dominates it. The Arch is elaborately decorated with swerving images of dancing Lao angels. Officials explained to me with a mild giggle that when Americans provided cement to build an air runway for fighter jets during the Vietnam War, the Lao people instead used it to build this wonderful arch. They were so proud of this.

As I passed the archway, my bicycle creaked to a halt before an imposing new building. Samane Souvannasao, the chief of cabinet of the People's Supreme Assembly (the Lao parliament) was waiting for me outside, wearing a construction worker's hat. He had grey hair and that French gentlemanly aura that many senior Pathet Lao possessed. The new assembly building was still under construction, which he was personally supervising (of course, as chief of cabinet, that was his job too!) He exuded pride, showing a brightly painted mural at the entrance, depicting historic and Buddhist places in the iconography of Laos.

Entering his office, he revealed passages of the new draft constitution. The words "People's Supreme" would be dropped in favor of "National Assembly," toning down socialist jargon as the nation prepared to adopt a market economy. But critical in the transformation was the question of property rights. The issue that nagged him was eminent domain, when the government had to confiscate property. In a communist society, that was easy, because it all belonged to the state anyway. But with new private enterprises, what to do? I suggested clauses allowing for compensation to owners at full fair market price.

But what was fair market price? There had been no real estate market since the Pathet Lao took over.

With the Soviet Union collapsed and China closed, the Pathet Lao leadership was faced with many questions, political as well as economic. They feared the crack-up that had occurred in Moscow when its model shifted from one economic extreme to another. They were curious about the middle way approach with which China was experimenting.

One night, when the streets of Laos were empty and very dark, a soft-spoken heavy-set official named Sisavath Sisane invited me to a dilapidated French villa tucked in a jungle grove. He held duel portfolios as executive vice-governor of the central bank, and vice minister of the Ministry of Economy, Planning and Finance. He was also Kaysone's illegitimate son. Inside the villa, they served the finest French food I had ever tasted in my life. Reserved for the elite, these tucked away villa restaurants were the Pathet Lao answer to Michelin dining. Sisavath asked me about the Soviet Union crack-up. Would China take the same road? Or would China reject "shock therapy," seeing how it had sparked the Soviet collapse?

China's 1987 Chinese Communist Party (CCP) congress became the reference. Deng had scrambled the rules of the game by stating that China was only at the "first stage of socialism," which would last "a relatively long period of time." He simply moved the goal posts so far back they were conveniently out of reach.

Sisavath just laughed and took another sip of Bordeaux. "Oh! Relatively long? It will be a very, very, very relatively long period of time. I am sure."

MONETARY SHUTTLE DIPLOMACY

Hanoi, 1993. A misty drizzle soaked the *cyclo* rickshaw drivers who were pedaling around the majestic lake. Mist lifted, exposing curve-roofed pavilions and delicate arching bridges as motorbikes zipped and zigzagged through the leafy tree-lined French-style streets encircling *Ho Hoan Kiem*, Broken Sword Lake.

A small boulevard led to a park-like setting with a single picture of Ho Chi Minh dominating the colonial-era building. As I entered the State Bank of Vietnam, a charming Vietnamese girl in a long *au sai* slit up to her waist, with flowing pantaloons over delicate sandals, met me at the front reception with its vast art deco iron-molded glass-inlaid ceiling.

The State Bank of Vietnam had invited me to Hanoi. They knew all about my work in Laos. Vietnam had vested interests there and an intricate intelligence network. The Vietnamese Communist Party liked to describe its relationship with the Pathet Lao as being as close as "lips and teeth." The laid-back Lao cringed whenever they heard this. The Lao people have a saying: "What the Lao will do for pride, the Vietnamese will do for money."

I had been invited to Vietnam to advise on money and to work directly with their central bank's foreign exchange department, run by a dynamic official named Ngyuen Doanh Hung. Hung frequently asked me to advise on foreign exchange issues, and so a kind of central bank shuttle diplomacy emerged between the State Bank of Vietnam and China's Foreign Exchange Control Bureau, borrowing legislation from China, and passing it to Vietnam. At the time, relations between the two nations were still strained from a 1979 border spat. But their systems were similar, so the two countries watched each other's reform maneuvers carefully.

In 1993, there was a Dong currency crisis. Ten dollars in cash could be traded for rubber-band-bound bricks of local currency. People would pile these bricks precariously on bicycles and take them to the market to buy vegetables. There was fear of further sharp devaluation against rising inflation.

In situations like this, sudden currency convertibility, as proposed by the shock therapists, is the last thing that is needed. The currency will certainly depreciate more, stimulating further inflation. People will go into the streets. Moreover, removing subsidies on key commodities at such a time, which was the "IMF medicine," would guarantee economic chaos. This is exactly what happened in Thailand and Indonesia during the 1997 Asian Financial Crisis.

There are certain central bank measures that have been proven to work in such a case: a mandated lending freeze, sharp interest rate hikes, and a drastic cutting of money supply. These were the same methods used by China's premier Zhu Rongji to rein in hyperinflation in 1994.

They are really administrative orders mixed with some fiscal levers. Some may argue that these are harsh measures that carry the shadow of state planning or at least state intervention, and therefore do not fit the neoliberal model.

But they work.

After the Dong currency crisis, Hung sat with me in his offices at the State Bank of Vietnam. The room, with its high ceiling and stone balustrade, overlooked the motorbike-buzzing street below. Like every room in the bank, a portrait of Ho Chi Minh dominated the space.

Hung offered to explain his analysis of the crisis. The relationship between the currency black market, devaluation, and rocketing inflation were connected to the sudden opening of the economy, the import of goods that people craved, and the subsequent relaxation of controls. People reacted by voting with their money. Speculation arose from excessive leveraging of opportunity against darker memories of stagnation and frugality. It was a formula for a financial crisis.

Carrying brick-like bundles of cash to the market recalled the wartime currency and inflation crisis, eroding people's confidence in the government. The central bank responded by cutting the money supply while reissuing newly denominated notes, in short, giving people less paper to carry.

To illustrate his point, Hung placed two Dong notes on the table before us, one in circulation before the crisis, another of recent issue. Each Dong note had a picture of Ho Chi Minh. But the pictures differed slightly. Hung pointed out wryly that on the note in circulation before the crisis, Ho's image was stern. On the later note, he was smiling. "You see, the people react based on how Uncle Ho looks at them!" He laughed.

Through black humor he was making a clear point. People's reaction to markets, inflation, and any financial crisis depend on emotional and psychological factors, not just empirical formulas.

You can have the best economic theory in the world, but if you do not understand people's emotions and psychology—driven by cultural, religious, geographic, and often very complex social factors under the surface—that theory may sound nice, but will be useless.

SHOCK THERAPY RESISTANCE

Back in Beijing, China's leadership began a gradual sequencing of steps that would ultimately lead toward the globalization of the Yuan. The approach would differ radically from the application of sudden currency convertibility preached by shock therapists and advocated by the IMF. The process would take two decades.

China's first step was to open many regional foreign exchange swap centers, where a controlled portion of local currency could be exchanged for foreign cash each day by businesses. The rate was set depending on who or how many enterprises came to trade that session. This was the precursor to a managed float that Zhu Rongji later introduced by closing and merging these centers into an interbank currency market.

In 1994, Pang Jiying from the State Administration Bureau of Foreign Exchange Controls, was sent by "boss Zhu" from Beijing to Shanghai. His mandate: open up a national foreign exchange trading center to replace the local "swap centers." He settled into his new office, located in an old neoclassical building on the Shanghai Bund, overlooking the thronging Huangpu River. My Shanghai office was just around the corner. Entering the building, I marveled at another 1930s art deco molded-iron-stained glass ceiling. Pang pointed to the designs so symbolic of another era that most Chinese people wanted to both forget and emulate. He then told me about Premier Zhu Rongji's plan: to turn the building into China's first interbank market.

Beijing and Hanoi, both facing similar predicaments, borrowed from each other.

The State Bank of Vietnam was grappling with how to securitize rural loans. How should it take collateral when all a farmer had were pigs? They might get fat (appreciate) or die (depreciate). The bank was at risk if it had a lot of pigs. These were real problems that bankers and borrowers faced at the grass roots. They could not be solved with theory. But they could be solved with microfinance.

Vietnam badly wanted a stock market as a threshold measure of success. Credit Lyonnais helped establish a securities market, inviting me as legal adviser. An anxious International Financial Corporation (IFC) (the World Bank's investment arm) intervened, presenting a thick bundle of legislation. Sure enough, it was the rules for the New York Stock Exchange, with the name New York replaced by Hanoi! The IFC insisted that this legislation be adopted, demanding secrecy during discussions. State Bank of Vietnam officials passed a copy to me immediately. What was the IFC thinking? In a land without private enterprises, it was simply a blind cookie cutter application of one system upon another, without thought.

Even if Vietnam were to adopt these fancy listing rules, there was nothing to list on the market! All of the enterprises were state owned. Working with Credit Lyonnais, we began the first privatization of a Vietnamese state-owned enterprise called Legamex.

But the government could not accept the concept of privatization. As members of the Communist Party of Vietnam, they just could not pronounce that word. I explained in a meeting that we would not "privatize" but rather "corporatize." It could run efficiently like a corporation, with shares owned by both state and private interests—not completely private. The term "corporatize" would come out of this meeting. Its Chinese equivalent, *gufenhua*, would later be used across China. Actually, in both Vietnamese and Chinese, the word is the same.

But that was not the end of Legamex's problems. Even though selected by the Vietnamese leadership as a "model enterprise," Legamex was riddled with corruption. After the due diligence results were submitted to the authorities, the management was arrested.

These are all just examples of how both systems were finding their independent paths toward fusion economics, while rejecting standard Washington Consensus formulas. They were adopting sequenced steps to address real problems.

It gave theory a reality check.

THE SEEDS OF FUSION ECONOMICS

The fundamental failure of ivory tower cookie-cutter models, for all of their theoretical perfection, is that they ignore local conditions, culture, mindset, and historical burdens. So many of these policies when applied to development, in the local context proved disruptive rather than constructive. Ironically, in 2008 the ricochet effect of these same policies would be felt in America.

Economics had lost common sense. It became ideology.

Sometimes the simplest solution is what really works. Let's bring common sense back into our economics. Think tank formulas and theory keeps politicians and academics pontificating, but don't help us common folk. It is time to tear down the ivory towers, find out what people in the street feel and need, and then do what works.

Yes, in the end, what shook up the fossilized thinking of proud Washington economists would not be the experiments in hermit Lao or emerging Vietnam, but the giant they all wrote off in 1989—China.

In the wake of Tiananmen, China cocooned conservative. But it observed everything occurring in these two sleepy backwaters, with minute attention to detail. Both Lao and Vietnam borrowed from China's cautious sequenced reforms. These measures proved a healthy alternative to the shock doctrine, sparking fusion economics. Their experiments would be recycled back to China.

In 1992, China embarked on fresh gradualist reforms. Within a decade, in the context of controlled experimentation, China would undergo massive economic transformation from poverty to wealth on a scale unprecedented in the history of our planet.

And fusion economics would change the way we think.

CHAPTER 3

RED GUARDS WITH CREDIT CARDS:
Merge Planning and Market the Fusion Way

CHINESE ECONOMISTS CHOOSE ONE FROM GROUP A AND TWO FROM GROUP B

Beijing, 1992. It was a cold, dreary late winter day. As I peered out through my office window, the city looked grey-yellowish and flat. Nobody could foresee that vast construction sites would sprawl in every direction over the coming years, devouring all that low-rise space. My office was located in the China World Trade Center, a single lonely modern tower rising over China's capital. A decade later, the China World Trade Center would be dwarfed in a vast sea of high-rises.

But in 1992, the building was almost empty. Only a few foreign firms bothered to keep a presence there after the Tiananmen crackdown. Working for Johnston Stokes & Master, Hong Kong's largest law firm, I was asked to return from Lao and Vietnam and reopen their Beijing office, which had been closed since 1989. My brief was to rebuild their China practice from scratch.

Staring out through the coal-polluted and dust-smudged windows, I was trying to visualize how to make this happen. There were no foreign investors. There was no sign of any business anywhere. My thoughts were interrupted as our Hong Kong secretary briskly opened the door to my office with a sense of tense efficiency. "Several Chinese officials are waiting in the reception to see you. They say they are your 'old friends.'"

Yu Xiaoyu, was stretched out on the reception's institutional blue couch as if he owned the place, accompanied by two other officials. Yu, a burly Beijing'er who exuded the confidence and crassness of a New Yorker, was personal secretary to the Minister of the State Commission for Reform of Economic Systems (going by the obscure acronym SCRES).

SCRES served as the premier's think tank. With far-reaching power to oversee other ministries in guiding the transition from planning to market, it was one of the most powerful organizations in the Chinese government.

Over steaming cups of jasmine tea, Yu whispered of changes and shifting power alignments at the top. Reformers planned for Deng Xiaoping to take a trip through southern China. It was clearly orchestrated as an emperor's grand imperial tour. Every Chinese would understand the innuendo of Deng's trip.

Deng's "southern inspection" was all about sending messages to open the valves of China's economy. Deng visited the special economic zones—capitalist experimental laboratories—that he had pioneered a decade before. Revisiting the zones, Deng unabashedly declared *his* experiment a success. He then called for the whole country to become a market economy.

Lashing out at conservatives, Deng took the upper hand. "Regardless of whether you call it capitalism or socialism, does it raise productivity?" Deng then pronounced China to be a "socialist market economy with Chinese characteristics." Up until that moment, officials were afraid to even utter the phrase "market economy." Now they had a green light to practice capitalism.[1]

When Deng declared, "To get rich is glorious," people took it literally. The tycoon as icon consumed the national psychology, replacing Confucius, Buddha, and Mao.

Everyone, including communist cadres, jumped on the business bandwagon. China began running more like a corporation than a government (hence the term "China Inc."). Investments poured in. An era of accelerated hypergrowth ensued. And soon everything got out of hand.

In China the ideological debate between socialism and capitalism had come full circle. Now it was buried. And the rest of the world would never be the same.

ZHU RONGJI: PRAGMATIC ECONOMICS

I first met Zhu Rongji in 1988. As Shanghai's charismatic mayor, he shook up the city's stifling bureaucracy. Zhu's first challenge was to bring in foreign investment. He called all of the departments together (that previously had refused to cooperate with each other), put them in a single room, and created a one-stop shop for investors. He called it the "investment dragon line."

I was invited to Shanghai as part of a Hong Kong American Chamber of Commerce delegation to understand how the dragon worked.

Zhu Rongji was connecting the discordant departments of China's fossilized communist bureaucracy to create economic efficiency where stagnation existed. The one-stop dragon shop he introduced into Shanghai was the nascent model employed a decade later in 1998 to coordinate China's industrial ministries opening the doors to foreign investment and ultimately the World Trade Organization (WTO).

It was one of those drizzly, misty, rainy days so typical of Shanghai. Zhu received us in the reception room of an old 1930s hotel, amid vintage red satin curtains and art deco chairs. The mood of Shanghai oozed with anticipation and apprehension, a city about to step from one era into another. Zhu arrived at the meeting a bit late, in a rush. We all stood up as he entered and took his seat in one of those overstuffed velvet chairs. Wasting no time, he encouragingly talked about his one-stop shop to make procedures smoother for everyone.

One Hong Kong business leader sitting next to me noticed Zhu was wearing hiking boots under his suit trousers. The Hong Kong businessman whispered snobbishly how in China even the mayor of an important city like Shanghai could not dress properly. Before ending the meeting, Zhu apologized for arriving late, explaining he had rushed from a construction site, which was the reason he wore hiking boots. As mayor, he was personally overseeing every investment project to assure it proceeded without delays, refusing any nonsense from any lethargic official who was holding up foreign investments. He was going to make the dragon work, and that point was made absolutely clear to everyone in the room.

But at that moment nobody could imagine that Zhu would become the single most powerful influence over China's transition from socialism to market, and the emergence of fusion economics.

Chinese New Year, February 1991, Deng Xiaoping visited Shanghai. "Some cadres think the planned economy is equivalent to socialism and market economy equivalent to capitalism. Capitalism has planning. Socialism also has markets," Deng declared emphatically spitting into a brass spittoon on the floor.

Deng himself was convinced that socialism had hit a wall. It discouraged growth and entrepreneurial spirit. At the same time, lessons from 1989 were still raw. Shock therapy had failed as a reform methodology. Deng wanted Chinese pragmatism, not American theory. The Soviet Union's collapse and the ensuing mess in Eastern Europe were stark lessons of exactly what China did not want. China needed its own economic model, not something fantasized in a Harvard classroom, which was irrelevant for China.

Instead of shock, Deng talked about gradual sequencing. He called it, "crossing the river by feeling the stones one at a time."

Across the Huangpu River bank from Shanghai's historic Bund, Zhu was determined to pioneer an international financial and trade zone called Pudong. As mundane as this idea sounds today, it was daring breakthrough stuff in China at that time.

Zhu's trusted deputy mayor, Zhao Qizheng, was mandated to create an ultra-modern city overnight. So Zhao needed foreign investment. When I convinced Swiss pharmaceutical giant Roche to relocate its Asia research and development center in Pudong, Zhao and I became best of friends.

Deng revisited the Pudong special economic zone during Chinese New Year 1992. New construction was underway. Deng then made a surprise visit to Beijing Capital Steel, a massive archetype state-owned enterprise on the outskirts of Beijing. Deng's visit rocked China's Communist Party when he announced, "Nobody in the central committee understands economics. Only Zhu Rongji understands economics!"[2]

The emperor's mandate had been given. By spring 1992, Zhu Rongji rose from Shanghai mayor to vice premier of China's powerful State Council, assuming the role of China's "economic tsar."

The era of fusion economics would begin.

THE CODED LANGUAGE OF ARCHITECTURE

In 1992, I lived in an old Chinese courtyard house in a narrow *hutong*, a Beijing alleyway lined with trees.[3] The courtyard was a state-run guesthouse, mostly for foreign experts. The Chinese working there as state employees were smiley friendly to foreign guests, but irascibly grumpy when it came to work. Despite its ancient charm, the place was always filthy, subsumed in dust because nobody bothered to clean it. None of the Chinese who worked there had any pride in their culture, nor could they care less.

The power and depth of China's architecture captured my imagination as coded language. Beijing's courtyard mirrors Chinese psychology: a zigzag entrance, blocked by a carved spirit wall. There is no straight way of entering a Chinese courtyard. Inside, the middle garden was the center of all activities. There was a strict hierarchy as to who lived where, fixed by the proportion of the buildings and height of the rooftops for the quarters of master, sons, daughters, concubines, and servants. It was all laid out in strict Confucian order, and everybody had their assigned place.

Somewhere in each courtyard there was a secretive back door.

It was so different from American homes that centered in a big lawn, where anyone from the street can see what is happening inside. Big frame windows expose the living room. When you enter through the main door, there is usually a stairwell that goes right upstairs to the bedroom, but everyone hangs out in the kitchen. And the garage is designed for at least two cars.

The logic became clear: architecture is the dialogue of a people with their environment.

In China, whether one is doing business or lobbying the corridors of power, everything functioned according to the architectural rules of a courtyard. It was a kind of Chinese cultural Da Vinci Code.

Throughout the 1990s, developers uprooted entire neighborhoods. Corruption played a big part in this. Government, developers, and banks cut a triangle of interlocking deals. People were evicted from homes where they had lived for generations. When they refused to leave, thugs on hire by developers, accompanied by police, beat them to disability until they relocated. Within one decade, Beijing's heritage architecture was obliterated on a scale dwarfing even the destruction during the Cultural Revolution. Tragic and shortsighted, the uprooting of neighborhoods and destruction of heritage architecture soon became a national trend as other cities followed Beijing's example.

Donald Trump would be very welcome here.

Great historic Chinese architecture, charming tree-lined alleyways, millennia of cultural values, all were bulldozed into oblivion and replaced by gaudy-looking facades and glassy showrooms for Ferrari and Porsche.

In the minds of many Chinese officials, this all represented progress. For them, the number of luxury brand cars stuck in gridlock was a tangible measure of China's economic boom and the success of their policies. China's hypergrowth trajectory was contaminating the environment at unprecedented speed and levels. Did achieving quantity of life necessitate losing quality of life?

China had gone from one extreme to another, from worshiping Mao to money. A new kind of fanaticism had been unleashed—Red Guards with credit cards. Discarding their own culture, traditions, and value systems, Chinese people lost their identity, absorbed and mesmerized by luxury Western brands that defined their new status. Western luxury brands had become the new opium of China.

Was this what modernization and globalization were supposed to be about?

I had come to China fired on idealism, wanting to help a nation transition out of poverty. Foreign investment achieved that, bringing both finance and technology. But I rejected the notion that modernization and globalization meant obliterating culture and dislocating communities. Could a neighborhood movement spark small business to preserve a community, giving it new vibrancy?

Many disagreed. I decided to try.

Over the coming five years, I renovated three courtyards, creating a small business in each of them. The government observed very closely my every move, sometimes with suspicion. But the idea caught on. Locals followed, restoring their courtyards and opening similar guest houses, restaurants, and coffee shop or tea house businesses throughout the neighborhood. We established the first private courtyard restaurant and hotel in Beijing's Eastern District. It had never been done before. Today, there are over 300 private boutique courtyard hotels in Eastern District alone. They preserve heritage, neighborhoods, and local culture. Eventually our neighborhood came under a city heritage preservation order.

I never thought we would actually win that battle. But it proved to me that pragmatic idealism works.

THE CHINESE ART OF CRISIS MANAGEMENT

Between the years 1992 and 1996, the freewheeling business atmosphere that Deng unleashed became a kind of Wild East. The valves on lending, money supply, and bureaucratic approval were wide open, and an atmosphere of condoned financial irregularity ensued and subsumed everything. Triangular relationships quickly formed between banks that lent funds to enterprises that invested in fantastical real estate pipedream projects that were quickly approved by local officials who were bribed with the bank loans. Investments became indiscriminate. The prevailing attitude was: who cared? The money all belonged to the government anyway.

So people had no fear of risk.

From 1949 through the mid-1980s China faced commodity scarcity. Even with money, there was nothing to buy. Deng's reforms sparked an unprecedented consumer economy, which gave producers a perception of demand infinity. State factories, inexperienced with market cycles, simply overproduced electronics and consumer goods en mass, flooding the market with oversupply gluts.

China's long pent-up entrepreneurial spirit had finally been released. But there was also a backlash. China became mired in a "triangle debt" conundrum. Banks loaned to enterprises for production. The enterprises then invested in real estate. Contractors used the cash to speculate on other projects. Everybody was trying to hit the jackpot. Investments were irrational. Production went into hyperdrive. By 1996, markets were flooded. Goods were in oversupply. Counterfeits filled every crack in price elasticity. Warehouses were overstocked. Receivables could not be collected. And debts could not be cleared.

In the 1990s, Zhu Rongji faced one crisis after another: hyperinflation, triangular debts, inefficient enterprises, bank insolvency, dilapidating infrastructure, and the 1997 Asian financial crisis. To top it off, there was (still is) a total lack of a social contract and trust between the government and the people, a leftover from the Cultural Revolution. The challenges were far more complex than anything America or Europe face today. No question, China was in much worse shape.

The sudden freeing of China's economy in 1992 stimulated rocket inflation, which hit 21.7 percent by 1993. Controlling inflation now became China's number one priority.

Zhu Rongji was then vice premier, holding portfolios for production and economics. But with no other leader able to tackle China's internal financial crisis, he personally took over the central bank as acting governor, while serving as vice premier. This gave him effective control over the banking and finance portfolios, as well opened the door for a series of experiments in combining planning tools with market that would become the foundation of fusion economics.[4]

Fusion economics really began in 1993 when inflation hit 21.7 percent. Zhu sacked the central bank governor, taking the reigns himself. Harsh controls were needed to steer the economy back onto some kind of rational track that could be managed. He introduced "Sixteen Measures for Macro-Economic Control," a policy document that unabashedly combined the monetary and fiscal tools of a market economy with socialist administrative controls.[5] To everyone's surprise, it worked.

The "Sixteen Measures for Macro-Economic Control" flew right in the face of neoliberal economists and shock therapy. Observers in Washington and Europe were stunned. Observers in Asia, Africa, and South America watched with gleeful fascination as this experiment unfolded, because it offered an alternative.[6]

Meanwhile, by the mid-1990s, a mishmash of "triangle debts" threatened to undermine China's reforms. With 300 billion Yuan in outstanding inter-enterprise credits, China's banking system was brought to the verge of collapse. By 1996, China's "economic Tsar" faced the crisis of cleaning up a mess of triangle debts and state-owned enterprise insolvencies that threatened to unravel the very reforms he was fighting for. A program of financial support to clear the debts, however, only stimulated more. It was not all that different than the 2008 financial crisis when bankers misappropriated Federal bank bailouts to grant themselves extravagant bonuses, while speculating with even riskier leverage.

When the cost of capital appears cheap, people do irrational things with their money, because at that moment everything seems possible and there is no sense of medium- or long-term risk. When deregulation allows financial institutions, government, and capital market regulators and real estate developers to join hands in profiteering without any guidance, checks or balance, the public will be ripped off. In an entirely twisted way, this is what happened in China during the mid- to late 1990s and in America a decade later.

However, in 1996, Zhu Rongji had had enough. He held a meeting that challenged the status quo—that snug relationship between regulators, banks, and real estate developers. Addressing everyone in the room, he banged his fist on the table and declared, "We will no longer call it triangle debt. Whoever spends money must pay for it. Whoever invests, pays. Otherwise go bankrupt!"[7]

Imagine what would have happened in 2008 if Treasury Secretary Hank Paulson had said the same thing to Wall Street? But he didn't.

Eighteen years later, I was standing among protesters at Occupy Wall Street, there was an eerie parallel between China's triangle debt conundrum of the 1990s and America's financial crisis of 2008. Effectively, we had created a decade and a half of seeming prosperity, when it was just a grand pyramid scheme of trading debt instruments alongside highly leveraged real estate developments. Many will be chagrined. Yes, it seems blasphemous to draw similarities between China and America. But some things about human nature remain consistent wherever you go. One of them is greed. The other is risk.

REENGINEERING THE RUST

As an investment lawyer, advising some of the biggest multinational corporations—Exxon Mobil, Ericsson, Roche, Bayer, Kodak, and Chubb—negotiating their first China deals and obtaining market entry, I was living on the inside of a massive experiment to re-engineer China. Every time a foreign company joint ventured with a Chinese state-owned enterprise, it meant restructuring the local partner.

My pet project was Power 28, a national detergent brand factory located in Hubei Province—smack in the center of China. It was the archetypal state-owned enterprise, run by a cunning but creative cadre-cum-mafia boss named Teng Jixin. Aside from making soap and detergent, Teng launched a spectrum of side ventures, from women's sanitary napkins, to bottled water, to karaoke dance clubs and restaurants. The enterprise was burdened with uncollectable receivables and awash in debt. But like most state-owned enterprises, the management could not have cared less. Risk belonged to the state.

The entire socialist system during Mao's time had been constructed around the notion of guaranteed employment. The "iron rice bowl" was ingrained in Chinese people's psyche. It was a source of immeasurable inefficiency. Zhu was determined to smash the bowl and release the commercial tenacity of Chinese, with foreign investors paying to lay off excess labor.

Foreign investors that were acquiring factories had to lay off vast numbers of redundant workers to make the businesses work. How to treat this on the books?

The answer came during a visit of Sanjay Bhandari, Asia's Regional Director for the Benckiser Group. He was expected to finalize bitter negotiations that had dragged on for months. Instead of letting him check into the hotel, Teng Jixin rushed us by police car to a crossroads where a new pedestrian bridge was being opened with full ceremony and marching band. The bridge was named after Power 28 because the enterprise had paid to build it. Teng was on the bridge waving to crowds, as if pretending to be Mao. Just as Mao had once invited Edgar Snow to Tiananmen Square, sending a message to Richard Nixon about relations with America, Teng invited us onto the bridge. Clearly he had a message for Benckiser headquarters. Sanjay asked what was the spectacle all about.

I tried to interpret the message. "This is Teng's way of finding a solution for our negotiation impasse. Power 28 has given a bridge to the people of Shashi. Now Benckiser must give financing to Power 28 for the workers."

Sanjay was stunned. "Is that what this parade is all about?"

"Yes," I explained. "It's all innuendo. You have to catch the gist because he won't tell you at the negotiating table. So it is up to you to figure out his meaning. That is the Chinese way."

So instead of sacking labor, Benckiser reemployed them. A second joint venture funded Teng's other ventures—such as sanitary napkins and bottled water—Benckiser only wanted the core industry detergents. This was China's first joint venture equity investment fund. Benckiser footed the bill, and Teng re-employed old workers.

This pioneering scheme went all the way to the top. Zhu's office was really interested at what was going down in Hubei.

HEAL AN ECONOMY: CHINESE VERSUS WESTERN MEDICINE

By retooling one enterprise after another, I inadvertently became the doctor of state-owned enterprise reform, and in 1997 was appointed to lead a task force blueprinting a nation-wide reform program. The experiment was to begin in Anhui Province, of all places. No surprise, as this was where free market reforms had started two decades earlier.

With a team of Chinese economists and officials, we began retooling enterprises in four sectors: iron and steel, cement, chemicals, and fertilizer.

These were Jurassic enterprises.

Huge debts were complicated by decades of tangled government funds from different ministries, cities, provinces, and the national government. After 40 years, these lines of capital were confused, tangled. Were they grants or loans? Who owned what?

Pig iron smoldered and rolled off the production line. Gas belched in all directions. "All of our equipment dates back to the 1960s and 1970s," explained factory manager Wang, shaking his head. "That's why we cannot make products that compete with Korean imports, unless we can buy the necessary technology. But that requires a huge capital injection. How to get such funds? No investor wants the social burdens we carry." Workers turned their heads and looked curiously. The unseemly presence of a foreigner was a rare distraction from the endless monotony of years on the same production line.

The enterprise supported schools, kindergartens, cafeterias, medical clinics, recreation centers, and retirement centers. A worker could be born, go to school, get married, work, live, and die within the confines of this enterprise without ever having to set foot outside. The enterprise was a city in itself.

"We have 50,000 people living here, including retirees and families of workers, all of whom we must support," explained Wang. "Actual workers are 20,000. To achieve maximum efficiency, we need 2,000 using existing equipment. If we upgrade the equipment, we need less."

The challenge was mind-boggling

When Mao took power, the state-owned enterprise actually solved many of China's postwar problems—housing, health care, employment, and industrialization. But by the 1990s, China's enterprises were uncompetitive. They had to get rid their social burdens. This required commercializing everything from health care to education, housing to insurance.

All of this needed regulation. At the time there was none. Ultimately, all costs would be passed on to the capital markets (but they hardly really existed either).

For example, removing the burden of housing required banking reforms in order to provide loans so that people could borrow money to buy their own homes, so that developers could borrow cash to actually build them. The need for legal collateral called for land and ownership rights, which also did not exist under socialism. In fact, the very concept of private ownership did not exist at all! Ultimately, this called for outright constitutional reform.

So in 1998, Zhu embarked on restructuring China's entire social structure. The commercialization of medical care and the introduction of pension funds meant reorganizing the insurance industry, which in turn called for comprehensive financial reforms. This thing was so complex, it could only be handled by adjusting each link in the chain in a sequential order.

Li Jiange, Zhu's monetary policy adviser, put it all in perspective. "The Washington Consensus is like Western medicine. It tries to cure the problem at its surface. We prefer Chinese medicine approach: examine the problem holistically and find the root cause. The Western medicine is a quick fix, but often has serious side affects. Chinese medicine is a longer and slower process. But it seeks the root of the problem. Often several causes are interconnected, so they must be solved together, but in sequenced steps."

This is really where the idea of sequencing began. Zhu recognized that none of the individual problems could be tackled in isolation. To reform the system, all issues would have to be confronted together, but in a logical order of layered priority. It was a complete rejection of market fundamentalism and shock therapy. Economists would later dub it "sequencing."

This was not lost on Western observers. One evening, Chile's ambassador to China asked, "What is this thing the Chinese are doing? It is capitalism without democracy. It is a communist party with full-blown capitalism. They are mixing up all these things. And they don't care. But it works."

He then took a sip of wine and laughed, "We are taught in the Western hemisphere, if you want capitalism, you must have democracy. If you have a communist party, you cannot have capitalism. China has taken everything we were taught, and mixed it up!"

He took another sip. "Do you realize how powerful this idea is? It is totally pragmatic and flexible.

"Why is it so powerful?" I asked.

"Because this unabashed mixing of economics without ideology, it is what Washington fears the most."

THE SOCIAL PSYCHOLOGY EFFECT ON A HERD OF SHEEP

As cups of hot *Longjing* Dragon Well tea were served and placed carefully on the table between us, I asked Premier Zhu Rongji how he balanced the odds when making key decisions on economic and financial policy. What did he actually consider in those critical moments when coming to a final decision?

Premier Zhu thought pensively for a moment, then replied with his characteristic directness, "Everyone knows, within economics there has to be a social-psychology effect. I call it the effect on a mass of sheep. If people are skeptical about your policy, even if it is correct, it will be difficult to implement and will be useless in producing any effect."

Frankly, I expected to get some lecture about an economic formula or policy framework. His answer was just down-to-earth stuff. The key was the importance of factoring psychology into economic policy. If people don't buy in, it is useless. So much economic theory is brainstormed by academics to win awards, but has little relevance to how a person in the street eats or lives their life.

Economic theory, for the sake of proving ideology, can be bad medicine for an economy.

In 1997, during the Asian financial crisis, the "IMF medicine"—sudden currency floats, convertibility, removal of grain and edible oil subsidies, with privatizations—further shocked nations like Indonesia and Thailand, with disastrous effects. People there resent the International Monetary Fund (IMF) approach to this day. The countries that refused this approach—Malaysia and China—managed the crisis well, but were rebuked in the Western media, because their approach did not fit the models.

Despite China's success in paving an independent path, market fundamentalism would continue to be advocated by Western academics and multilateral institutions in the Washington Consensus ambit. It remains the accepted mainstream economic view to this day. But these views have lost ground throughout the developing world since the 2008 financial crisis.

They have also lost credibility at home. Today, economies of America and Europe are debt ridden and rudderless. Politicians are clueless. It is clear that political leadership has been reduced to adopting very short-term remedial measures just to stay in power.

At the time of this writing, the world has turned upside down. Through direct investment, debt, and equity purchases, China has pumped an estimated EUR 200 billion into rescuing Europe from the euro crisis. With $4 trillion in foreign exchange reserves, underwriting $1.2 trillion of America's debt and holding over one-fourth of US treasury bills, China has become America's and Europe's de facto central bank.

China has effectively replaced the IMF as the world's lender of last resort.

PART II

PRAGMATIC IDEALISM:
Compassionate Capital, Stakeholder Value, and Social Enterprise

How can there be laughter, how can there be pleasure, when the whole world is burning? When you are in darkness, will you not ask for a lamp?

—The Buddha

A new era is dawning upon us of social enterprise and impact investments. We need to consider the bigger picture in each thing we do, because everything is interconnected. Imagine economics without greed. Picture doing business and making a profit for the sake of others and a good cause rather than just to gratify oneself. Maybe in the end, this is more gratifying.

Does this sound like a revolution in values?

It is time to introduce new concepts such as: "stakeholder value" (judging a company by what it does for the community and environment), "compassionate capital" (investments that have positive community and environmental impact) and "conscientious consumption" (consumers exercising their choice of values by choosing what to buy or boycott).

Sure, investment should be for profit. But it can also be for a wider social good. Business with the right focus can help preserve communities, empower the marginalized, and protect the environment. Just as market and planning are not mutually exclusive, neither are doing business and social good.

Small businesses are providing a practical way to support meaningful social and environmental programs. This trend, which is now occurring on many continents at once, gives rise to a fresh notion. Business does not have to be motivated by profit alone. It can provide jobs while achieving a vision, supporting a social cause, or creating a sense of community. There are many different and creative ways to help people and protect the environment. Business can be one of them. Social entrepreneurship is more than a trend. It is spreading everywhere.

Today, these new "social entrepreneurs" face challenges. Aid donors cannot place them in a box. Sufficient start-up or growth financing is difficult to obtain. Financial institutions don't recognize them, obviously because they are not fast-tracking to initial public offering. But why does every start-up have to try to go global? Does it make anyone happier? Better or more successful? Maybe it is more important to contribute to one's community by being a part of it.

We cannot rely only on gross domestic product and other growth-rate statistics to measure what we have achieved. So what is true development? Quantitative measurements of success do not reflect quality of life. Protecting community, culture, local identity, and the environment may be true development. Moreover, it could prove to be the next global economic, business, and financial driver.

CHAPTER 4

THE TAO OF SHANGRI-LA:
Learning Social Enterprise from Nomads and Monks

THE CHINA BUBBLE TURNS INVESTORS INTO LEMMINGS

Beijing, 2002. The lobby of the Grand Hyatt in Beijing was buzzing. The World Economic Forum was in town for its 2002 spring session. Everyone who was someone in China was there. In the chandeliered lobby of the Grand Hyatt, the China bubble was inflating fast.

I had second thoughts.

From an insider's view, China's large-scale reforms were complete. State-owned enterprises were on their way to becoming global multinational corporations. China had entered the World Trade Organization (WTO), which had set an irreversible roadmap for China's market economy. Economic integration with the rest of the world was inevitable. Exchange and interest rate issues would continue to grab media attention. Western politicians would focus on them. Would China appreciate or depreciate its currency value? These were technical questions—valve tightening—not real reform.

The trillion-dollar question was, will China's leadership establish social values that can make their economic achievements sustainable?

China had broken from the classic economic development formulas of the West. Its economic success proved those Western formulas were fossilized. But deep contradictions seized Chinese society. Excessive aping of globalized brands and the quick money craze consumed the nation's psyche. The thrift, patience, and long-term planning that had made China's reforms successful were largely lost in the process, ironically threatening to unravel what had been achieved. In the wake of its successful reforms, China was embarking on policies of super-high growth. The environment was totally disregarded. Within a mere decade, these policies would transform China into the world's second-largest economy and single largest emitter of greenhouse gases.

Values of conspicuous consumption were encouraged. And they went too far. Amid the excitement of change, a rapid social deterioration occurred. Corruption, on a scale possibly unprecedented in human history, rotted every aspect of Chinese society. All ethics had gone. Acquiring as much money as possible and showing off one's wealth were the overriding ideals of the day.

The cause was clear.

Having come out of the Cultural Revolution, when everyone wore army rags and being poor was proletariat chic, it was natural for China to swing to a brand-conscious conspicuous consumption model. China leaped from extreme Maoism and it fast-tracked market reforms, epitomizing capitalism, then taking it to a new extreme. Amid all the bubble and buzz, a coolheaded question had to be asked. Were China's economic achievements sustainable?

I began to think about what had brought me to China in the first place.

Chinese philosophy—an amalgam of Buddhist, Taoist, and Confucian principles had once framed life as an integrated whole between man and nature. After the Great Leap Forward, the Cultural Revolution, and 20 years of the dragon chasing the dollar, a rhythm of life once in balance with itself had been broken. In China's overconstructed debauchery-oriented cities, this philosophy was nowhere to be found. It had become extinct.

Could China's traditional values still be alive, somehow embedded among its ethnic minorities? That might sound like a strange thing to say, but much of what we think of today as Chinese Han culture actually comes from Mongolians, Manchurians, Tibetans, and other ethnic groups who ruled large portions of what constituted China over the past millennia.[1] So with traditions all but wiped out, what occurred was that certain core values remained with those ethnic groups from which they probably derived in the first place. I would soon have an opportunity to go to western China and find out.

CHINA'S SPIN DOCTOR

It was 2002, and China was embarking on a fiscal spending program. Zhu wanted to create domestic consumption to counter the reliance on exports. That meant developing China's interior and not only focusing on the coastal cities. Infrastructure investment would "open the West just as America opened its west too!" explained Zhao Qizheng, minister of the State Council News and Information Office. "Now, how can we use media to positively influence investment into China's western regions?"

A debate had erupted between several counties in Yunnan Province, Sichuan Province, and the Tibet Autonomous Region over which region could "legally" use the name "Shangri-la" to promote tourism. In the end, Diqing County in northern Yunnan Province was "awarded" the official "Shangri-la County" label, with the caveat that everywhere else in western China could use the name Shangri-la to promote tourism, as long as it made money for the local economy.

That is how China's central government made deals with its regions.

This decision was academically based on statements in James Hilton's book *Lost Horizons* and exploration notes by Joseph Rock, the first *National Geographic* bureau chief in Southwest China, who spent 18 years in Diqing County and the Lijiang area. I would learn years later that Shangri-la is a Western ill-informed misspelling of Shambhala, a core Tibetan concept of a future realm, where spirituality rises above materialism. Ironically, the Chinese government was flogging off the name as a gimmick to churn up tourism dollars.

I had known Zhao back when he was vice mayor of Shanghai serving under Zhu Rongji. When Zhu came to Beijing, he brought his trusted lieutenants. It was one team.

"Ok," I said, testing the limits of China's newly found media tolerance—basically Zhao's tolerance. "If you give me authorization to make a documentary film and it is just a travelogue—no politics—then I will hitchhike across China's remote western regions, followed by a documentary crew, and create a new image for China's west—young backpackers and environmentalists. Think like America's West in the

1970s, Hotel California, and all that." Thinking about the debate, I added, "Let's call it 'Searching for Shangri-la'. Will you agree, and grant me this permission?"

Zhao nodded, and arranged all the permissions.

I was stunned, never expecting this answer. It came without any expectation. That night, returning home, I took off my tie, hung up my suit, and began looking for mothballed hiking boots.

I was determined to find Shangri-la!

NOMADS AND MONKS SHATTER OUR ECONOMIC ASSUMPTIONS

The reality was, I knew nothing about filmmaking. Now, I was about to become producer and director without any script or film crew.

So I caught up with Ai Jing, one of China's top pop singers. We met at Beijing's first Starbucks. Ironically, this Starbucks was located in the nostalgic Friendship Store, where I had once shocked my Chinese hosts by spending one dollar on a Coke as an exchange student fresh off the plane in 1981. Now Starbucks was thronged with Chinese youth.[2]

I told Ai Jing about the permission granted by Minister Zhao to film in Tibet and across minority regions of western China. She understood the difficulties of media in China. "It is quite unprecedented, a unique window of opportunity," she exclaimed, offering to help.

Ai Jing got on top of the project. Within less than a week, she had assembled a first-class team. San Bao, China's most popular music composer, himself an ethnic Mongolian, agreed to write the entire soundtrack. Dou Yan, one of China's most experienced cameramen in Tibetan regions, led the cinematography team. Ai Jing was there to give artistic advice. The only thing I had to do was ask, "Where is Shangri-la?" With film crew in tow, I began hitchhiking and asking for directions to Shangri-la.

During the years 2002–2004, I made two films in Tibet. "Searching for Shangri-la" and "Shambhala Sutra." Neither film would air on Chinese television or in mainstream theaters. But in the end, that did not matter at all.

To me, the journey had been more important than arriving at the destination.

The films became less relevant than the people I met along the way. Four in particular were deeply inspiring. An Sang, a Tibetan artist, helped establish a factory for disabled artisans. Ethnic Bai dancer Yang Liping ran a performing arts program to protect hill tribe culture. Uttara Crees, an Indian environmentalist, was protecting biodiversity through ecotourism. Each was a pioneering social entrepreneur.

But the person who shattered all the economic assumptions was the monk Jigme Jensen, who established a yak cheese factory to help nomadic communities, while reinvesting profits into nomad schools.

THE MONK WHO OUTSMARTED THE HEDGE FUND MANAGERS

Our jeep splashed across icy rivers trickling down from melting glaciers. We drove deeper until there was no road, and then continued across grassland. As we entered the next valley, I noticed a monk in saffron robes across the river, waving. We pulled up to where he sat on a rock, head shaven except for a small mustache and goatee. His smile widened over his goatee, stretching to pointed elf-like ears, "Are you by chance looking for Jigme Jensen's cheese factory?" he giggled. "This is why you came here. You think you are searching for Shangri-la. Actually, you are looking for our cheese factory!" He broke into laughter.

With our overreliance on technology, the human ability to have intuitive knowledge of events and changes has been diminished. Instinct is on its way to becoming extinct. Living close to the earth, Jigme Jensen sensed our arrival and sent one of his monks to find us.

With a flourish of his hand, the monk led the way. A snow peak hovered over the crest of mountain above. Eagles flew so close, I felt I could touch them. A freezing cold river ran before us. We followed the river, then, crossed it, stepping upon stones, one at a time, as there was no bridge.

In contrast to everything around, a tiny factory building stood before us. Ironically, it had been built with seed funding from the Trace Foundation, which had been established by the daughter of famous hedge fund manger George Soros.

Tibetan workers stepped from the factory door to greet us. Dou Yan began filming immediately. Then another saffron-robed monk stepped forward. This was Jigme Jensen, the head of the yak cheese factory.

I was flabbergasted. A factory so utterly remote, so totally lacking in logistics, made no sense to my logical Western business mind. It had taken us days to find the place. So I asked in blunt frustration, "How can you make cheese in a factory away from markets, transport, everything? You are not near anything!"

"We are near the yaks," explained Jigme nonchalantly. "You see, we make yak milk cheese."

Over the coming days, Jigme Jensen would change the way I think about cheese, yaks, mountains, people, and education. More importantly, he would shatter all of my assumptions as to what constitutes a good business model.

His factory was simple. There were only three large rooms.

Before we entered, Jigme asked me to put on rubber boots and a white lab coat and face mask as if I were entering an operating room. "We must keep international health standards here when making yak cheese for export," Jigme explained with a flourish of his hand as if he were about to wipe Dutch Gouda off the market.

Sure enough, entering the little Tibetan factory was like stepping into a cheese factory in the suburbs of Amsterdam. The same techniques were applied. Yak milk was churned into heated vats and settled into molds. It solidified on wooden racks in cool rooms. I was convinced. Jigme Jensen was making real cheese.

Only one question remained. "Why here?"

"We need to be close to nomads who bring us fresh yak milk every morning and every evening. They bring it through this door," said Jigme, pointing to a side door leading to the room with the hot churning vats.

The factory was nowhere near any point of distribution. There were no roads in the middle of nomad country, in mountains within the heart of a sea of wild grasslands.

"I don't worry about distribution," Jigme explained, "because I do not want to manufacture cheese in a place that might be inconvenient for nomads."

It still didn't make commercial sense. How do you get the cheese to market? Why build a factory here just to provide convenience to nomads making yak milk deliveries?

"But that is just the point," Jigme insisted. "You see, they all live in mountains, in yak felt tents at high altitudes. They cannot leave valleys so easily. So by our having the factory here in the mountains, they can deliver yak milk every day, even twice a day. In this way, the milk is assured to be fresh."

I still did not understand this. "You can raise yak on farms near a factory, near a city, or a point of distribution, right?"

"Wrong. It would not be wild yak milk," Jigme sighed, "that is, milk from yaks herded by nomads. My real purpose is to help nomads."

Now I understood what was driving Jigme.

Jigme explained that the nomads, being herdsmen, traditionally had no income. Now, with economic change occurring everywhere, they needed cash to replace trade for goods. By purchasing yak milk every day, Jigme was providing income, without affecting their traditional lifestyle. In fact, he was not changing their traditional means of livelihood, but supporting and strengthening it.

China's official government policy insists that nomads be settled in apartments and assimilated to live like Han Chinese. The government pressures nomads to sell off their yak herds and tries to persuade them to make a down payment on a township apartment, borrowing the rest from a bank. Lacking the skill set to compete in a highly structured Han Chinese society, nomads are often unable to find work. Crammed into cement block living quarters, these proud people who herded flocks over vast ranges for generations, slip into alcohol, family abuse, and depression.

The Chinese government argues that nomads should be resettled in townships so they can receive proper medical care and education. However most government-run clinics in the region are poor, operating at something below sub-Saharan African conditions. What's more, Chinese education is alien and irrelevant to nomad children.

Jigme's response is to reinvest cheese profits into building schools. He pointed in the direction of another valley. "Tomorrow I will go to that valley to determine plot lines for the walls of a new school. It will be built with the proceeds from yak milk cheese!" By bringing enterprise and education to the nomads, Jigme was offering nomadic communities a far more advanced and conceptualized approach to sustainable development, both meaningful and relevant to their livelihood.

That said, Jigme still had to overcome the logistical challenge of distributing cheese from his isolated factory. Every day, he would fill up a jeep with round cheese blocks, driving through rivers and mountain mud to Maduo, a Tibetan town of teahouses and beer halls that looked like a scene from an American western like *High Noon*.

At Maduo, monks from Jigme's monastery would load the yak cheese onto lorries and vans, to truck it over a winding road for the

15-hour journey to Xining, Qinghai's main city. From there it would be transshipped to Beijing and other cities of China, and on to Europe and North America, where yak cheese was the ultimate for très chic cocktail parties and wine-tasting circles.

Meanwhile, Tibetan nomads earned cash and kept their traditional lifestyle.

Jigme explained that since he had established the cheese factory, nomad income in the surrounding valleys and mountains had increased, reinforcing rather than disrupting their traditional lifestyle. In Jigme's mind, preserving nomad life had far-reaching impacts beyond simply maintaining traditions. He saw nomad existence as integral to the survival of a delicate, endangered, biodiversity system.

Yak grazing patterns, tens of thousands of years old, are essential to the balance of nature in this area. The biodiversity, permafrost, and glacial cycles of the Qinghai-Tibetan plateau account for the source of water from down glacial river flows, for China, South Asia, and mainland Southeast Asia.

THE INVESTMENT IMPACT OF A SOCIAL ENTERPRISE

The next morning, we rose early to the patter of horse hooves as nomads delivered fresh yak milk outside the factory's side door. Then, with a flourish of his saffron robe, Jigme led me to his jeep. He sat up front, while another monk drove. I squeezed in-between two other monks in the back, and realized I was the only one not wearing saffron. We bounced down the narrow trail. My film crew followed two jeeps behind.

Jigme pointed excitedly. "See that tent in the distance? There are two young children in that nomad family. Do you see that tent there?" He pointed in another direction. I could barely see a tent on the horizon surrounded by tiny dots, yak. "There are several more girls living there. None of them has any opportunity to go to school because they are nomads. I will bring the school to them. They will be my students."

We drove into another valley where several workers were painting wall lines on a rounded, flattened parcel of grassland. Jigme jumped out of the jeep and strode over to them. Pointing to where he thought the lines should be drawn, Jigme was more like a construction site boss than a monk. The workers adjusted the line to his satisfaction. The classrooms would be bigger.

The cliffs of a sharp-peaked mountain rose above the valley, attracting Jigme's attention away from the work site. In the rock face I saw dots of dark color. "Those are caves," he whispered. "Monks used to meditate there. Good location for a school."

But why not build the school closer to town? The children can go there and stay in a dorm. They can return to their parents on holidays. It would be so much easier.

"You see, their parents all live in the mountains, in yak-felt tents at high altitudes. They cannot leave the valleys so easily. So by having the school here in mountains, they can go to school every day. Their traditional lifestyle will not be affected. I do not want to build a school in a place which might be inconvenient for nomads."

Within an hour or so, we arrived at the gated entrance to a compound. Within, stood a newly built Tibetan-style building with glass windows and doors. A monk unlocked the clean glass doors and nodded in deference.

On the first floor, Jigme led me into a physics lab full of modern equipment, past a chemistry lab, and into a small library filled with Chinese and Tibetan books. There were copies of sutra text in a cabinet. There were also copies of American books, even Disney cartoons for kids. "Tibetan children like Mickey Mouse," Jigme casually noted as he led me upstairs.

On the second floor we saw classrooms filled with computers and the latest Internet equipment. Qinghai was online! Jigme explained that his school was offering nomad children 24-hour global Internet access for free. "They can come here after class and go online. We encourage that. They can be connected to the world from our little school in Qinghai."

Jigme went on to explain, "It is the first private school in this region, meaning we have had no government funding support. So we did it on our own. Our school welcomes any nomad children to attend regardless of ethnicity or religion. We have Tibetans, Muslims, and Manchurians. At our school, education is free. It is all paid for with cheese."

This page intentionally left blank

CHAPTER 5

THE POSITIVE ENERGY BANK:
Quantum Economics Taught by Lamas and Bodhisattvas

THE AGE OF KALI: TURNING POSITIVE INTENTION INTO INDIVIDUAL ACTION

Lhasa, 2002. Gongar Airport is constructed on the banks of the Brahmaputra River, the mother river of India. Tibet's melting glaciers are the source of water that nourishes many rivers in Asia: China's Yangtze and Yellow Rivers; Southeast Asia's Irrawaddy, Salween, and Mekong; South Asia's Indus, Ganges, and Brahmaputra. On my arrival in Lhasa, I was impressed by the power of the Brahmaputra's rushing waters. Sadly, in the years to come I would observe these waters becoming less and less. By 2010, the Brahmaputra alongside Gongar was a mere creek with Sahara-type sand dunes on each side, the direct effect of global warming.

Having taken the first flight out from Beijing, it was still morning when we arrived. Dou Yan started filming as I climbed into one of the waiting jeeps. Even though it was midsummer, the air was thin and cold from the high altitude.

Dou Yan suggested we begin by visiting the Tara temple. There are 21 Tara female deities in Tibetan Buddhism, each of which can remove a different obstacle. It was local custom to visit the temple when arriving in—or leaving—Lhasa.

Upon entering the temple's inner chamber, I found myself staring at the penetrating composure of the female deity Tara, whose significance would become increasingly important for me in years to come. The hand of White Tara, reaching out to help others, has an eye on it, the message being that seeing and observing suffering is the first step, but is not enough. It must be accompanied by practical action to remedy the problem. This hand would become the symbol of our future social enterprise, "Shambhala Serai."

I rang the number a friend had given me. It was the home of a famous lama or *Rinpoche*.[1]

"Yes, Pemba here," a voice answered. "Rinpoche is now in Lhasa. Tomorrow I will bring you to see him."

The next day, Pemba and I met for the first time.

He took me to Rinpoche's house, a quiet Tibetan courtyard beside Chakpori Medicine Hill—the place where Tibetan medical science originated during the seventh century. The hill was covered with *longda* prayer flags. Hanging prayer flags is a very core part of Tibetan culture. The prayers are carved on wooden blocks. When the monks print prayers on colored flags—each color represents a universal element—they recite prayers with deep intention, transferring positive energy to the flag itself. Flags are hung across mountain passes, rivers, or key natural energy centers or cross-vortexes. When the wind blows, it spreads the positive energy embedded in the printed prayers, in all directions.

Chapkpori has an impressive cliff on the *lingkuo*[2] pilgrimage route. Hundreds of people prostrate there every day. The shear rock is carved with an infinite pantheon of Buddhist deities, painted in the brightest of colors. Staring at this vast cliff mural, I couldn't help thinking that on the one hand the deity images are very traditional, but on the other hand, as an abstraction, the mural is quite modernist. Modern art, with its emphasis on color juxtaposition, in its finest epoch, might just reach this level of expressionism.

Ancient arts, ethnic tradition, and indigenous people possess many ideas and ways of doing things that are holistic and modernistic at the same time. Actually, the two are not necessarily in conflict. In many spheres, indigenous knowledge compounds what we have, because we have forgotten or ignored what they achieved. We should not be cajoled into thinking that what we do or have is modern.

Just because we can type something into a computer or play on an iPhone, does that really make us all that modern and intelligent?

Within a few moments of short conversation, Rinpoche would shatter the assumptions I had been brought up with and change my way of thinking.

"Most people are focused on material life," Rinpoche explained. "They are very busy keeping up with the material, stressed and very unhappy. Money and wealth create an illusion of satisfaction, but usually create more suffering. With more things to possess, more to take care of, comes more suffering. Materialism will temporarily make you happy. People always want more. We call it desire. Satisfy yourself, with just enough money, enough things, without pursuing more. Then you will be happy. Otherwise, you will never be satisfied."

"Shangri-la is a misspelling of the term 'Shambhala.' An author named James Hilton wrote a book called *Lost Horizons* about a lost kingdom in Tibet, without knowing what he was writing about," Rinpoche laughed. "Hilton never even visited Tibet, or Asia for that matter."[3]

Rinpoche explained that we are living in the *Kali Yulga*, or Age of Destruction. It is prophesied as a period of human short-term self-interested desire to control the earth's resources, and blind pursuit of material greed, causing cycles of war, poverty, reactive terror, new incurable diseases, and resource exhaustion and environmental desecration, which stimulate unprecedented natural disasters. In short, it is a period in which humans suffer from their actions.[4] Shambhala, by contrast, is a future realm of peace, equity, and environmental respect. Shambhala arises out of the destruction from this Kali era, which we are now in.

"We can journey to Shambhala through meditation, dreams, or our every day living," Rinpoche continued. "Our world can become Shambhala, if we have this intention. But only *we* can make it happen. By turning positive intention into individual action."

THE POSITIVE ENERGY BANK: EARN INTEREST ON WHAT YOU GIVE

In the center of old Lhasa lies the Jokhang Monastery, a major religious site in Lhasa. Built in the seventh century by Songtsan Gampo, the Tibetan king who unified Tibet, it holds the sacred Jowo image of Buddha, personally blessed by Siddhārtha Gautama Buddha, some 2,500 years ago.

Every day, pilgrims wait in line for hours just to glimpse the Jowo. Thousands of pilgrims prostrate at the door of Jokhang, throughout the day, and often into the night. They send positive energy in the form of prayers, through their intention.

It is said, if one makes a wish to the Jowo, it will be granted. A skeptic would call it superstition. But I have tried this many times. It works. I started to wonder why.

Maybe the many good intentions, in the form of positive energy electrons, have accumulated at this power vortex. It could be seen as a kind of positive energy bank.

Think of it this way: text messages can be sent through space, via a satellite and back down to earth. That means a message is traveling vast distances by electronic waves, just like a radio signal, relaying an intention. If we perceive text messaging as just a mechanized extension of our mind, then all of this makes perfect sense.

It certainly makes sense for anyone studying quantum physics.

Actually, through the empirical process we categorize what is "scientific" and what is not, putting each into a separate box and labeling it, thereby underestimating the power of our own mental thought process.

This was one of the deepest lessons that I learned from the lamas of Tibet. Mind power can be vast and interconnected with our universe, that is, if it is released.

With that in mind, let's think of a pilgrimage site as a positive energy bank. Energy borrowed must be returned, presumably with interest. This can come in the form of good deeds to benefit less fortunate others. Among all philosophies of the Himalayan region, almsgiving is beneficial merit or good karma. It means positive intention is extended to others. Something one does for others will return. If one receives, one should give. It all comes down to the question of intention.

It is the economic law of positive karma. It redefines the concept of quantum economics.

At the entrance to Jokhang Monastery is an image of the Tibetan protector spirit Jambala. He is rotund, bearded, and holds a mongoose in his arms that spits jewels from its mouth. Jambala is the protector of assets and wealth. He is a popular spirit that is often seen in places of business and in the reception areas of many Tibetan-run backpacker guesthouses.

Chinese visitors often mistakenly call him the "god of wealth" and ask him to grant fortune and make stock prices rise! The Tibetan Buddhist way of understanding is somewhat different.

Jambala protects assets and wealth, but wealth carries greater social responsibility. One can have resources, but one should not use these selfishly or wastefully. The whole point is that these resources should be extended to help others less fortunate. In most Himalayan philosophies, there is a notion of community over self. Individual lives come and go, but the community can be sustainable.

In other words: give when you get, because you get when you give.

COMPASSIONATE CAPITALISM AND THE ECONOMICS OF THREE BODHISATTVAS

Passing many prostrating pilgrims, I entered the heavy red gate of Jokhang Monastery, smothered in the smell of incense and yak butter oil. I crawled up a narrow staircase to the rooftop, looking for Nyima Tsering, the mercurial abbot of Jokhang, famed for taking ancient Buddhist ideals and putting them in an entirely modern and practical context. Many young and far-thinking Chinese were inspired by his outspoken views. Rich Chinese sought his guidance when they realized wealth was not the only answer. Chinese officials were jittery over his moral stance on economic and environmental issues.

Nyima Tsering was on the rooftop of Jokhang, overlooking the doorway where pilgrims come to prostrate. The surrounding mountains were covered with snow. They gave the golden rooftops with their curving lines a sense of loftiness as if the entire place were a palace floating above the clouds.

He offered yak butter tea.

"The monks are too busy sweeping up cigarettes and Kodak film cartons left by the tourists," he complained. "They have no time for meditation. This is becoming a problem that is interfering with the process of concentration. How can monks help visitors seeking answers, when our monks are too busy cleaning up the garbage visitors have left behind with their questions?"

When asked how to find Shangri-la, Nyima Tsering responded, "The question is not how to find Shangri-la, but how to seek it back. In the race for economic development, we build factories and modernize technology and chase money. We lose our human nature, human morality, all polluted. People throughout the world are now questioning the current status quo. Why? Because materialist consumption did not bring more happiness; rather, it brought many frustrations. Balance is missing. To have economy, industry, and Western modernization is not enough. If we lose the human side of our world, in the end, we will have to find Shangri-la and bring it back."

We walked around the monastery's circumambulation path, lined with enormous brass prayer wheels, containing sutras tucked within. Each time the wheels are turned by pilgrims or visitors, it has the same effect as reading the sutra. The more the wheel is turned, the more the prayer is repeated. In this sense, Jokhang is always surrounded by the whirling energy emitted from concentric prayer spinning. Tibetans, while deeply pious are also pragmatic. Nyima Tsering explained, "Prayer wheels must be turned clockwise, not counterclockwise. Clocks cannot be turned backwards." The word "revolution" in English literally means a complete 360-degree turning of a wheel, or the completion of a cycle. The notion of a "Peaceful Revolution" is about positive cyclical transformation.

Here on the top of the world, one monk's voice dared to challenge the fundamentals of a world order, which he saw as not assuring shared prosperity, but rather shared self-destruction.

Nyima Tsering leaned forward and poured more yak butter tea. Was this Tibetan politeness, or was he making a statement by filling the cup to the point of overflow?

"Too much material wealth is being spent on war and mutual deceit to conquer others. If governments were to adopt values of spirituality as a moral basis of action and combine them with rational materialism, then we would all be moving in the direction of a real Shambhala."

Of all the people I would meet on my journey, it was this mercurial monk abbot of Jokhang Monastery who would put a collection of philosophical ideas and practical observations into a broader context. He was the one who allowed me to connect the dots. One day, his ideas would turn into a fresh economic paradigm: the Himalayan Consensus.

With a flourish of his saffron robes, Nyima Tsering then brought me to a shrine room at the end of a corridor. There were three images of Bodhisattvas.[5]

Nyima Tsering explained the function of each one. "The one in the center is Avalokitshavra, who represents compassion. Manjushuri, on the left side, represents wisdom, and holds aloft a sword to cut ignorance at its root. On the other side is Vajrapani, representing power. He holds a *dorge*—like a thunderbolt. He has the power to shatter obstacles and illusion."

Nyima Tsering explained how all three are needed—together. "Expressing compassion emotionally, or mindlessly, without rational pragmatism and sufficient resources, achieves nothing. Maybe in the end it even creates problems for others. On the other hand an individual or nation may have economic power and technological know-how. But without compassion, then both the power and technology will be misused."

Nyima Tsering taught me to prioritize these ideals as expressed in the form of the three Bodhisattvas, to keep them in balance and to use them together: wisdom and power with compassion. This framework, he explained, can be applied to everything. From government administration and economic development, to just living one's life on a personal level, in both caring for others and caring for oneself.

The idea of "compassionate capital" would come from this explanation.[6]

This page intentionally left blank

CHAPTER 6

CREATING SHAMBHALA:
Building a Social Enterprise on Top of the World

ECONOMICS ENLIGHTENED

Lhasa, 2005. It was already 9:30 a.m. But the narrow whitewashed adobe alleyways of Lhasa's old city were just beginning to awaken. That is because things start later in Lhasa. While clocks are set to Beijing time, local people follow the sun.

At 3,600 meters above sea level, breathing becomes difficult. Having just arrived the night before, I still felt wheezy from the altitude, as if everything were in slow motion.

Stopping for breakfast at a food stall selling *palip*, Tibetan flatbread. "How much for one flat bread?" I asked the woman.

"Five *jiao* (fifty cents)," she said, smiling.

As I pulled five Chinese ten-cent bills from my pocket, three children rushed up. They tugged at my sleeves, hands held out, begging.

I handed the fifty cents to the stall lady. Smiling, she leaned over and gave each begging child one ten-cent piece. "Now go," she told them. "Leave the foreigner alone."

The kids ran off giggling.

Stunned, I quickly ran the economics through my head. She had sold me Tibetan bread for fifty cents, but had given most of it away to the begging children. With only twenty cents in her hand, she was technically covering the cost of the dough and keeping the same amount she had given each child for herself.

In most cities of the world, locals might easily cheat money from an unwitting newly arrived foreigner. But giving it to begging children, leaving just a margin over break-even? This sudden glimpse into Tibetan thinking challenged my economic assumptions.

While following two documentary expeditions in search of the mythical kingdom of Shambhala (Shangri-la), I had been granted a rare audience with Nanqin Rinpoche, then the highest-ranking surviving tantric practitioner in Tibet. Elderly and frail, his long white beard gave him a noble look. He sat on a raised dais, wrapped in warm robes against the evening cold, in a room heaving with incense.

"Where is Shambhala?" I had asked. Knowing it is a metaphysical state of mind rather than an actual place, I clumsily asked what meditation technique could zoom me there on a cloud, as if I were about to board an airplane.

With a mystical look in his eyes, he had nodded and then responded. "It is not anywhere. You cannot find it by searching. You cannot go there through meditation either. It is through compassionate action, giving to others, that we can create a better world. We can visualize the future through meditation. But without action, it is useless. Only through each person's individual action every day, bringing that vision to become reality, can we arrive in Shambhala. There is no other way."

This is when I stopped searching.

Inspired by people I met during my three-year journey making documentaries in Tibet, I decided to move there. Closing my investment consultancy, I acquired an old three-story Tibetan house in Lhasa and began to create a social enterprise.

The house was located in a narrow alleyway in the Tibetan quarter called the *Barkor*, after the famous circumambulation route that wrapped around the central Jokhang Monastery. Every day the route was thronged with devotees from all over Tibet who made it a pilgrimage route. Radiating from the market, a labyrinth of alleyways connecting whitewashed stone and adobe buildings formed the old city.[1]

The Chinese did not like this neighborhood. They kept to the new commercial area of the city, sprawling with karaoke, nightclubs, brothels and massage parlors, every kind of Chinese restaurant, and cheap electronic shops. The Chinese section lay to the west of the Potala Palace, while the Tibetan section was to the east. The two worlds faced off in stark contrast to each other. I found myself living in an all-Tibetan society where the rhythm of life and tradition remained more or less intact, as it may have centuries ago.

I awoke each day to the sound of prayers being chanted just outside my window. Nuns sat in groups collecting alms from passersby. "Begging" or "almsgiving"—depends how you look at it—represents another set of economic relationships. Everywhere throughout the Barkor, nuns and monks sit in groups along alleyways and chant mantra or read sutra. They receive alms from people passing by. Often it is just small change, but they need this to live on. Chanting begins early in the morning and lasts into the evening. An immediate Western reaction might be to label this as "begging," which has a negative connotation. However, it is not begging.

The chanting represents a service, in the form of prayer. In a Tibetan context, this is a service no different from what might be provided by a doctor, psychotherapist, or lawyer. Passing pedestrians are busy with their daily work. Maybe they do not have time, or they forget to say their daily mantra and prayers, which are an integral part of Tibetan life. However, by giving donations in the rush to get from one place to another, they gain the benefit of those chants and prayers being done for them along the way.

In the realm of Tibetan thought, these prayers can ward off negativity by spreading positive energy. Tibetans share a deep religiosity with their environment. One intimately faces life and death on a daily basis due to extreme weather changes on the Himalayan plateau. In a practical sense, protector prayers can remind one to take precautions and act in a caring and thoughtful way. Certainly avoiding accidents is more cost effective than going to a doctor or lawyer afterward.

Again, if we apply quantum physics, it all makes sense. It is the economic law of the interconnectivity of everything—the economic quantum hologram matrix.

When I spoke with Chinese officials and even those Chinese researching Tibetan issues, there was a terrible disdain for such practices as full-form prostration while reciting mantra. The standard comment was "These Tibetans spend too much time prostrating before temples and not enough time engaged in productivity." The Chinese view was that only high productivity could maintain social stability, as everyone would become wealthier and busier, consuming material goods or collecting brands. They were shocked when I suggested that 50 reps of full prostration might be a better workout than going to a fitness club. To me, Tibetans were living holistic lives long before health clubs existed. Again, it was another way of looking at and understanding the ways people live, work, pray, and understand their own place in the greater scheme of things.

THE SOCIAL ENTERPRISE PROJECT

Pembala joined me to work on the social enterprise project. We had met while filming "Searching for Shangri-la" in 2002. Together we turned the old Tibetan courtyard into a nine-room boutique hotel, with restaurant and teahouse, restored in a period style of the Thirteenth Dalai Lama (1876–1933).[2] Himself a carpenter, Pembala assembled a team of 30 Tibetan artisans from his hometown outside Lhasa, a village known for wood craftsmen and painters. His father had been a woodcraftsman, and the art had been passed from father to son. When the building next door was for sale, we acquired it as well. Now with the two buildings running the length of the alley, we had a full street side, and we added shops and craft studios.

Architecture represents each ethnic group's dialogue with their own environment, and is critical to cultural identity. China's government had for decades embarked on policies of destroying local architectural style en mass, replacing it with faceless cement structures. Such nation-wide uniformity assured lack of individuality by uprooting each community's identity. Of course, before communism in 1949, China was a nation with vastly diverse local cultures, each with its own architecture, customs, language, and way of life—now all gone. Only in the remote ethnic regions of China's west did cultural individuality still breathe.

Over the years ahead, only local artisans were engaged in our restorations. Doing everything in a traditional manner, we kept as much of the original buildings as possible intact, using old materials to rebuild new sections that were collapsed or damaged. Even when purchasing paint, we sought pigments ground from stone.

We heard of a stone-carving master who lived in the Nechung Monastery, on a hill just outside the city that historically houses the protector oracle of the Dalai Lamas. We found him one October afternoon when the mountains were radiant with red leaves, sitting cross-legged behind a pile of *mani* stones, each bearing a Tibetan mantra that he had inscribed himself. We asked him to carve deities and auspicious symbols on stones. The designs had been carefully selected and approved by Nyima Tsering and Beru Khyentse Rinpoche. We would insert them into the walls of our hotel as decor. Over six years, he would do all the stone carving for the three hotel properties we developed. For each project the designs became more complex. By becoming his patron, we provided steady income that supported his art. Soon his carving became famous, as many came to our hotels to admire this work.

Craftsmanship in Tibet is still taught through oral tradition from father to son, master to apprentice. Yet with so much steel and cement construction these days, such skills will soon become extinct. Our team of Tibetan craftsmen worked with us for six years, completing four hotels, three medical clinics, workshops for the disabled, and a school.

In the late afternoon, the workers rested. Sitting in a circle, they sang and drank *chang*, Tibetan liquor. These were joyous moments filled with laughter. Then they picked up their tools and continued working until dark, singing the whole time.

In Tibet, the concepts of work and relaxation were not in conflict. They blended into a way of life.

One morning, when construction of the courtyard hotel was nearing completion, a little girl from the countryside showed up at our door. She had wide eyes, long hair down to her waist, and only a basic fifth grade education. Her name was Gusan. She offered to help clean up the construction debris.

The site was a mess, but Gusan cleaned like crazy. Emerging from my partially finished room each morning, I found Gusan sitting in the sun on the veranda studying English. Everyday before starting work, she asked how to pronounce a new word.

When the hotel opened, Gusan stayed on, cleaning rooms, always practicing English. She graduated from room cleaner to room inspector. Her English improved. She then started working at the front desk, and soon managed the reception.

"Treat people as if they were what they ought to be and you help them to become what they are capable of being," were the words of eighteenth-century German philosopher Johann Wolfgang von Goethe. It became our motto.

House of Shambhala would become the first licensed "family guest house" in the old section of Lhasa. Its example sparked a wave of heritage house conversions. Some became fancy boutique hotels, others just tiny family inns. Regardless, Tibetans were able to utilize old buildings for a new purpose, protecting their architecture and reinvigorating their neighborhoods.

We opened our doors expecting mostly foreign clients. But after the 2008 riots that swept over the Tibetan plateau, restrictions on foreign travel became very tight. To our surprise, more Chinese began staying with us, wanting to experience Tibetan culture, probably due to the surge of Buddhism that was now filling the gap in a society that had become devoid of spirituality after decades of communism. During the day, many Tibetans doing *kora* circumambulation in the old city would stop by our hotel to visit the shrines we always kept lit and have sweet milk or butter tea.

House of Shambhala became a micro-model for development. There was no theory. We just did it by interacting with people and working from the ground up. Through the process of doing and creating, we embarked on what would become a social enterprise.

THE ECONOMIC INTERCONNECTIVITY OF EVERYTHING

Awaking each morning to the sound of worshipers reciting mantra while passing along the alleyway outside my window, I would buy Tibetan flatbread from the lady who gave her profits to wandering street children.

At the alleyway crossroads of *Tsongsikhang* market, dried Tibetan cheese was piled high at stalls. The fragrance of red chili and yellow cumin overflowed from the wooden trays of spice vendors. This juncture between alleyways was an ancient traders' market, in unbroken service since the seventh century when the city was first built. Nomads from Kham, wearing chunks of amber and turquoise around their necks and red tassels tied to their hair from which coral pieces dangled, chatted into dusk, excitedly trading semiprecious stones, saddles, and pelts. All of this occurred daily, just minutes from my door. I observed each day how every aspect of the kaleidoscope of color in these alleyways was actually part of an integrated economy. The success of our social enterprise would depend upon joining that integration.

During afternoons, Pembala and I walked through the neighborhood, visiting artisans in their shops, asking if they wanted to work on our products. Together we designed everything we needed for this little hotel. We sketched pencil designs on scraps of paper for the artisans. Only traditional materials were to be used.

Soon the whole neighborhood became stakeholders in Shambhala.

When creating coffee cups, plates, and bowls for our first restaurant, we traced the source of Tibetan ceramics by talking with migrant vendors squatting in the alleyways selling earthenware. The source led to a village three hours from Lhasa. Here the earth was deep red. The pottery village specialized in ceramic vats to store *chang*. However, production was in decline because Chinese-manufactured plastic and aluminum products were cheaper. With no money in pottery, young people left to find work in cities. We suggested modifying the natural shape of traditional ceramic vats and storage bowls to create cups, plates, and vases for shampoo and bath lotion. With three hotels and three restaurants under conceptualization, we kept the villagers quite busy revitalizing their craft. The best thing about the plates and coffee cups was that no two matched at all. It was all just pure art.

The restaurant tearoom was decorated with antique door panels collected from western Tibet during the filming of "Shambhala Sutra." When it turned out that guests were keen to purchase and collect them, we made reproductions small enough to pack in a suitcase. Before we knew it, the entire neighborhood was making them.

We had sparked an artisan revival without even knowing it.

Tibetans live by a natural rhythm. There was no separation in their minds between the spiritual and material worlds. Their thought process is intrinsic. Time is somewhat irrelevant. For instance, the word *guongda*, "afternoon," really means anything from lunchtime onward, including all night. Things flowed without specific context or deadlines. By living in the old city and interacting with Tibetans each day, I was making a conscious effort to step out of our Western preconceived rational thinking box.

Stepping into their world was like swimming into a rich yet dimensionless void in which the intrinsic senses become key to navigating the crosscurrents of interconnectivity. My own concepts of time and space changed. It became clear how even what might seem on the surface to be a small inconsequential thought or action could have the potential of colossal impact. Within this context, I had a realization. The inspirational value of even a tiny micro-project, if successful, could have transformational implications on a global scale.

I began to think about the economic interconnectivity of all things. Whatever was happening in our neighborhood was intimately connected with the sustainability of the Tibetan plateau, and in turn global climate change. All things were interconnected, in ways that often were not apparent, but always present.

By restoring traditional homes as small family businesses, shops, teahouses, or guest lodges, people would not have to move out, as developers wanted, and some as government officials insisted. The neighborhood could have an economic platform that would evolve and sustain culture rather than change or break it. People would continue to live in the old neighborhood, buy yak butter for their tea and family shrines. The nomads in Amdo could continue herding yak. And the patterns of grazing that had kept balance in the grasslands for millennia could remain.

WEAVING RUGS TO SAVE TIGERS

One afternoon, Gusan accompanied me to the market. It was a large two-story building on the circumambulation route. Inside there were many wholesale and retail dealers, selling everything from plastic turquoise to rugs. We went up to the second floor and looked at the rugs.

I found a tiger rug.

The pattern matched traditional motifs I'd seen in books on the subject. "This is the one we want to buy," I exclaimed, and began bargaining. She gently grabbed my sleeve and pulled me aside, whispering in my ear, "Why do you want to buy that? It is not made by Tibetans, but by Chinese."

I was stunned. "But it is a traditional rug, right?"

"No," she whispered even more softly. "It is a traditional design. The rug is made by Chinese, in factories either in Shanghai or Guangzhou." She nodded toward the salespeople. "They are all Chinese dealers. They will not sell Tibetan products. All of these products sold by these dealers are coming from the Chinese cities, not from Tibetan regions. They are all machine made, mass produced. Look," she said, leading me back over to the rug, touching it with an open palm that was already well worn from years of work as a child. "This is all synthetic," she sighed. "It is not real wool. The dye is chemical, not natural pigment. Why are we buying a Chinese-made rug, when Tibetan weavers have no work and are losing their traditional artisan skills?"

I was taken aback by this instant lesson in local economics and pondered it for a moment, staring at the Chinese dealers who were pushing with peppery voices the wonderful characteristics of their rugs.

We immediately went back to Shambhala House, and found Pembala on our sunny terrace sipping yak butter tea. Together we brainstormed a plan to revive Tibetan rug weaving.

Pembala explained that his wife was once a rug weaver who had won awards for her skill. But the average salary of a rug weaver was only about RMB 300 (less than 50 dollars) a month. She actually made more money selling cigarettes at *Tsongksikhang* market than weaving rugs. In any case, the local rug factory had been forced out of business by growing inflation, flat wages, and a rapidly dwindling traditional rug market due to Chinese mass manufacturing. How could it compete with the Chinese machine-made synthetic rugs with their cheap chemical dyes?

We did our own market survey. After visiting all of the shops in Lhasa's main tourist sites, we estimated that 90 percent of Tibetan-style rugs for sale came from other cities in China. Of those "real" Tibetan rugs on the market, most were imported from Nepal, made by exiled Tibetans. Locally Tibetan-made rugs were actually quite rare.

In the old days, tiger skins symbolized protector spirits. They were used to wrap sutra boxes, as meditation mats, or were hung on temple doors as a wrathful warning to demons. Tibetans prized such skins, respected and cared for them. Using tiger skins sparingly, Tibetans maintained a cycle of balance with and respect for their environment. Such skins were passed down through generations and carefully guarded.

The Himalayan mountain range and foothills were the tiger's natural habitat until the nineteenth century. The British Raj organized expeditions for tiger trophies and bounty hunting. This led to wholesale decimation of the Himalayan tiger, disrupting entire cycles of environmental balance within a very short time.

At the outset of the twentieth century, the Himalayan tiger was all but gone. Responsive to changing conditions, Tibetans began weaving tiger rugs instead, which displaced past hunting practices. This natural evolution was driven by need and adaptation to changing environmental conditions. The tiger rug pattern emerged from this lifestyle evolution. It became increasingly popular as Tibetans replaced real tiger skins with woven ones. By doing so, they adjusted lifestyles to rebalance unnaturally distorted environmental conditions.

We decided to start a micro-weaving enterprise. Pembala bought metal frames used for weaving, and our woodworkers made wooden turnstiles for wool. We set them up in one of our shops and engaged women from rural villages who had rug weaving skills, but no other education. Soon we had a little rug-weaving cooperative called Save the Tibetan Tiger.

One of our staff posted on the wall of our shop an old tinted picture of British Raj hunters with pork chop sideburns and waxed mustaches accompanied by Indian scouts with their guns posing grandly over tiger carcasses. The staff wrote under the picture, "The British Raj hunted tigers, Tibetans wove rugs. Buy a rug. Save a tiger!"

All the wool came from nomadic herdsmen. At our workshop, girls pounded natural dyes, mixing them in big copper vats, and then took them to the rooftop, to hang the freshly dyed wool in the vibrantly strong Lhasa sun. Guests, who climbed the rickety wooden stairs to our rooftop garden for a view of Potala Palace, often found themselves walking into a kaleidoscope of colors from the strings of wool being dried and spun on wooden turnstiles into tight balls. The tiger rugs were woven on the premises. Today, tiger rugs adorn each room in House of Shambhala and our second hotel, Shambhala Palace.

The tiger rug project achieved many goals. We were reviving local artisan skill sets, while empowering women with a sense of cultural identity and self-respect through employment. In a sense, the tiger rug project went beyond artisan revival.

It reminded us to adjust our own lifestyle needs to world conditions as others destroy our environment.

THE SILENT POWER OF EMPOWERING THE DISABLED

I visited Anu for the first time during the winter 2006. It was a cold morning. Sharp sunlight streamed through the window of her tiny room. Anu was an elderly Tibetan lady. She lived alone on the upper floor of a traditional Tibetan-style courtyard home. She was crippled at age four when a tractor ran over her leg, severing it. She never married, and had no children

Anu used a crude wooden crutch to move about her apartment. Her place was simple and bare, except for a Buddhist shrine and her old Singer sewing machine. She pointed to the machine and explained that she liked to sew.

Wrapping a few pieces of black cloth around my hand, I indicated a head with horns. Could she make a yak puppet for children? I was certain children would love this. And if we succeeded with a yak, well, we could then make a goat.

Anu made 30 puppets that quickly sold. Hotel guests wanted more. We purchased sewing machines and soon had a collective of puppet makers with disabilities. We added puppets for other nomadic animals such as the wolf and mastiff dog. Two volunteer Montessori teachers helped write a book about each animal's role in the delicate ecology of the Tibetan plateau, published in three languages—English, Tibetan and Chinese—and illustrated by local Tibetan artists.

We called the workshop the Tibet Children's Initiative. It empowered marginalized handicapped individuals and raised children's awareness of environmental issues.

Empowering the marginalized became the main motto of Shambhala. In fact, almost none of our employees had anything beyond a fifth-grade education. Most were women. Half of the employees were disabled. As restoration on other buildings got underway, our workshop expanded. Every pillowcase, bedspread, curtain, and lantern in the new hotels would be handmade in this workshop.

One day, Pembala and I found a woman named Dhondup Lhamo sitting alone on a bench, struggling to sew. We tried to speak to her, only to find that she could not speak or hear. Using simple sign language, she led us through several narrow alleyways to a Tibetan house where she lived with a couple who had raised her. She had been abandoned as a child because of her disability. She was raped as a teenager and gave birth to a child, with no means of supporting herself or the child. She was hoping to find work and wanted to learn how to sew.

The next day, Semola, the head of our workshop (himself disabled in one leg) began to teach her how to sew. She learned to embroider the image of the helping hand of White Tara. It was the same deity hand I had first seen in 2002, at the Tara Monastery along the road from the airport to Lhasa. An eye upon the palm observes suffering, and fingers extend, reaching out to help.

She loved that motif and began to sew it on everything. It became our logo.

CREATING THE REALM OF SHAMBHALA IN DAILY LIFE

The House of Shambhala was more than a hotel. It became a kind of community center. All items in the hotel—curtains, napkins, bedspreads, blankets, pillowcases, lanterns, laundry bags, toothbrush holders—everything you can imagine that is used in a hotel operation, was made in our own workshop for Tibetans with disabilities. The old building had storefronts facing the street, and workshops behind. According to an old map of Lhasa, the site of our workshop was once a teahouse run by a nunnery.

My whole mindset had changed. Awakening each morning in Lhasa to the sound of chanting in the street, looking out over the snow-dusted mountains surrounding the city, my thoughts were not about how much money we could make or how to spend it on lifestyle, but rather how many eye operations we could fund, how many more children could be placed in our school, how many more disabled we could bring into our workshop. It gave me more personal gratification to see the positive impact that our small enterprise was having on other people's lives than just thinking about profit. Of course, the business had to be profitable to achieve what we were doing. Yet the two were not in conflict. In fact, there was no duality. This is where the lessons of monk Nyima Tsering and the economics of three Bodhisattvas came in: view everything as multidimensional.

Between 2006 and 2012, our workshop for Tibetans with disabilities opened craft lines ranging from textiles to clothing to turquoise jewelry to lanterns. Their products were either used in our hotels or sold in our shops. In addition we undertook projects for local medical care (Empower the Monks as Medics[3]), fundraising for blindness eradication (Let the People See[4]), and education (Give the Children a Chance[5]), administratively supported through our hotel operation.

A social enterprise evolved from our collective experiences. A business can be profitable, while protecting local culture, environment, and even pioneering social programs.

During the same period, we also opened three more heritage hotels. Shambhala Palace was located in a restored lama's palace only a five-minute walk from House of Shambhala. In another ancient pilgrimage city, Gyangtze, we undertook the first restoration of a building in the old quarter, setting an example.

But the most challenging project was located 4200 meters above sea level in a canyon of hot spring pools considered sacred. These hot springs had been granted to a village of disabled nomads. Under government policies of settlement, they had been previously located in an area where upstream mining contaminated their water supply. Out of 500 villagers, 300 were disabled, the majority being women. As compensation, the government offered them the hot springs to run as a "resort." Of course they had no idea how to run a resort, so we partnered with them.

To create the new hotel was a bigger challenge than expected. We wanted the building to blend into the surrounding mountains. The topography meant that it would have to be scaled alongside the edges of the canyon. Of course, traditional Tibetan architecture could achieve this. They had been building monasteries on cliff edges and precipices for millennia. When we discovered developers tearing down an old building in Lhasa, Pembala decided this ancient edifice would be perfect if it could be moved to the cliff site. Our team stayed beside the site and took the ancient stones and wooden pillars one by one, as the developers torn them down. We saved and numbered the materials. At the canyon they were reassembled as our hotel.

A center was built within the hotel grounds to provide programs ranging from incense to yogurt making to yak fur processing and fine wool for sweaters. We also installed a clinic on the hotel premises with a monk as doctor offering medical treatment to nomads and pilgrims. By 2012, the doctor was receiving sometimes up to 40 people a day. He asked me to go raise funds to build a hospital. At the time of this writing, we have completed the first phase, a 20-bed ward.

However, none of this was easy going. Just prior to Beijing's hosting the 2008 summer Olympics, our projects were interrupted on March 14 when Lhasa erupted in ethnic rioting against Chinese rule. The rioting became violent. A kind of "Tibetan Intifada" tore across the Tibetan plateau. From Tibet, the disturbances spread north, south, and east through the provinces of Gansu, Qinghai, and Sichuan.

As the crackdown got underway, tourists were expelled.

With no tourism during Tibet's warm summer months, everyone joined hands to restore the then newly acquired lama's palace, which was dilapidated and badly in need of caring restoration. Within a year, the Shambhala Palace was completed. True to a lama's palace, the building looked like a monastery rather than a hotel. Shambhala Palace opened its doors in 2010, and has been thriving since.

It was actually a monument to the determination of the Tibetan people to hold onto their culture even under the most difficult and degrading of circumstances. In the years to come, I would see that this applies to all people everywhere, whether Tibetans, Chinese, Jews, Palestinians, Afghans, Kurds, Africans, Native Americans, African Americans, or any race or nationality. The result will always be the same.

People's culture, heritage, and ethnic pride are core to their soul. If you pour cement on grass, the stems of grass will eventually rise through and crack the cement. Spirituality and soul, the collective unconscious of a people, cannot be bought by materialism or uprooted with infrastructure. As Nyma Tsering taught, spirituality can be more powerful than materialism.

Don't kid yourself. The "we can make them like us" idea does not work. All the aid programs in Afghanistan and Iraq did not eradicate any of the cultural prerogatives of the people there. The depth of one's culture and pride in ethnicity are always present, sometimes waiting and dormant, until a crack allows them to rise up. Trust me, they always will.

By restoring ancient buildings as heritage hotels (powered with solar energy), a micro-model for community development was created on the top of the world. Ecotourism as a business protected local architecture, in turn providing community social support in the form of medical clinics, workshops for the disabled, and a school. Each heritage hotel is a profitable business that itself protects local culture. Moreover, it gives people self-pride in running a business while making a positive impact on their community and environment. That is the essential idea behind a social enterprise. It is not something that needs a fancy definition, an economic formula, or a measurement matrix theory. It is only as simple as what I have described here.

If it can be done in Tibet, it can be done anywhere.

PART III

DIVERSIFIED LOCALIZATION:
Empowering People Brings Sustainable Security

Buddha renounced politics to go sit under a tree. Now it's time for Buddha to get back into politics, not sit under a tree. Because the trees are all being cut down.

—Ian Baker National Geographic *Explorer and Author*

Sustainable local economics and grass roots community development are a basis for water and food security, prevention of ethnic violence and terror, in both the developing and developed world.

Maybe our economic assumptions have been wrong. People are not necessarily motivated by greed alone. People's strength of ethnic identity and cultural pride are equally important as their material development. Maybe we need new measurements of satisfaction and success.

The Himalayan Consensus presents a fresh economic paradigm that does not recognize any one model or economic theory. It is drawn from collective experiences across the Himalayan region. The Himalayan Consensus approach is flexible, seeking solutions from local wisdom in the context of changing global conditions. Examples are Bhutan's concept of 'gross national happiness' and Bangladesh's micro-finance. People need micro-finance as much in Detroit as they do in Dhaka.

Himalayan values are based upon the great philosophies of this region: Hinduism, Jainism, Buddhism, Islam, Taoism, and Confucianism. Each emphasizes community over individual, greater social benefit over self, and the importance of helping those less fortunate than you. At least those are the core principles.

Indigenous people are regional custodians of the environment. Their lifestyles embody valuable local wisdom, a living knowledge that can protect our environment. Never has this been so important as now. Our planet faces crisis of water and food security due to climate change. Indigenous wisdom and holistic approaches are badly needed in our economic equations.

Sustainable economics is the best prevention of violence and terror. People turn to extreme measures when they have no outlet to vent their frustration. Conditions of poverty, ethnic marginalization, or loss of resources – such as food and water – can precipitate this. So changes in our financial system are badly needed. Get funding to local businesses. That is the fastest way to empower and enrich communities. It is not all about capital markets that endear a few people to cash in for the short term. It is about the rest of us, our children, their children, and the long-term health of our planet.

Experience shows that when people are marginalized with no hope of improvement, and have no outlets to vent their frustration, extremism arises. This is what the Himalayan Consensus seeks to prevent.

CHAPTER 7

THE DISEMPOWERMENT FACTOR:
Stop Terrorism at Its Root

FIND THE CAUSATIONAL EFFECT OF EXTREMISM TO CHILL IT

Islamabad, 2007. On January 26, 2007, I was at the Marriot Hotel coffee shop in Islamabad where it was rocketed by a large explosion. People dove under tables. Within minutes, media and military swarmed into the lobby. It was the first suicide bombing to hit Pakistan's capital in five years. I had been sitting smack in the center of the targeted zone.

This was the actual Marriot Hotel bomb attack that was later depicted in the Hollywood blockbuster *Zero Dark Thirty*.

I survived, thanks to a thick wall and a security guard, who was tragically killed. Later it was revealed that a young suicide bomber had tried to enter the hotel lobby through the parking lot. A suspicious security guard stopped him, and that brief delay saved my life.

The bomb was timed.

Minutes after the bomb attack, Momin Aga, then secretary to the mayor of Islamabad, showed up at the hotel. Chaos unfolded in the lobby as military, police, and journalists swarmed in, all trying to find out at once what had happened.

Momin was perplexed and lost as to what to do. I was the only American in the place. One phone call after another came ringing in on his cell. "Where should we go?" he asked, not knowing himself.

"Let's go to the bazar," I suggested. "I can bargain for rugs."

He was shocked. "At a moment like this?"

"Believe me, it will be the safest place in the city. Let's go."

Fifteen minutes later, Momin was still receiving frantic calls. I sat cross-legged, on a pile of rugs, quietly observing steam rising from a cup of spiced chai, in a bazaar overflowing with ornately embroidered Punjab pillows.

Thoughts of Lhasa arose from the steam in the chai cup.

Incense rose before a shrine. It permeated the space and clung to the sound of pilgrims shuffling by, paying homage to the Bodhisattva images within the shrine. Inside Johkang Monastery, enigmatic monk Nyima Tsering sat before the altar of Avalokitashavara, the Bodhisattva of Compassion. He explained, "All matter and events in our universe are interconnected. Each effect has its cause. If you disenfranchise a people, they will not sit back and take it. They will come back for revenge. It will take one form or another. This is the law of causational effect. Every action has a counter-reaction. If your action is positive, their reaction will be more positive. If your action is negative, it will breed more negativity. If violent, it will be revenged."

An Asian view of history sees events as cyclical, not linear. According to the monk's interpretation, we are in a vicious cycle that can only end if the cycle is broken or brought to conclusion. Compassion rather than anger can achieve this. Otherwise, it will just continue, even escalate.

As Nyima Tsering once observed, "Some of our world's leaders think by crushing one nation after another, terrorism can be eliminated. Think about it. Does this make rational sense? If you look at what is really happening, it appears the more they try to crush the problem, the more it multiplies. Intelligence and resources should be used to cure disease, alleviate poverty, and address our social ills. Then terrorism will not arise, because there will be no reason for it. So this endless creation and use of weaponry represents abuse of our human intelligence, not its rational application."

My attention returned to the bazaar, and the fragrance emanating from a hot cup of chai. The chaos of what was happening a few blocks away was already gossip in the bazaar. Cell phones kept ringing.

I thought about the young suicide bomber who had almost killed me. Washington think tanks are running all kinds of complex scenarios to figure out how to combat terrorism. Has anyone in these highly paid organizations bothered to ask a very simple, commonsensical question:

why would a young man, with his whole life ahead of him, wish to end it so abruptly?

The only explanation: he had no hope in his future.

ECONOMIC EMPOWERMENT BRINGS A SENSE OF SECURITY

Shortly after the bombing, Riza Mohammad Khan, then Pakistan's foreign secretary, summoned me to the Foreign Ministry. "Terrorism happens not because people have a political agenda, but because they have no hope," Khan explained. "They have been marginalized from society. When the international media demonize their only beliefs, they have no choice left but to become radicalized."

"It is more important to get rid of poverty," Khan sighed, touching the problem at its root. "In Pakistan we are struggling with poverty and looking at alternatives. A new value system is required, calling for closer international cooperation and more balanced trading relationships involving a shared-help development model." He then thought for a moment, staring into a delicate porcelain cup of milk tea on the table before us. "We need better management of the globe. We will destroy it, if we are not careful. We are now a global village."

In the days that followed, I tried to understand what had happened. Why, at that moment, did the suicide bomber attack my hotel? I was the only American within the targeted zone at the time of the explosion. Was his martyrdom in response to something that I, as a symbolic American, had done? The answer, lay in an event earlier in the week.

An American drone had bombed an Islamic *madrassa* school. Flying into Pakistani air space from across the Afghan border, its mission was to kill suspected Taliban members. Eighty children lost their lives. There were no Taliban anywhere nearby.

Why were madrassas targets of American drone attacks?

Many children studying in the madrassas are just street kids. Their parents, often poor, are busy trying to eke out a living. They cannot watch or discipline them. By sending their children to religious schools, they hope the kids will get a social structure that the family cannot provide.

The curriculum comprises religious studies, because the madrassas are not equipped to teach anything else. So when children emerge from the madrassas, they are enriched with Islamic religious knowledge, but lack practical skills necessary to support themselves. Without a sustainable livelihood, they either work in a madrassa—if that is at all feasible—or instead work for a religious organization with a cause.

They are economically disenfranchised and also acutely aware that the Western media belittles their heritage and beliefs. Angry, they turn to the mosque for psychological security and reassurance of identity. It becomes their way of life.

By bombing madrassas, America incubates new generations of potential terrorists. Relatives of the young victims might be expected to use whatever tools available to try and avenge their deaths. By continuously targeting Islamic schools, coalition forces in Afghanistan are almost certain to guarantee an increase in the number of suicide bombers, not a reduction.

Madrassas are seen in Washington and depicted in Western media as hotbeds of fundamentalism. Yet despite all the highly funded think tanks, nobody has thought about how these schools could be turned into incubators of social harmony rather than violence.

A fraction of American taxpayer funds could be used, through appropriate local foundations, to support social work and vocational education. People could be empowered by establishing local cottage industries through the extensive social network of religious schools. What are the costs?

According to the Central Asia Institute, $5,000 is sufficient to support an existing school in Pakistan for one year. It costs $50,000 to build a school and insure its operation for five years. The Maria Helena Foundation supports a women's vocational school for $1,000 a year. A temporary field hospital in Pakistan costs $11,830.

The American taxpayer spends a lot of money on drones that bomb madrassas. The cost of making a Reaper drone runs between $10 and $12 million, while a Predatory drone costs $4.5 million. Just to fly a drone on reconnaissance costs $13,000 per flight hour. Each individual bomb dropped on a madrassa costs between $31,000 per unit for the Jadam bomb and $19,000 per bomb for the Paveway.

All the bombing is useless. We have ignored the most basic equation in all this. Economic empowerment brings a sense of security. People could have a life to look forward to and a means of making it happen. Of course, not all poor and disenfranchised people turn to violence. However, a clear pattern does seem obvious. When any group or people are marginalized—both in terms of identity as well as economy—they may turn to desperate means. Empowering people economically and with the means and respect to preserve and evolve their ethnicity and culture identity will not stop all violence and terrorism, but it will certainly reduce a large part of it.

Should we dare to question the use of American taxpayer money to bomb impoverished schools in Pakistan, when America is sinking in a debt black hole? At the time of this writing, $6 trillion has been spent on wars in Afghanistan, Pakistan, and Iraq. Has this contributed to America's domestic security? It certainly does not help our financial security. The more America bombs Pakistani madrassas, the more Pakistan as a nation and people turn to China as an ally. Meanwhile, to fund our military adventurism, the US Department of the Treasury is turning to China for credit. For the cost of one drone mission to bomb a madrassa, how many vocational schools could be financed in Pakistan?

A mere piddling of the vast funds spent in the drone war that is killing children could be used to provide vocational skills and give them the means to a future worth living for. Then, fewer people might hate us. Actually, most people beyond the Beltway would probably agree—especially within our own military complex—as it is our poor who end up fighting these wars, not the rich. Preventing extremism through economics may prove less costly in the end than fighting it once everything has spun out of control.

But the American government does not sufficiently finance vocational schools for its own people back home.

COMMUNITY EMPOWERMENT THROUGH ZAKAT

Lahore's labyrinthine streets are filled with mixed smells of spices and exhaust fumes and the noise of motorcycle rickshaws. Kamrin Lashari, when previously serving as mayor of Lahore, brought back to life historic neighborhoods and restored the city's heritage-rich old quarter, the Moghul city. He revitalized ancient markets, turning them into modern, open-air pedestrian boulevards with hygienic food stalls and diverse crafts,

Back in Islamabad, as mayor, Lashari was supervising the restoration of an ancient mosque beneath a cliff dotted with Sufi meditation caves. Lashari's vision was to reempower Islamabad's surrounding rural villages with cottage industries and sustainable-tourism development.

Between 2007 and 2009 across South Asia, I was exchanging experiences on social enterprise and community empowerment with political leaders, environmentalists, nongovernmental organizations (NGOs), and social activists. Each individual was creating a holistic economic approach. Each envisioned a new economic paradigm to sustain our planet. The ideas that would become the Himalayan Consensus evolved during this time I spent with these individuals. A few principles emerged:

> *—Ethnicity is core to people's identity. It should be cherished for its individuality, not homogenized into a melting pot.*
> *—Cultural preservation can contribute to sustainable development.*
> *—Culture can only be protected and evolve if supported through economics.*
> *—Micro-finance can serve this purpose. It can empower the marginalized.*
> *—Supporting small, localized businesses can regenerate communities.*
> *—Our global financial architecture needs to change so that it can support the small and medium, not only the large.*

Core to the Himalayan Consensus are the powerful philosophies of this region—Islam, Buddhism, and Hinduism. Each emphasizes empowerment of the less advantaged. Almsgiving—prevalent in Hindu, Buddhist, and Islamic traditions—is a basic social and moral responsibility, recognized across the Himalayan plateau.

Zakat is one of the Five Pillars of Islam. The Koran states very clearly in section 2:177: "Piety lies not in turning your face East or West in prayer...but in distributing your wealth out of love for God to your needy kin; to orphans, to the vagrants, and to the mendicants; it lies in freeing the slaves, in observing your devotions, and in giving alms to the poor."

Underlying this is the construct that the individual belongs to a greater community and must contribute to that community's well being. The community in turn helps the individual. Both are interconnected.

Reza Aslan, one of America's leading Islamic scholars, and author of the book *No God But One God*, explained, "2.5 percent of one's income is zakat. It's not the same as 'charity,' which you can and should give. The idea of *zakat* focuses not on the person who is receiving the alms, but on the person giving them. It is not charity, but virtue. In Islam, which is very community based, everyone is responsible for everyone else. *Zakat* isn't about distributing funds, but rather about the strongest in a community taking care of the weakest."

"The Western notion that the weakest are in that position because they are not working hard enough or are not determined enough to succeed is not valid in Islam," Aslan explained. "The weakest are the responsibility of the strongest. There is a sense of obligation; the strong in the community are obligated to take care of the weak in the community."

When visiting the United Nations International Labor Organization (UNILO) in Islamabad, Donglin Li, a Chinese who headed the office, asked about the bomb explosion. Li then spread the numbers on a table. UNILO statistics revealed, during the previous decade of unprecedented prosperity, unemployment hit young people the hardest, marginalizing 86.3 million youth. In 2007, youth represented 44 percent of the world's total unemployed. Most are between ages 15 and 24, which is the prime age range of suicide bombers.

He then recalled a story. "When my tire was flat in Pakistan's countryside, many villagers came to help. I offered money but they all refused. In Islamabad, I have a papaya tree in my garden, but nobody steals the fruit. I think it has something to do with Muslim intercommunity support."

Muslim intercommunity support was key to a UNILO program in Pakistan that addressed poverty and children's rights. Li explained how UNILO introduced a US$15 million anti-child-labor fund to boost parental incomes and get children out of work and into proper schools. The program provided training in parallel with micro-finance. The aim—to empower poor through self-employment—combined with a self-confidence-building support system.

The program was not about aid, but lending without physical collateral. "Our scheme involves a village community of 20 to 30 people to create 'collective collateral,' which is a social rather than financial guarantee," explained Li. "Through this grassroots networking, our lending-return program enjoys a 95 percent success rate."

Li sighed: "GDP growth should create employment, but it often expands the income gap. World productivity increased 26 percent over the previous decade. However, the global number of those enjoying employment rose by only 16.6 percent. Income gaps continue to widen at accelerated rates."

"Because of globalization, the rich become richer. But the poor should not become poorer."

PEOPLE WHO CANNOT WORK TO GET OUT OF POVERTY, WILL FIGHT THEIR WAY OUT

Kathmandu, 2007: A motorcycle picked me up. It deposited me on a crowded street corner. There, someone flagged a taxi.

The taxi took me to another congested street corner. I was confused at the crossroads. Then someone else appeared. They guided me to a house.

Looking up, a scout leaned from the window. He sent a signal. Someone then appeared from the driveway. They directed me into an alleyway. I followed.

It seemed to lead nowhere.

This process continued until, lost in the labyrinthine slums of Kathmandu, I finally arrived at a nondescript safe house. It seemed empty except for the armed guerrilla guards in position on the balconies and stairwell.

I figured this must be the right place.

I was led into a room that was empty except for a table and a few chairs. A single cup of spiced tea was placed on the table. I stared into the tea. Minutes later, the silence was broken by walkie-talkie static, followed by a bustle of activity in the hallway outside. The door burst open. Pushpa Kamal Dahal, known as "Prachanda" (the "sharp one"), the elusive leader of Nepal's Maoist party, entered the room and gave me a big bear hug.

The Maoists had forged a decade-long revolt and guerrilla struggle. During the war years, Prachanda stayed in southern Nepal, often crossing the porous India border clandestinely to find sanctuary. His elusiveness, and the surprising success of the guerrilla struggle, made him a living legend. After surrounding Kathmandu, his guerrillas, in an unusual compromise, put down their arms and agreed to enter Nepalese politics as a legitimate party.

They sought power through elections rather than guns.

"We want democracy for poor people and suppressed groups. We want real change for the whole society—both commercial and agricultural," declared Prachanda. "Create democracy in mountainous areas in order to rebuild rural infrastructure and roads. And we want to establish an infrastructure that is consistent with an independent country."

Maoist? The whole vision sounded more like Deng Xiaoping.

The Maoist leaders were far from radical, contrary to assertions in the Western press. They were driven by a strong commitment to remedy the economic distortions in their country. After fighting for a decade, the Maoist leadership wanted peace and the alleviation of poverty. China's approach interested them because it unabashedly combined socialist and capitalist tools. They sought a middle path for forging a "new society" that would combine market forces with social responsibility.

On the other hand, they feared the dilution of culture and values. They were keenly aware how ethnic minorities had become so quickly marginalized throughout China. They firmly wanted Nepal to remain ethnically diverse, to thrive on the richness of its own heritage and identity.

My hosts wanted a fresh perspective. They were keen to understand China's success story and how it could be applied to Nepal.

However, it could not.

The conditions between the countries were so different. China had a massive labor pool of 1.3 billion, and a vast coastline. In the early stages of development, Overseas Chinese populations in Hong Kong, Southeast Asia, and Taiwan were eager to establish contract manufacturing in China's coastal cities. China also had a relatively liberal policy toward foreign investment, at least compared with most South Asian countries at the time.

These conditions provided China with the economic base for export processing—to become a factory to the world. None of these conditions existed in tiny landlocked, mountainous Nepal, whose population was scattered in hill and mountain hamlets.

"I don't want to follow blindly the International Monetary Fund (IMF) and World Bank, either." Prachanda explained. Rather they sought alternatives to the IMF and World Bank. In studying China's example, it inspired them to want their own model, based on local conditions and circumstances.

Prachanda, leader of Nepal's Maoists, seemed to be a political pragmatist, not an ideologue. For Westerners, the idea was anathema. So why did Prachanda, a highly educated member of the Hindu Brahmin elite class, of all people, choose a term like "Maoist" for his political movement?

It had a lot to do with his constituency—the impoverished.

Seeking answers, I contacted Ian Baker, a *National Geographic* explorer and author of numerous books on the Himalayan region. He lived in Nepal for decades, and could offer insights.

"It is totally inevitable for a cause like the Maoists to arise in Nepal," Baker said as he outlined the country's political geography. His Kathmandu home was filled with books and maps from explorations. "Apart from name, it is largely a rural-based revolution of people who have been marginalized from Nepal's development and evolution. Western donor countries who channel aid money through Nepal's royal family create an entire culture of corruption, against which the Maoists are rising up."

Bauburam Bhattarai, second in command of Nepal's Maoists (in 2011, he became prime minister), responded similarly. "U.S. aid-funded projects that lasted only for periods of five years created distorted development, which fueled conditions for revolution in the countryside." Bhattarai reflected how misguided programs supported by the United States Agency for International Development (USAID), the World Bank, and the IMF had twisted development, often focusing on top-down infrastructure projects that benefitted corrupt government elites without even reaching the intended recipients. In the view of the Maoists, these institutions contributed to cyclical poverty, providing their movement with its widespread rural support base—the disenfranchised

These highly educated political leaders saw in Nepal's rural mountain villages and urban slums a fertile nesting ground for the dispossessed. By adopting imagery of China's revolution, they simply borrowed a proven model for galvanizing the marginalized. They organized cells throughout Nepal that could convincingly speak a common language to the poor at village and urban levels. These networks could paralyze the infrastructure of Nepal, using peaceful civil disobedience.

These mass rallies, were intoxicating daylong demonstrations that brought bustling Kathmandu to a standstill. People filled the streets with a fusion of Hindu-revolutionary dance, songs, and vitriolic speeches. Hundreds of thousands rallied with red flags to support guerrilla fighters who performed martial arts with traditional curved *Gurka* knives against the rhythm of Nepalese drums while village girls gracefully tossed flowers. These demonstrations repeatedly made the point to Kathmandu's elite Brahmin political and business community that the Maoists controlled the street. There was a reason for this. Some 40 percent of all Maoist party members were women. Traditionally subservient and encumbered, the Maoist movement psychologically empowered them. They in turn gave it broad popular support[1].

The Maoists as a political force had come in from the cold. At the height of tensions in 2007, Prachanda called me into a breakfast meeting at a nondescript Kathmandu backpacker guesthouse. The temporary government coalition faced collapse; he threatened to return to the jungle and take up arms again if his demands for the king's abdication were not met. The Maoists were antiroyalist.

But events turned. By December, the monarchy was toppled, and the king kicked out of his palace, which was turned into a museum. The following year, Prachanda was elected prime minister.

ECONOMIC DISEMPOWERMENT AND IDENTITY LOSS

Prachanda again summoned me for a meeting, this time at the prime minister's official residence. His question: to borrow or not to borrow from the World Bank with all of its conditions? What had China done?

Nepal, like so many underdeveloped countries, seemed caught between choosing the Washington or the Beijing Consensus. Washington offered democracy with purse strings attached. Multilateral aid brought with it dependency and alien economic models with dysfunctional application to real conditions on the ground. The Maoist decade-long revolt was already a rejection of this status quo.

China opted for foreign investment export promotion policies. It matched foreign investment with infrastructure commitments to encourage inbound capital, which grew. Nepal was suffering from rolling blackouts, an oversubscribed mobile phone system, and transport clogs. China could invest in hydropower (which they had done in Pakistan), mobile communications, and roads.

Whether in Pakistan or Nepal, the violence conundrum cycle is one of cause and effect. Extreme violence arises when people are economically disempowered and ethnically marginalized. Likewise, political revolt occurs when people are pushed off the edge. Economic empowerment and the means of self-reliance are keys in reducing terrorism and violence. The problem needs to be addressed at its root.

REFLECTIONS FROM THE GODDESS OF SMALL THINGS

Leaving Nepal, I stopped in India to visit acclaimed activist Arundhati Roy, author of *The God of Small Things*. We met in her sunny New Delhi home with sounds of the city roaring in the street below, just outside her plant-filled balcony.

Reflecting on my experiences in both Pakistan and Nepal, we shared views.

Roy spoke with conviction: "Perhaps they [the marginalized] wonder how they can go on a hunger strike when they're already starving? How they can boycott goods when they have no money to buy any goods? How they can refuse to pay taxes when they have no earnings? People who have taken arms have done so with full knowledge of what the consequences of that decision will be. They have done so knowing they are on their own. They know that the new laws of the land criminalize the poor and conflate resistance with terrorism."

Meanwhile, she criticized the blind application of gross domestic product (GDP) as a measure of national economic success. "Economists cheering from the pages of corporate newspapers inform us that the GDP growth rate is phenomenal, unprecedented. Shops are overflowing with consumer goods. Government storehouses are overflowing with food grains. Outside this circle of light, farmers steeped in debt are committing suicide in the hundreds. Reports of starvation and malnutrition come in from across the country."

"Dangerous levels of malnutrition and permanent hunger are widespread these days: 47 percent of India's children below three suffer from malnutrition; 46 percent are stunted, about 40 percent of the rural population in India has the same food grain absorption level as Sub-Saharan Africa. Today, an average rural family eats about 100 kg less food in a year than it did in the early 1990s. The last five years have seen the most violent increase in rural-urban income inequalities since Independence."

Roy rejected the aid approach—which she viewed as an extension of a past colonial system. "We need to redefine the meaning of politics," she said. "The 'NGO-ization' of civil society initiatives is taking us in exactly the opposite direction. It's depoliticizing us, making us dependent on aid and handouts."

Leaving her apartment, I walked through the streets of New Delhi. Smells of frying samosas contrasted with fast food restaurants, and rickshaws competed in the streets with BMWs. What is best for people, intrusive fast-track globalization or protective ancient tradition?

I decided to visit the hermit kingdom of Bhutan and look for an answer.

CHAPTER 8

THE HIMALAYAN CONSENSUS:
Happiness, Micro-Finance, and Community Development

TRADITIONAL VALUES AS NEW MEASURES OF SUCCESS

Thimphu, 2007. The Buthanese capital is precious, almost like a European village built on the side of pine-crested hills, only the houses are not chalet but Bhutanese-style stone and wood, and the hilltops dominated by *Tsong*, Bhutanese castles with thick high walls and layered arching rooftops. *Tsong* contain a monastery that serves as combined government, religious, and community center for a region or town. Thimphu's main street runs parallel to the river, from which side alleys with traditional markets spread. In autumn it is brilliant, and the colors of late fall spread gold and purple.

Bhutan is extraordinarily beautiful, but the Thunder Dragon Kingdom's most famous export item is an idea.

The term "gross national happiness" (GNH), was first coined in 1986 by Bhutan's fourth King, Jigme Singye Wangchuck. He used the term in an interview with the *Financial Times*. Deflecting criticism over the closed Himalayan kingdom's isolation and Bhutan's low gross national product (GNP) rate, the monarch made his famous statement: "Gross National Happiness is more important than Gross National Product."[1]

The concept shattered traditional economic assumptions. It touched a chord with people worldwide, challenging conventional measures for individual and national success. GNH questions economic assumptions that underlie the post-Bretton Woods order. It presents a potential paradigm for reevaluating the way we measure economic achievement and corporate values.

Moreover, it has implications for how we measure the way we spend our lives and how we use our time.

Classic measures of success include a company's growth or a nation's gross national product. For an individual, it might be how many homes, cars, or luxury brands they have collected in a lifetime.

Ironically, as early as 1968, Senator Robert Kennedy questioned the gross domestic product (GDP) matrix, saying to the American people, "Our gross national product counts air pollution and cigarette advertising... the destruction of our redwoods and the loss of our natural wonder in chaotic sprawl.... Yet [it] does not allow for the health of our children [or] the quality of their education. It measures neither our wit nor our courage; our wisdom nor our learning; it measures everything, in short, except that which makes life worthwhile."[2]

GNH questions what the point is in accumulating a home, a car, and lots of brand-name goods, when one is miserable and frustrated paying debt. What use is the new home or car, when you open the door to the new house and the air outside is polluted?

GNH is about the freedom to choose and feel good without having to think in terms of strict material quantitative dimensions. While academics across the globe are struggling to find a matrix to quantify it, GNH simply defies measurement.

HOLISTIC ECONOMICS

At the United Nations Educational, Scientific, and Cultural Organization (UNESCO) office in Thimphu, Dasho Meghraj Gurung, a Bhutanese of Nepalese descent is a board member of the Bhutan Studies Center. He put GNH into perspective:

"To understand the genesis of GNH, we must go back to the essence of our traditional culture. Our own cultural construct was greatly influenced by Buddhism. Within this context, people have already internalized everlasting happiness—an abstract notion of how to free our life of suffering. Most traditional people accept this.

Remember, what Buddha said: the individual must find his own path. We can give his meaning a modern twist. Development is like this. We need a new paradigm to regenerate values."

"After all we are not so Shangri-la," he admitted with a shrug. "In 1971, my cousin went to Japan and came back with dollars, which I had never seen before. So, I went neoliberal. But we cannot sustain that. Economics comes down to the whole issue of need. All of us are need driven—the need for security, sustenance, love—an economic constant since the beginning of humankind. So, how to satisfy needs? Happiness can transcend this."

Dasho Meghraj Gurung shrugged again and smiled. "Never approach this issue with 'I have all the answers,' because you never do." He tilted his head: "This is the problem with neoliberalists. They believe they have all the answers. They do research, but in the end they create their own reality, because what they believe in becomes their reality."

Professor Lungtaen Gyatso, director of the Institute of Language and Culture Studies at the Royal University of Bhutan, a practicing monk, expanded on this view.

"Because of our tiny population, we fear cultural erosion. Globalization is moving toward a monoculture. We want to stick to what we are. When we talk about GNH, we are talking about our values. Preservation of our culture is important to Bhutanese. So the government, in the name of GNH, is trying to educate our people in cultural survival."

He gave an example of how the GNH framework affects policy. "Plans are on the rise for our ore industry. While this will bring in billions of dollars in material and economic benefits, we must ask two commonsense questions. First, what will be the environmental impact—will it degrade or compromise the environment? Second, how will it affect our traditional cultural system? If this industry makes people's living conditions more difficult, or causes dislocation, or has a negative impact upon their homes and lifestyles, then we will hold back the project!"

Then he added as an afterthought, "The natural environment plays an important role as part of GNH. The global economy is in crisis, and degeneration of our environment is a global concern. Bhutan can contribute to the world at large by serving as a model of environmental protection."

STATISTICS DO NOT DEFINE HAPPINESS

The Bhutan Studies Center is in a long log-built lodge alongside a river, beside a *tsong*. Next to the *tsong* is a cremation ground, smoke rising from smoldering bodies as ashes drift slowly along the river's current.

Thsheing Phuntsho, a researcher at the center, introduces four pillars of GNH: economic development, environmental preservation, cultural preservation, and good governance.

The Bhutan Studies Center has come up with a Bhutan Development Index, which covers nine indicators: 1) psychological well-being, 2) time use (amount of time devoted to work, leisure, religion), 3) health, 4) education, 5) culture (diversity and resilience), 6) governance, 7) community vitality, 8) ecological diversity and resilience, 9) economic living standards.

The center verifies these indicators by carrying out field studies throughout Bhutan. "Whatever test we run, it does not come up to our expectations," complained Thsheing Phuntsho with a shrug. "There are 19 different dialects in Bhutan." Even in a country as small as Bhutan, what constitutes happiness varies between different dialect groups.

By putting happiness into a matrix, the Bhutan Studies Center runs the risk of falling into the very empirical measurements of Western economic models it seeks to break away from. The whole point of GNH is that it places spiritual needs on par with material ones, de facto rejecting traditional measurements of economic, national, and personal success by calling for a new economic paradigm.

The notion echoes the words of Lhasa's philosopher monk Nyima Tsering, "As we enter the twenty-first century it is clear materialism alone does not bring human happiness. Under our current system of greed, people are wasting resources to chase illusionary brand images. The result: more wars of destruction to control those resources, in turn accumulating more negative karma. Remember, spirituality can overcome materialism."

Thsheing Phuntsho looked across the river from the Bhutan Studies Center. He nodded in the direction of a cremation ground on the other side, near the *tsong*. Black and grey ashes were smoldering. Smoke twisted upwards, gracefully evaporating into a blue sky above.

"During our study and research," Thsheing Phuntsho sighed, "that cremation ground reminds us about the impermanence of all things."

THE PRIME MINISTER WHO DARED TO BE HAPPY

"I have never supported moves to develop the GNH concept in a quantitative manner." Bhutan's Prime Minister, Lyonpo Jigmi Y. Thinley spoke with conviction, sitting cross-legged on a woven mat, wrapped comfortably in a traditional Bhutanese robe.[3]

"You cannot quantify the causes of happiness," explained the prime minister. "Living with happiness is the most important element to be measured. To quantify is to adopt the same economic approaches that we are seeking an alternative to!"

Across the world, institutions had begun to research new measurements of economic success. GNH conferences were happening everywhere. It had all begun with a simple statement in the *Financial Times* in 1986. Thinley explained, "The concept of GNH emerged with the fourth King of Bhutan. His Majesty was dissatisfied with the progress of developing countries, by their inability to choose their own path."

When he looked at the models of industrialized countries that called for relentless growth, the King felt that material goods didn't necessarily produce happiness. Happiness is defined by the mind and body, and moreover by the right to choose a sustainable form of development."

Thinley reflected on the social impact of conspicuous consumption. "When the market ethics move in, who is to deny that a better standard of living can arise? But is that how we define quality of life, by 'you are not buying enough of this and that, so you need to buy more?' GNH suggests that maybe there are different kinds of markets."

GNH is a policy of equitable and balanced distribution of the benefits of development for all spectrums of society," suggested Thinley.

I asked him, "Could the Himalayan Consensus offer an alternative economic paradigm?"

"Why not?" the prime minister responded immediately. "In fact, it is already happening. Yes, the compulsion is powerful in this region. "We need a clearer worldview—one that increasingly supports a holistic approach. We need to redefine globalization and bring in some new dimensions that relate to the finite world in which we live. We need to live, produce, and consume more consciously, and bring world responsibility back into the globalization process."

THE POOR NEED BANKING, THEY DON'T HAVE COUNTRY CLUBS

"There is nothing more powerful than an idea whose time has come." The words of Victor Hugo were inscribed on a red banner welcoming Professor Muhammad Yunus, "banker to the poor," to the Bangladesh Embassy in Beijing.

It was 2006, and Yunus was speaking at a micro-credit conference in China's capital when the news broke: he had won the Nobel Peace Prize for pioneering micro-credit. The Bangladesh Embassy was holding a reception to celebrate. Ashfquar Rahman, Bangladesh ambassador to China, telephoned, asking me to join the reception. That night, over a *banana lassi*, Yunus told us the story of how he pioneered micro-credit.

"In 1974, I found it increasingly difficult to teach elegant theories of economics in the university classroom while a terrible famine was raging in Bangladesh. Suddenly I felt the emptiness of those theories in the face of crushing hunger and poverty. I wanted to do something immediately to help people around me."

Yunus was shocked to discover a woman who had borrowed less than a dollar from a moneylender, becoming indebted to produce goods for him at prices he fixed. Yunus then made a list of moneylender victims in the village. When complete, it had the names of 42 people, who had borrowed altogether 27 dollars. Stunned, Yunus offered the cash from his own pocket. From this simple act of liberating a small group of women from indentured servitude, he created the concept of micro-credit and founded Grameen Bank.[4] Based on this experience, Yunus evolved an entire system of noncollateral lending to the poor, intricately crafted around the structure of Islamic village society in Bangladesh. For most impoverished people living in a country with a per-capita income of $128 per year, access to just $10 or $20 can change their lives for the better.

"If I could make so many people so happy with a tiny amount of money," Yunus explained, "why shouldn't I do more of it?"

THE RESTRUCTURING OF GLOBAL FINANCE STARTS FROM A CORRUGATED HUT

Yunus invited me to Dhaka the following year to visit Grameen Bank's rural branches and village lending centers, which organize women into village peer groups. The Muslim village social network provides a structure for noncollateral guarantees. Each person in the group guarantees the loan for the others, creating a social guarantee with the bank. Loans may be given without collateral.

"The poor always repay their loans," Yunus said. "If someone trusts a woman with what represents a lot of money for her, she will work very hard to repay it." A borrower's social prestige is at stake if they fail to repay their loan. Repayment amounts are very small, weekly installments are affordable. Moreover, a poor person sees what the rich have and fail to use. For that reason, they are more determined to make the most of each opportunity given to them.

Grameen operates with a small bureaucracy, low costs, and flexible policies. This "village" approach tailors lending to the needs of an individual. Bank managers consider problems of individual borrowers, how a loan impacts their family and life. This is the antithesis of traditional banking—bureaucracy, inflexible credit criteria, and cold customer relations.

Yunus took institutionalism out of banking.

A Grameen village lending center consists of a pavilion with corrugated iron roof and benches. Borrowers congregate weekly in groups of five women. Each group elects a leader who collects interest payments for the branch manager. Branches are simple offices in a town near the villages.

Women borrow small amounts to set up a tiny business, ranging from fish and poultry breeding to betel nut harvesting. A micro-loan will allow a family to purchase a small rice paddy and begin self-sufficient farming. Small repayments are made at these lending center meetings.

Such gatherings are more like village get-togethers. Women come with their children, joke, gossip, and then report on the loan repayments within their circle. Most of Grameen's borrowers share similar stories and dreams. They strive to have a solid roof over their heads, their children in school, and their own business to improve their lives.

Measurements of success are straightforward.

Since Yunus received the Nobel Peace Prize in 2006, the IMF and World Bank have also begun to acknowledge the power of bottom-up economics. Their traditional emphasis on top-down infrastructure projects (from which self-appointed advisers and favored contractors reaped profits from soft loans) had left both institutions largely disliked in the developing world.

But it really took somebody like Yunus, who achieved celebrity status, to bring attention to grass-roots economic efforts, which so many organizations and individuals are undertaking across the developing world.

Yunus pointed out that organizations like the World Bank and IMF often do not bother to consider factors such as transportation costs, price hikes, the cost of staple foods like rice and grain, or the affordability of education. Any tiny shift in these factors, resulting from policies they may insist upon, can disrupt or even destroy the lives of those whom they are supposed to help.

"With all of our economic theories, we forget the environment, forget people, forget culture, and destroy anything to make money," Yunus said sadly. "There is an inherent fault in economic theory, which creates an artificial human being who knows how to make money because maximizing profit is the sole basis of business. But human beings are bigger than just money. The compassionate, caring human who jumps in to help others is being is left out. So in economic theory, the only ones left are the people making money. Economic assumptions forget the compassionate people."

On hearing this, I realized the core principles of the Himalayan Consensus were evolving. Small local businesses can alleviate poverty, while empowering people with pride in themselves. But the challenge for localized start-ups to succeed, or scale, is financing. Micro-finance offers a solution. But it is just one example of an approach that works. There are many variations, including community banking, small enterprise seed investment, and socially responsible venture capital, which can be applied in various ways depending on local need and circumstance. They are all out there, but can't work effectively because the current financial architecture renders them "alternative."

Changes in our global financial system are required to allow capital to flow to them.

Whether in Dhaka or Detroit, creative approaches toward banking, finance, and venture capital can address the needs of local business entrepreneurs who contribute to their communities. It is not all about globalization and listing websites on capital markets.

The dichotomy between the talking heads, Wall Street, the Treasury, the Fed, and the four big tech companies (Facebook, Twitter, Yahoo, YouTube) and the rest of the country is shocking. "The America That Works," as *The Economist* put it,[5] is calling for capital to run or start up real businesses in communities. America is screaming for real stuff: infrastructure finance, community banking, local loans for vocational support. Give us investment bankers with vision.

When I was in Dhaka, I did not expect to stand in Wall Street exactly four years later, offering spontaneous sit-in lectures on microfinance to occupying protestors. No one in the towering offices above us could imagine that the process of global financial restructuring had started from a Bangladeshi village, in a corrugated hut.

IT'S TIME TO PUT POVERTY INTO MUSEUMS

A small amount of money can go very far in transforming one's life, if spent in the right place, in the right way. If a family can build up its own business—say, opening a tiny roadside shop—Grameen will lease them a mobile phone. They can then use the phone to provide public telephone services, thus becoming a mini call center. On the back of micro-credit, Grameen offers education loans and pension funds. Step-by-step, a family can work its way out of poverty and into a sustainable business.

Some 58 percent of Grameen's borrowers have moved out of poverty, a phenomenon the bank tracks and measures carefully. Even here, Yunus provides new criteria. Instead of the mainstream institutional approach, which uses annual per-capital income to determine whether people have shifted above the poverty line, his organization asks harder, more relevant questions: "Do you have a roof over your head, warm clothes for winter, safe drinking water and sanitation? Are your children in school?"

Yunus has even extended his idea to help beggars become entrepreneurs. In Grameen's Struggling (Beggars) Members Program, "members are not required to give up begging, but are encouraged to take up additional income-generating activity such as selling popular consumer items door-to-door, or at the place of begging." This weans beggars away from begging and conditions them to begin a self-sufficient business. Yunus's approach breaks all the rules. Under the same Struggling Beggars Members Program, the first rule is: "Existing rules of Grameen Bank do not apply to beggar members; they make up their own rules."

"Since economic textbooks don't recognize the poor, there are no supportive institutions and policies to help them. As a result, the poor go out and create their own jobs." Yunus has declared his personal mission is to put poverty into a museum.

DEVELOPMENT WITHOUT VALUES IS USELESS

Colombo, 2007: At the entrance to a Buddhist monastery, a monkey had descended from the trees to look for fruit among offerings. A young boy approached the monkey, who fled.

"Why is the animal afraid of me?" the boy asked a monk standing nearby.

"Because you are different from him," responded the monk with a smile. "Don't you realize? That is the problem with everything!"

Athuraliya Rathana was no ordinary monk, but rather the founder of Sri Lanka's influential opposition political party (Jaikahelo Urumiya) that claims 5 percent of the nation's population as members.

"How do we eradicate poverty? What is the cause of poverty?" Athuraliya Rathana asked rhetorically as he poured a cup of steaming Sri Lankan black tea. "Globalization is important, but we need balance. We need a common agenda to protect our environment and defeat the materialist dictatorship of multilateral organizations."

"The modern age needs a new set of aesthetics, values, and morals to replace the old," Athuraliya Rathana explained. "Western people around the world are not satisfied with their material gains. So they are coming to Asia for spiritual gain. Today is an era of material imperialism. Meditation is not enough. Academic practice is not enough. Ritual is not enough. We need political force using spiritual force to create a new world."

"A year ago, I went to China," Athuraliya Rathana said. "I visited the markets there and met some people. I noticed there are no ethnics and the people are not happy. They are rather like machines. They have huge, marvelous cities in China, even bigger than New York. But I think nobody there is happy. China has no ideology. The changes have brought only material gains. China is obtaining international power through capital and investment, but not through its cultural authority. If the Chinese try to embrace a Buddhist way of life, they will become a real giant."

Sri Lanka's approach differed from China's, by not emphasizing urbanization. Instead it seeks to empower villages with its own sustainable economic systems. It also rejected the World Bank's approach, seeking a middle-way path of its own.

"The World Bank said that our old buildings were underutilized, and that the people should be moved to the urban areas and their land given to multinational corporations who could then take over the village and redevelop the land. They claimed it was a question of economic efficiency," explained Sri Lanaka's President Mahinda Rajapaksa, when we had met in Beijing a few months earlier. The result was, "We then had slums and many social problems, such as rising crime and drugs."

Instead of hyper infrastructure development, Sri Lanka focused on building good schools and hospitals in villages, the president explained. Before, children did not even eat breakfast. The Sri Lankan government now provides these meals free to village youngsters. Such initiatives serve to address core tangible needs, while rooting people in their villages. In turn, this stimulates local growth and community.

While providing infrastructure to rural areas, Rajapaksa sought local solutions to development, consolidating the garment and textile industries in the countryside. However, he drew the line at creating artificial consolidated townships, the way China had done. Sri Lanka instead allowed villages to evolve naturally.

Rajapaksa challenged and even openly confronted the World Bank's model by supporting micro-initiatives that revived the village as a source of people's economic livelihood and psychological comfort. Rajapaksa argued for the importance of keeping village social structure intact, so values can evolve from traditions. Where traditions are maintained, people can return at any time and feel at home.

"We have to provide for the practical needs of the people, not what some theorist thinks," Rajapaksa explained.

Sri Lanka refused offers of infrastructure aid with strings attached. Instead, it invested in infrastructure relevant to its people's own needs. According to Rajapaksa, "Government infrastructure in rural areas reaches the villages where no previous infrastructure existed. At the village level, people need better roads. Then they will start to move back toward the village rather than crowding into the cities. How people choose to live is something they have to decide for themselves. It shouldn't be decided by politicians, the World Bank or the IMF."

Rajapaksa smiled. "There are simply different international approaches. People need to retain their values. Without their values, development is useless."

A MONK TOLD ME...

Still at the temple with monk Athuraliya Rathana, I reflected on my journey. Traveling across the Himalayan region of South Asia, the emergence of an alternative approach became clear. Time spent exchanging experiences with a broad spectrum of leaders in South Asia—whether heads of state, social entrepreneurs, NGO workers—was critical in crystallizing the idea that a set of alternative approaches could converge into a fresh economic paradigm and, moreover, that these alternatives had the potential to represent a new mainstream.

Bhutan's concept of GNH provided a fresh way of measuring success, not by quantity of consumption but quality of happiness. Bangladesh pioneered micro-finance and presented another way of banking and finance that did not just cater to the rich, but helped the poor—and even beggars—through profitability. Sri Lanka demonstrated practical ways in which the countryside and village communities can develop without urbanizing and can modernize without losing its traditional values, which are equally important as economic development. Nepal demonstrated how cyclical poverty fuels revolution and violence. Pakistan underscored how the extreme marginalization of economic conditions and identity gives rise to terrorism.

The Himalayan Consensus began as an amalgamation of ideas from social enterprise, gross national happiness, and micro-finance. Three principles emerged: 1) protect ethnic diversity and identity, 2) work through local business, which requires community finance (meaning, change our financial system to support real businesses), 3) encourage business to be a stakeholder in community development and prioritize environmental protection.

This was the early framework calling for a new economic paradigm. In the coming years, it would grow and its set of principles evolve with the creation of the African Consensus and integration with other independent progressive movements in Russia, Europe, and finally America.

Monk Athuraliya Rathna could foresee all this. He called for a global movement that coalesced from many disparate and not yet coordinated grassroots initiatives.

"Some monks retreat to the forest," said Athuraliya Rathna, explaining a tradition common to yogic practitioners. It symbolizes discarding worldly and material illusions, a journey to inner peace.

A traditional monk regularly retreats to the forest for prolonged periods of meditation. However, Athuraliya Rathna is no ordinary monk, but a political leader. "Meditation is good for spirituality. But without the use of common sense, it cannot achieve anything. Without common sense, we cannot impact society. Why only go to the forest?" he asks rhetorically amid temple grounds wafting with incense. Then he spoke as if issuing a mandate.

"Hatred and greed are our common enemies. We have to defeat them using people's power. Organize all people, not only the poor, but the rich as well. They also suffer. They have luxury and palaces, but are spiritually poor. If you can do that, then I can go back to the forest again."

This page intentionally left blank

CHAPTER 9

THE AFRICAN CONSENSUS:
Community Empowerment to Prevent Violence

FEEDING THE HUNGRY DRAGON: CHINA AND AFRICA

Dakar, 2011. The smell of ocean mixed with the heady fragrance of Senegalese incense. Spectrums of clothing from the street swirled like a kaleidoscope of colors amid the ever-present intoxicating hypnotism of pounding drums.

At the home of China's ambassador to Senegal, the finest Chinese food was served. Fresh fruit and Oriental sweet cakes were placed on the table by Chinese waiters wearing starched white gloves. Without warning, one of the embassy protocol staff entered the room. He had a worried twist to his eyebrow. "Egyptian president Muhammad Hosni El Sayed Mubarak will address the crowds," he whispered into the ambassador's ear.

The Chinese ambassador stood up immediately. With a graceful gesture of his hand, he suggested that I join him in the adjacent living room. A thin yet spry gentlemen, Ambassador Gong had nearly two decades of postings in Africa, serving in over half a dozen countries, and was extremely informed about this continent. China, unlike America, was closely following developments in all corners of Africa at all times. It had its eyes everywhere.

The ambassador invited me to dinner fully briefed that I had been an adviser to his government during the transition from socialism to market, and to other Asian countries during their critical reforms. We spent the evening talking about the relevance of China's development experience to Africa. He felt some aspects could be borrowed, but not all. Africa's development experience will be unique unto itself, just as China's was, he observed. The cultural, geographic, and demographic factors are just so different.

Of all the points discussed, he was especially interested to know why I had called for an "African Consensus" at a rally of over 100,000 people from the top of a truck the day before, as activists poured through the streets of Dakar for the World Social Forum. Essentially, he wanted to know what I was *really* doing in Senegal.

Moving to the living room, we sat down on large elegant couches. A flat-screen television dominated one wall. On television, we could see frenetic throngs occupying Tahrir Square in Cairo. Mubarak was about to speak. Anticipation oozed out from the television screen into the room.

Turning to Ambassador Gong, I asked diplomatically, "Does this bother you?" pointing to the television set. "What I mean is, what do you really think of all this?"

"I find it interesting," he responded with a cool yet pursed look on his face. Then almost as an afterthought he quickly added, "We in China are observing it with care."

Taking this as a cue to press a bit more, I asked, "Are you worried about something like this happening in China?"

"It won't," he responded with emphatic confidence, offering three reasons. "First, there is a lot of corruption in these countries. We do not have corruption. Second, in these countries the people are very poor. There are no poor in China. The people are now rich." Then with a sense of sternness, but almost as an incomplete thought, he added, "Most important is the third reason—We do not allow Twitter or Facebook in China."

THE ART OF PRAGMATIC DISOBEDIENCE

Rokhaya, an African woman in her mid-thirties, hands waving, greeted me at Dakar airport, with a powerful warm hug. I had arrived in Senegal to attend preparatory work for the 2011 World Social Forum being hosted there. Dressed entirely in bright orange, with a matching orange bandanna tied tightly around her head, she laughingly introduced herself, "I will be your assistant while working in Senegal." I sensed she had already taken charge of everything. Under her laughter, I felt a hint of hardened activism in the things she said and did.

From 2011 onward, we entered a decade of protest. The world would witness the emergence of many independent movements, working separately, yet in parallel, toward building a new global consensus. In sub-Sahara Africa, the process was beginning in Senegal.

Rokhaya introduced me to Mamadouba. "He will advise you during your stay in Senegal. There are many things you may not understand about West Africa. He will guide you." She then presented Miniane Diouf and Charles Owens, professors at the very liberal Cheik Anta Diop University, and leaders of the World Social Forum in Africa.[1].

The World Social Forum (WSF) is the antithesis of the World Economic Forum (WEF), the club of politicians and business leaders who meet annually in Davos, Switzerland.

Whatever the trends, it seems the entire agenda and tone for business and media is set at Davos. It is a high table session that puts everyone onto the same page of what is politically correct to say and do in the year ahead.

The WEF is exclusive, expensive, and very elitist. It is unquestionably the convention of the 1 percent.

By contrast, the WSF is grassroots, populist, embracing, and open to everyone. It is the counterconvention of the 99 percent.

WSF held its first meeting in Porto Alegre, Brazil, in 2001. In many ways it evolved out of the "anti-globalization movement" that first came to light during the riots that disrupted the 1998 World Trade Organization ministerial meeting in Seattle.

WSF has been criticized as a disorganized cultural circus. To some extent this is intentional. WSF wants to be flat in hierarchy—not elitist, maybe a bit anarchical. It consciously avoids offering specific answers to the problems it identifies. It is all about free speech and free flow.

Senegal, as host of the 2011 World Social Forum, wanted to present a blueprint for change. Instead of just criticizing and attacking, it wanted to put forward ideas that are positive and proactive.

Africa, for all of its problems, was pioneering its way out of poverty, corruption, and internal violence. In the shadow of failed aid programs and dysfunctional governments, real change was coming from the street, led by civil society. Across Africa, NGOs and "people's social action" groups or networks were creatively addressing social problems. Many had set up side business ventures to support their programs.

The consensus in Africa: multilateral and Western donor aid programs had become ineffectual, and often corrupted by government. The byzantine bureaucracy of Western aid administrators frustrated people in the field. It infuriated those in the street.

Rokhaya was a social worker who treated postwar traumatized children. Her husband was an AIDS activist. I often visited them at their home. They lived in a small but very cozy apartment in Dakar's medina. The entrance was through a very narrow winding staircase that twisted into the coolness of an adobe corridor above the street sounds. Rokhaya explained their sentiment. "Open that door each day and step into the street. There is so much poverty everywhere. You have no choice but to become an activist."

For many, setting up a business to support a social program often proved more efficient than applying for aid. Unlike aid, business could provide ongoing revenue stream. Civil society found it was almost easier to make the money, rather than apply for it.

Against the backdrop of revolution in North Africa, we were launching an African Consensus in the sub-Sahara. The image was compelling, but the message was lost on Western media. They did not connect the dots. But the revolution spread, becoming an engine of change. Not only for Africa but also Europe and America.

Revolutionary imagery brings people into the street, a lesson taken from Nepal's Maoists. The upward grass-roots expression of frustration and anger is powerful and can shake institutions. But it does not necessarily build new ones.

Activism needs pragmatism.

That does not mean selling out idealism. It means putting ideals into practice and actually changing the things that one is protesting against. This can occur on multiple levels, through different initiatives.

Protest and civil disobedience is a great means of communication because it slams issues at the media and right into the face of the public and politicians. But protest alone is not enough. Saying, "destroy the World Bank" or "end corporate greed" makes a dramatic point on television. But realistically, multilateral institutions and corporate greed are not going away any time soon.

So while people protest, quiet and persuasive lobbying is also needed. The intention should be to spark internal debate within an organization like the World Bank and then push for policy change, or change the status quo by establishing an alternative multilateral institution driven by players from the "south" that can prove things can be done better.

Similarly, boards of multinationals must be persuaded to adopt energy efficiency measures to cut carbon and establish meaningful corporate community investments that go beyond the superficiality of "corporate social responsibility," which more often just amounts to some budgeted handouts to different charities.

The same approach applies with government. Most of the time, their think tanks are not thinking. But businesses are. Change the mindset of corporations, and the politicians who need their funding for reelection will follow, obediently.

Ultimately three stakeholders—civil society, business, and government—have to find their own consensus. This begins with clear communication on issues that offer realistically achievable paths or solutions. Then change occurs.

This is the art of pragmatic disobedience.

WHEN RAP GETS POLITICAL.

"We don't want to suffer anymore. We just want to eat some more…" are hip-hop lyrics of Didier Awadi, Senegal's most celebrated rapper.

He now leads the African Consensus.

I first met Awadi at Center Bopp, a community center in a poor section in Dakar's medina. The neighborhood is famous for one thing – drum making. There were rows of drums along the roadside—every size imaginable, intricately carved, made of wood and leather, lashed with tight rope. The sound of their beat filled the street.

Center Bopp was a simple three-story concrete building, with a large field full of kids playing basketball. The field was just dirt, no fancy watered grass or asphalt. But the kids were not just shooting hoops. Laughing, they were playing basketball with the competitive spirit of tournament training. Upstairs every afternoon at five there was a karate class.

That is the new spirit of Africa.

Center Bopp was chaotic, thronged with French and African youth clicking away at laptops. Breakout meetings were already happening in the open corridors. Phones rang incessantly. People crammed to register. The stairwells were packed with activists, NGO representatives, and reggae singers. Everyone wanted to have a program within the forum, a sit-in, teach-in, or sing-in.

Awadi stepped into the room.

A large man with dreadlocks, he was West Africa's biggest celebrity rapper. His music was highly politicized, often going to the extreme of fusing scratchy recordings from speeches by Africa's pan-African leaders with electronic rap on a synthesizer. His latest album was called *Presidents of Africa*.

Artists congregated on the rooftop garden of his studio, which was located on a dusty road deep within Dakar's medina, jamming all day and night, synthesizing African and electronic instruments. His online media team networked his aspirations and ideas across the continent. African Consensus did not have a website, only a Facebook page. The studio buzzed with creativity. Posters of African leaders hung on the walls of corridors throughout the studio.

Awadi was anguished that Africa continues exports raw commodities to those Western powers that once colonized them, still buying back the finished products. "It is still colonialism," he said, "a detrimental hindrance to growth."

Awadi shared the vision and aspiration of leaders like the Ghana's founding president, Kwame Nkrumah, who first articulated pan-Africanism as a movement. Africa needs economic development. Barriers between nations must come down. He envisioned a unified Africa. More specifically, that meant an African monetary zone, a continental free trade zone, and value added manufacturing within a North American Free Trade Agreement-type arrangement.

He saw the African Consensus as a vehicle to advance these goals.

Pan-Africanism ran like a circuit connecting everyone I met from the continent, no matter which country, tribe, or language grouping they came from. It was a singular identity vibe that transcended these differences and connected each individual to the continent and to being African. It was a special, albeit amorphous oneness that was not shared in any other region of the world that I have lived or worked in. This powerful impulse spread from the Sahara to South Africa, across a vast space. It also carried an anticolonial, anti-western institution, anti-outsider-interference emotion.

The pantheon of African leaders whose posters hung all around Awadi's studio brought this into sharp focus. Each had advocated a form of African unity. It seemed that everyone recognized that the resources both natural and human of this continent were a powerful force. But that force remained asleep. Key African leaders who advocated pan-Africanism were sidelined, forced down from power, or assassinated. The historical demise of each leader was in one way or another linked to resources and Western commercial exploitation of them.

While colonialism had ended, the old colonial powers kept strong commercial and strategic interests in their former African colonies, and did not approve of individual leaders standing up to that. Moreover, in the mind of most Africans, Western powers had no interest in seeing a unified or economically integrated Africa. Certainly economic integration and the taking down of trade and other barriers between states would allow the continent to evolve more efficient economies and alleviate poverty. All this somehow seemed threatening to some leaders and institutions in the West. Many in Africa felt that Western leaders paid lip service to ending poverty in Africa, but in fact had another agenda. Western economic interests certainly were not losing out from Africa's backwardness.

Awadi admired Thomas Sankara more than any other African president. Sankara was the leader of Burkina Faso (formerly Upper Volta) from 1983 until his assassination (possibly by French agents) in 1987. Awadi saw in Sankara a martyr standing up against French neocolonial interests. Awadi named his own recording studio "Sankara Studio," in homage to his favorite African revolutionary leader, who was known for his distaste of luxury and corruption. Sankara was also ahead of his time by promoting health and women's rights.

Awadi wrote songs about Sankara and even visited the late president's family in Bukino Faso. They gave Awadi a T-shirt that Sankara had worn. One night when sitting in his living room, I asked Awadi why he did not frame the T-shirt and hang it in his home or studio. "Because sometimes I like to wear it," he responded in a low voice. "It gives me strength."

MULTILATERAL AID IS DYSFUNCTIONAL, AND BUSINESS IS MORE SUSTAINABLE

An African Consensus Resolution drafting committee was initially composed of Senegalese NGO leaders. Soon others joined from across Africa as they arrived to attend the WSF. We met at a Senegalese think tank called the Center for Research of Society and Economy. It was located in an old French villa, with motorcycles crowded outside. Everyone gathered in a meeting room with a long rounded wooden table. As the call to prayer echoing from hundreds of minarets across Dakar subsided, Miniane convened the meeting and presided over the drafting. Awadi arrived at the first session, dressed in army fatigues, wearing a Che Guevara beret complete with a red star.

A document emerged that articulated a framework that became the African Consensus. It started with the following line: *"The African Consensus does not turn to any one model or economic theory. Rather it is draws from collective experiences across the continent where local knowledge proved successful in creating pragmatic solutions to development challenges."*

The African Consensus presented several core principles borrowed in spirit from the Himalayan Consensus: preserve ethnic diversity and local identity; do this through business not aid because aid is spent once, but business can be self-sustaining; business should give back to the community and protect the environment.

A month later, attending an Economic and Social Council (ECOSOC) meeting at the General Assembly Hall of the United Nations, Jeffrey Sachs, the father of "shock therapy," talked enthusiastically about getting every child in Africa online within a decade.

One of the African NGO leaders on the same panel spoke out. "Our children don't need to be online by 2020," he remarked. "We don't need to teach our children computer skills."

Most Americans would be shocked by such a statement, thinking it is shortsighted or just not "in touch." But actually we are the ones who are out of touch.

"We need basic irrigation skills," explained the NGO leader. "Can you transfer to our youth basic irrigation engineering? That is what we need. We need basic farming skills too. We want to be able to grow our own food. Is that too much to ask for? We don't necessarily need our children to be playing with computers. Anyway, they cannot afford them. Please don't assume that our children are online. In most places there is no Wi-Fi. We don't have Internet either. Actually, we don't have electricity. Oh, and by the way, most days we don't have water. Do you now understand? That is why I want to start with basic transfer of irrigation skills for our children. We can talk about Internet later."

WATER IS AN INALIENABLE HUMAN RIGHT AND OUR BIGGEST SECURITY THREAT

At the drafting meeting in Dakar, a tall woman draped elegantly in African robes, hair tightly bound in a wide bandanna, exuded dignity and pride. She was an activist from an organization known as Rhaddo, which combatted human trafficking and the abuse of women and children. Their leader, Alioune Tine, was a peace broker who had been a key mediator in a number of conflicts, including those in Darfur and Cote d'Ivoire (Ivory Coast). She asked if I wanted to meet him.

Tine's face lit up, and he hugged me upon entering the room. Tine already knew all the details of our drafting session. "I have had many meetings today," he explained. "I am sorry I could not be there this afternoon." He then pointed to the door. "Many people come through that door asking me to mediate disputes. I had both sides of the Darfur conflict, right here in this room." He then chuckled and shook his head. "I support the African Consensus. We need a new consensus."

The African Consensus gradually became the main theme of the 2011 World Social Forum. It touched upon a common sentiment that linked a broad network of activist groups and NGOs into a common platform. Over the days that followed, the African Consensus movement was launched through a series of press conferences and rallies.

After one of those energizing rallies, Tine, speaking softly, voiced his concerns. "It is one thing to launch African Consensus at the World Social Forum. But what's next? We must bring this idea up further. Integrate into the African Union system," he said.[2] "So far, this is a Senegalese initiative. It must be broader, to represent NGOs across our continent. We should bring our draft resolution to the African Commission on Human and People's Rights in Gambia at a congress of human rights activists from across the continent. NGO leaders from all 54 African countries will be there this April. If they adopt this draft resolution, it will become the African Consensus Declaration."

Tine thought for a moment. The sound of waves rippled the nearby shore of the West African coast. "The African Consensus is an important step for us," he added. "It is more than an economic development paradigm. It can be a framework for peace."

Tine's point was that the root of violence lay in poverty. Conflicts between ethnic groups in Africa were not necessarily over cultural differences or even religion. They were over the question of controlling resources, whether diamonds for wealth or water for survival. The issue was the same, and so was the solution: economic empowerment of people.

"Violence will be on the rise," he warned. "Because of climate change, the Sahara encroaches upon our people in sub-Sahara Africa." He listened to the sound of waves.

"Remember, for Africans, water is a basic human right."

COMBINE TRADITIONAL WISDOM WITH
MODERN EDUCATION AND HEALTH CARE

Together with Mamadouba, we drove out of Dakar through crowded towns, poor villages, from paved to dirt road. Finally, there was no road. Our jeep rambled across low bush. We were driving into the desert along the Mauritania border. We were searching for nomads.

They in turn were searching for water.

Mamadouba squinted into the horizon. "I think they must be over there. We came this way the last time I was here."

It all looked the same to me. Low bush. Sand.

The family of nomads we were looking for were Mamadouba's relatives. Mamadouba came from this desert, born here in a tiny thatched hut, sheltered from the sun, wind, and sand. One could not imagine Mamadouba's simple background when visiting his Dakar office on the top floor of the National Assembly building where he serves as political and strategic adviser to the third highest-ranking man in the Senegalese government.

As a political leader, Mamdouba is the vice president of the district of St. Louis. He is also the head of the Podor subdistrict. Podor is a nomadic region in the harsh desert. Mamdouba lives most of his time in Dakar, where he can lobby for the region, but returns to Podor every weekend. "I was born in that kind of hut," he said, pointing to a shelter woven of bush branches so low one needs to stoop down and crawl in to enter. His relatives came out of the hut to greet us.

"It was education that brought me from here to the National Assembly," he explained. "I started in a simple village school. It only had a tent. I studied hard anything and everything I could get my hands on. It enabled me to go to university. And so my life changed. Now I want to bring that change back to my people. So I am dedicated to building schools here in the desert."

As we visited one such school, class was just being dismissed. Kids rushed over to talk and joke with Mamdouba. There was hardly anything in the classroom. Simple benches and desks, a chalkboard—that was it. The teachers pulled him to the side to discuss their curriculum.

"If I can bring a child to graduate from here and go to a university," Mamadouba explained, "I will have already effected a great change."

We then visited two clinics he had established nearby, one specifically for women, and a third under construction. He pointed out how modern medicine could be grafted onto traditional. In rural or nomadic regions, the *marabou* traditional medicine men—what Westerners deride as witch doctors—still retain strong credibility with people. Rather than fight their powers, why not use them constructively? Bring modern medicine. Train them, respecting their traditions. And let the *marabou* merge the powers of dispensing modern medicine with their spiritual and psychological cures.

Jeffrey Sach's Earth Institute supervises Millennium Village projects throughout Africa. In the cavernous confines of the Columbia University Library, staff at the Earth Institute explained how they introduced Western clinics into their village projects that were completely separate from traditional holistic practitioners. The two approaches were so divergent. Did they have to be?

The idea of merging traditional thinking with modern medicine first came to me in 1988 when trekking among hill tribes along the northern Thai and Burmese border. In my backpack I had brought those very same simple magic tricks I had had in China, and performed them for the villagers. Then they started to bring me sick children asking for cures. Not knowing what to do, I tried to give out whatever little medicine I had in my backpack. This was not the right thing to do, but there was little choice. One of the village leaders came to me and explained that the people believed I was a wizard and had a cure for the children. Then leader asked if I also had the power to deflect bullets. I firmly said, "No!"

This incident reveals how wizardry and medicine were long ago merged in the human psyche. But through our own evolution we separated the two. Through science, we began to ignore the holistic, and in the end even forgot about the psychological power of our own minds and the role that thought processes can play in balanced healing.

Rokhaya reflected her own experience of using traditional wisdom during posttrauma counseling for children who had survived conflict in the Congo. Many had been guerrilla fighters, in reality armed teenage gangs. They shot each other randomly, often without cause. The killing went beyond logic. Those children who survived the nightmare were themselves responsible for child genocide. "All the USAID counseling didn't work," explained Rokhaya. "Then we tried something which goes way back in African tradition."

She showed me a simple leather box. It had tribal motifs carved into the leather. I opened it. There was nothing inside. "What's this for?" I asked.

"It is what we call a memory box," she explained. "We have them all over Africa. You see, in life, there are many things that we cannot deal with. Maybe there are problems that cannot be solved, or trauma that we cannot forget. So you take the problem out of your mind like this." She reached to the top of her head as if grabbing something inside and yanking it out. Grasping that something that could not be seen, she placed it in the empty leather box, closing it quickly.

"The idea is to put it here. To not think about it until you are ready. Not to worry. It will not escape or go away. But when you are finally ready to deal with it, and actually open the box, well, maybe it will have already gone, or the situation may have changed. That is our traditional way of dealing with such things. It cannot solve everything. But certainly, it did help the children with their post-conflict trauma."

She then presented me with the box. I have kept it on my desk ever since. It is quite full.

THE TEACHING OF A DRY WATER WELL

Mamadouba's jeep stopped at another village. Under a grass woven canopy in the village center, women were weaving mats of natural fiber. They presented a rainbow of colors in their robes, giggling, laughing, and weaving. "These are our traditional mats. In the villages, we spread them on the floor of thatched huts or shelters in the desert. In the towns and cities, we still use them on the floor of new homes made of cement. They are natural, cool to sit on, and convenient. When you need to clean them, just shake or brush them off. It is that easy. Whenever we sit as a family, to eat or rest, we use these mats."

Mamadouba then shook his head. "But today, the traditional art of mat weaving is disappearing. Chinese have brought plastic mats with them. In fact, Chinese traders flood our market with their plastics. Because they are cheaper, people now buy them. Women are losing their weaving skill. More seriously, their sources of income are disappearing. As they stop weaving, a sense of community is broken as well. The women gather during the day with their little children, to gossip and weave. It was a way of life. Here in Podor, I am trying to bring that back."

Rokhaya explained how Mamadouba had systematized a common village practice in Senegal, where women would organize themselves into groups to produce traditional handicrafts. Sale of the crafts supports social projects in the village such as vaccines for kids, the purchase of books, and so on. Different women take the lead in organizing each project, on a rotating basis. Mamadouba had simply scaled their grass-roots efforts, making mat weaving a social enterprise.

Mamadouba's projects reminded me exactly of what Shambhala was doing in Tibet.

Driving his jeep further into the desert, we arrived at another nomad's village. Here yellow mud bricks were being piled upon each other. The shell of what would soon become another clinic was taking shape. After discussing the construction and measuring the width of walls and doors, Mamadouba sent instructions. He was followed at every step by village leaders dressed in crimson blue, vibrant yellow, and white robes. They listened intently as he described how the next stage of construction should be. This is how Mamadouba spends every weekend. That is why there is progress in Podor.

Then together, followed by the village leaders in flowing robes, we walked across the sands to sit on mats woven by village women, under a thatched canopy. Before sitting, I took off my heavy boots and realized, aside from Mamadouba, I was the only one wearing shoes.

The village chiefs came to Mamadouba with their problems. "The younger village leaders should better respect their elders. I was offended by one from the other village. You should have him killed," said one sarcastically. Another complained about someone who was stealing his sheep. Mamdouba navigated these issues diplomatically, diffusing tensions, turning anger to laughter. But there was one problem that he could not laugh off. It was the single burning issue that affected everyone: scarcity of water.

One elder chieftain made his point perfectly clear. "What are you going to do about my wife? She is no longer as beautiful as before. Her hands are becoming rough. Why? Every day she must walk twice the distance as before, to get water. She must then carry the water. The old village wells that we have used since the time of my great grandfather's father are now dry."

TRADITIONAL WAYS PRESENT NEW APPROACHES

What Mamadouba had achieved in his district of Podor reflected many experiences in Tibet. However, in Namibia, this approach went beyond experiment, to transition on a nationwide scale.

Until 1989, Namibia was subject to apartheid, controlled by European Afrikaans. There were 6,500 private farms covering 5,000 hectares in average size. The government embarked on a program of purchasing land from white owners, which it would redistribute to local disadvantaged communities.

Namibia is rich in resources. But under apartheid, these resources were state controlled. Villagers did not benefit. Torn by war, they saw no benefit in protecting animals, and poaching flourished. Namibia's animal population was depleted.

After apartheid, the new government offered a comprehensive plan for sustainable ecotourism, supported by the World Wildlife Fund. The plan: return tribal lands to the villages and empower them as wardens of their own nature conservancy. Traditional villagers were once hunters, so they were able to track animal movement patterns and bring tourists to see them. By running ecotourism lodges, they could make more money providing full-service safaris than they could from taking bribes from poachers.

Here three stakeholders—NGO, government, and community—worked together for positive change.

"In the beginning, local people did not have a clear concept of how a conservancy would benefit them," explained the conservancy leader—effectively the village chief. "But once they had tangible results, people understood the importance and positive impact a conservancy could have."

Conservancies are run as an ecotourism business offering safari lodge services. They also become community centers for the villagers who are members of the conservancy. These centers provide education and medical treatment while addressing issues such as HIV and water management.

The entire model is based on the structure of a traditional village. Local people were once custodians of the land and environment. They hunted according to their own rules, knowing that conservative hunting assured the replenishment of species for the next generation.

The influence of environmentalists offering business solutions changed government policy. New legislation empowered communities to have authority over wildlife. That meant the communities had ownership of the problem. They saw wildlife as an asset, rather than a detriment to their livelihood. The conservancy movement empowered local people to make their own decisions about their resources.[3]

To date, 59 established conservancies cover 16.8 percent of Namibia. In fact, 1 out of every 8 Namibians now lives in a conservancy. In addition, over 30 new conservancies are forming, and should be fully established in the near future.

All money earned goes back to the local community, not the state. The community runs partly as a village, partly as a business. The village members are effectively shareholders in the business. The government levies a 15 percent tax on safari game trophies (hunted legally with a license) and a 35 percent corporate tax on revenue from the safari lodge.

Mongolia and Nepal are now studying the Namibian conservancy model. The underlying principles can be applied anywhere in the world to empower and benefit people.

AFRICAN CONSENSUS AS A FRAMEWORK FOR NONVIOLENCE

By April 2011, I joined Awadi and Tine in Banjul, the capital of Gambia, where the African Commission for Human and Peoples Rights is headquartered. A congress of NGOs from across the continent was to convene. Following Tine's advice, we sought to bring the African Consensus Resolution before the NGO forum and turn it into a continent-wide declaration.

Over 200 NGOs from all 54 African countries were present, including many of the organizers of Arab Spring protests in Tunisia, Egypt, and Libya. NGOs of all strands represented a cross-section of interests, from fighting torture to sexual equality, democracy, and the right to clean water and food. It was a powerful gathering of leaders who were dedicating their careers and lives to fighting for human rights.

We began to redraft the African Consensus Resolution with input from many others. Awadi suggested we boil it down to two pages, preferably even one. We added new language, emphasizing the role of traditional wisdom in medicine but also economics:

> *In our era of measuring success by industrial growth and consumption alone, we have ignored traditional systems of wisdom that prioritize environmental balance and quality of life.... But development economists and multilateral institutions largely ignored traditional*

knowledge in favor of imported economic models often unconnected to realities on the African continent. The African Consensus declaration calls upon these values in establishing an economic development approach that suits the realities of Africa.

He shook his head. "Too wordy. If you can't rap it, nobody gonna understand it."

Both Awadi and Tine strongly believed that the African Consensus could become a framework for advancing peace. Cote d'Ivoire and Libya were erupting in crisis as we worked on the document. Tine then drafted out in the document a three-point framework for understanding the rise of violence in Africa:

Ethnic violence often arises from competition to control scarce resources. The problems associated with the alienation of ethnic groups must be addressed at their root cause. Economic empowerment ultimately is at the root of the problem.

In the Himalayas, Africa, and many regions of our planet, ethnic violence arises from conflicts over the control of resources. In most cases, the issue is ultimately economic. Likewise, terrorism arises when people are deprived of their economic rights and when their identity is marginalized. In short, they are pushed to, or over the edge.

The African Consensus Declaration was adopted by the African Commission on Human and People's Rights NGO Forum, in Banjul, Gambia, on April 27, 2011.[4] It articulated three fundamental human rights: the right to one's ethnic identity, the right to cultural sustainable development, and the right to water, crystallizing the point that economic empowerment is a valid framework for prevention of violence and terrorism.

Didier Awadi spoke again and summed up the aspirations of all those present (finally happy to rap it in one sentence): "Africa does not have poverty. Africa has been impoverished."

PART IV

THE NEW EARTH CONSENSUS:
Community Consciousness and Planetary Survival

Anarchism really means people working together outside of the structure of the state to meet people's needs... media promotes the idea that anarchy means violence and mayhem. Actually it only means adults taking responsibility and accountability. Anyway, I think most people know the difference between "right and wrong" much better than the authoritarians who fear our freedom.

—*Anonymous European Blogger*

We need a new financial architecture based on environmental economics to address infrastructure conversion from fossil fuels to renewable energy as the next global economic driver. It is the biggest challenge our planet faces if we want to have a planet on which to live. And our global youth have to lead us.

Three decades of neoliberal market fundamentalism has cemented shopping malls over communities and made junk food omniscient and price competitive, while putting America's pioneering community spirit in a museum. Europe followed this model.

Change will not come through either elections or long-winded speeches. It will happen through the revitalization of communities and giving back to people what is theirs: the opportunity to empower themselves with their own businesses. This is not a question for televised debate between political parties. It is the vital issue of how to "re-pioneer" America through its own communities. For Europe, austerity is not the answer. It is about diversified localization, the reempowerment of communities, and the creation of new smart growth through investment in energy efficiency and renewables.

Community rejuvenation, the return to our roots, the repossession of our ethnic identity, these are all parts of the same equation. New measures of success also play a part. They are breaking the conspicuous consumption conundrum that eats our planet's resources and widens social and income gaps.

More people are beginning to realize that our planet is not sustainable the way it is being handled. This means the financial architecture needs to change. We need to stop thinking only capital markets and return to the basics, supporting small and community-based businesses. This means a shift from monolithic globalization to diversified localization.

Climate change is the biggest security threat to our planet today.

Our planet's survival requires a slowdown in the process of climate change. This can only occur by reducing actual $CO2$ emissions, not trading them for remaining air space to pollute—what activists call "green wash." This will require massive infrastructure investments in grid conversion from fossil fuels to renewable energy.

It is not a question of theory, but the survival of our planet.

CHAPTER 10

OCCUPY YOUR MIND:
The Peaceful Revolution Comes to America

VOICES OF GLOBAL DISSENT UNITE: SAY "NO" TO GREED

New York, 2011. Unprecedented numbers of protesters were out in the streets. But protest wasn't enough. A rational economic paradigm and agenda was needed to get us out of the mess we were in. Moreover, unlike all the protests I had observed in other nations, this was occurring in my own. I had a responsibility to be there. This was my fight.

The drive into Manhattan from LaGuardia Airport underscored the problem. Empty buildings and run-down neighborhoods reflect a nation whose leaders are not looking ahead to the future.

There is no reason for America's airports, bridges, roads, and transit systems to be falling into decay. We have only our inertia to blame for allowing politicians to wreck this country. The ignorance of policymakers in America seemed infuriating. No wonder everyone was just pouring out into the streets.

The taxi driver offered the latest news. "There were more people arrested today. The protests have spread."

"How far?"

"Several parks, and now the crowd is moving into Times Square." The driver laughed. "More arrests will happen."

Detecting an accent, I asked where he was from.

"Egypt."

That evening the Occupy movement had called for global protests. From Taiwan to Rome and Sydney, people were pouring into the street that day, voicing outrage. Was it the beginning of a new earth consensus?

Occupy Wall Street had set its sights on Times Square. The police had cleverly cordoned off all the street thoroughfares to break up the crowd. Lines of police blocked storefronts, warning protestors, "Keep moving and don't block the stores." The New York City Police Department is adept at cleverly using traffic flow and antiloitering ordinances to prevent a critical mass from gathering in any one place, as the Chinese were good at brutally crushing any form of dissent or protest.

ZEN AND THE ART OF SUBWAY INFRASTRUCTURE MANAGEMENT

Born in Manhattan, I felt very much at home. Strangely enough, this was not because I was back in the Big Apple. Rather the sights and sounds of the city came from all the other places I had lived since leaving New York as a kid.

As I entering the subway, the familiar sound of a Senegalese drummer banging out rhythm from a carved wooden drum echoed. From the woodcarving style, it must have come from the drummers' market near Center Bopp in Dakar.

Riding an antiquated, graffitied, squealing subway train in New York contrasted with the gleaming ultramodern, superclean subway systems you can ride in Asia. Why does our government not spend stimulus package funds on infrastructure upgrades to create jobs for many, instead of using the same funds to bail out a few rogue hedge fund and investment bankers?

As I came up from the subway at Wall Street, the iconic golden bull had been cordoned off with metal barricades used for crowd control. Police stood uneasily around it, on alert. The image of that bull in a cage—seemingly behind bars—was packed with symbolism.

Did a golden bull under police protection represent the Wall Street titans' fear that the people in the street might take their treasure?

Or did it symbolize a more populist sentiment: that the titans of Wall Street and their political backers in the Federal Reserve and the Treasury should be put behind bars?

I walked past Charging Bull, and the surrealist juxtaposition struck a chord. By afternoon, protesters invited me to give a speech in front of that same 11-foot-long bronze bull condemning "irrational consumption," demanding that our Federal Reserve and Treasury "get back to basics," and asserting that the 99 percent represented a "new American consensus."

The next morning, there were no Senegalese drums in the subway. This time, the station was filled with the sound of a *guzhen*, a stringed Chinese instrument and flute. In New York, Chinese students played music in the street for small change. In Beijing, their government had bought much of America's Treasury notes, thereby propping up the US government, which runs at a $16.370 trillion deficit, borrowing $4.8 billion each day.

I listened to the music and thanked the Chinese girl who was playing it, dropping three quarters into her *guzhen* case.

"Oh, please keep this," she said, handing the three quarters back to me. "It is too little for us to use. You may need this change for the subway."

THE NEW AMERICAN REVOLUTION IS REDISCOVERING VALUES AND COMMUNITY

Before it was named after a real estate tycoon, Zuccotti Park was called Liberty Plaza Park. The mood of protest in 2011 felt retro-1960s, the Age of Aquarius. In those days, people in the "Village" read poetry, smoked pot, condemned the Vietnam War, and called for a new era based on a higher spirituality than the postwar materialism of their parents. Young girls wearing headbands and dressed in flowing tie-dyed skirts were determined to change the world by eating whole wheat, sprout sandwiches. It all felt just that good.

Forty years later, it all looked so familiar. An almost flower-child-like euphoria intoxicated Zuccotti Park. There were hippies and the homeless, the jobless and disaffected graduate students, PhD students from Columbia, and concerned people from across the spectrum of America. Among them were those who have been marginalized and those who fear that they will be. Occupy represented an America that had been let down and had come out to vent its frustration. It was an America that felt deluded and ripped off.

There was an energetic pulse that vibrated across the lines of political party, race, and class. It drew everyone who gathered in the street, and those watching from their televisions and laptops, into a matrix of common sentiment. I had never felt so American before in my whole life. I realized that feeling has nothing to do with the Super Bowl or Thanksgiving turkeys. It is all about Lexington, Concord, and Shay's Rebellion.

Many groups, activists, and political parties had congregated there. While drawn into the vortex, all of them wanted to ride the energy of protest for their own cause. But no one group could harness the Occupy force, because by its nature it was spontaneous. Even the organizers realized they were roughriding a many-headed hydra moving without a single direction.

An older disheveled man, holding aloft a Chinese flag, condemned China for taking American jobs. A sharply dressed younger man—perhaps an out-of-work professional—called for abolition of the Federal Reserve and the Treasury Department. There were hundreds of disparate voices calling for change that President Barack Obama had failed to deliver. Many jobless persons held signs, wanting to tell their stories to anyone willing to listen. There were unemployed veterans and peace protesters. The plethora of opinion and style of protest merged the 1930s Great Depression protests with the hippies at Union Square in the 1960s, with Hyde Park added on Sunday. To a great extent, the diversity of opinion kept the movement energized. This spectrum of voices had been missing from the American political debate and media for too long.

There was no core group of organizers, but rather clusters of people working together. People came and went, but somehow there was a kind of consistency to it. Many firmly believed that they were about to create a new society with new rules of conduct, new age economics, and a fresh, all-inclusive participatory political system. They called it "consensus democracy."

It was not really about a set of ideas or agendas. They all agreed something was wrong and our system was dysfunctional, but they did not want to put forward any solutions. In fact, there was almost a knee-jerk reaction against any specific demands or a solution to address their grievances. Everyone talked about "occupying space" as being the very core of their movement. But nobody asked, "What happens when the government moves in and reclaims the space?"

Jason, a self-acclaimed anarchist, explained, "We want to keep the momentum behind our movement. If we can get through the winter, then we will be really strong by spring." Many firmly believed that. Then it rained one night. The next morning, homeless people huddled in their shelters, while student organizers were in McDonalds having breakfast. The crisp autumn days were numbered. Another New York winter was soon approaching.

A sharp split emerged between those who felt the time was ripe to make specific demands and an agenda, and the vast majority, who feared that any demands from one group would alienate those in another.

This division would be the fatal flaw of Occupy.

Rachael, a young graduate student leading "think tank" sessions—group talk-ins to vent frustration—explained: "I need to establish my values first. Once I have values, then I can figure out what my demands are going to be."

All of this exposed a vibrant section of America that was frenetically groping for values. At one end of the park a designated "spiritual tree" served as an ecumenical site for prayer. Throughout the day, people meditated, burned incense, undertook exorcism, did yoga, and sought a higher level of values. Because it was all-inclusive, Occupy gave them an identity. This was the power of the movement.

THE OCCUPY "BRAND": PEOPLE'S MICROPHONE AND TEMPERATURE READING

Embedding myself with Occupy Wall Street, I saw parallels with Yan'an, also a political utopia from another era and continent. Yan'an is where Mao created his ideal commune during the revolutionary struggle of the 1930s and 1940s. Students across China flocked there, dreaming of building a new society from scratch. A brilliant self-promoter, Mao used Yan'an as a theater upon which an ideal future society was enacted in miniature. It was all about social equality and mission. But when scaled nationally after 1949, it fell apart because it was not practical.

Occupy activists sought to create an ideal world right at street level under the towers of Wall Street. Their whole point was to prove that there was another way.

Basically a small village was being operated in Zuccotti Park. Remarkably, the various service committees coordinated their interservices between themselves without any offices, salaries, or infrastructure, and reported to the General Assembly (GA), which was the highest governing council, effectively a mini-parliament.

Zuccotti Park became a well-organized community. The food committee set up a clean and efficient kitchen to serve street sleepers, but anyone could eat there. The food was healthy and good. There was a sanitation and garbage committee. A library was established in one corner of the park. A media network and Internet center were running a news stream all day. A medical clinic was established in another corner of the park. Even though all of these services were being provided daily to hundreds of people amid the chaos and confusion of ongoing protest, it all functioned like clockwork.

Mayor Michael Bloomberg should have provided these services to the homeless a long time ago.

Each evening from 7 to 9, everyone gathered at the GA regardless of weather or events. Anyone who showed up could participate.

The GA was the highest body charged with approving any plan or idea that would become an Occupy Wall Street action or position. But its membership could change at any time. The GA met on the steps along the Broadway side of Zuccotti Park, across from the towering offices of Brown Brothers and Harriman.

Occupy effectively set up a government-in-exile with no leaders, no parties, and no Speaker of the House. Everyone participated and helped out. The New York Police Department banned the use of loudspeakers, so everyone just repeated to someone else what the speaker was saying, and in that way everyone could hear it. This method was called "The People's Microphone." Because of the need to repeat what was being said, everyone actually listened. That's very different from what goes on at congressional filibuster sessions.

Moreover, because of the repeat factor, the speaker had to be clear, articulate, and to the point. There were no long-winded speeches. This was very unlike Congress where legislation written by lawyers, leaves nonlawyers unable to understand it. Most congressmen do not bother to read the legislation they are adopting anyway. That opens the door to corporate lobbying, and that's where money kicks in to control the process. At the GA, people understood what they were voting for.

At Occupy, voting was done with hand signals called "temperature readings." This was more about building consensus rather than an absolute black-or-white, yes-or-no vote.

Each protest group occupying public space in other cities of America, under the Occupy franchise, operated according to the same rules, each with its own GA. At its height, Occupy effectively formed a shadow government, or a political process run in parallel to the national process, even if just as an experiment. By holding a general assembly on the street, where anyone could attend and participate, they upstaged Congress.

An immense political theater had opened its curtain. But the news media never got this point. As a demonstration, Occupy was a vast sprawling masterpiece of living installation art spreading from New York to California, pantomiming our political system.

The quixotic irony is that Occupy was a celebration of our diversity as Americans and the strength of that diversity when it comes together as a force for common purpose. At Zuccotti Park, it was not just a few hippies and homeless people that the mainstream media portrayed. Occupy represented a microcosm of America. From the Left to the Right, blue collar to white, they were all there expressing both frustration and anger. There were war veterans and peace activists, Free Palestine activists and Hassidic Jews, strait-laced Americans with multiple masters degrees but no jobs and street kids deprived of education altogether. Labor unions and organic farmers, communists, socialists, libertarians, anarchists, evangelist Christians, Hare Krishnas, American Indians, school teachers, rap singers, Sufi drummers, right-left-center and the complete spectrum of everything in-between were there in full force.

They spoke their mind about how badly our politicians with their Wall Street cohorts have messed up America. They said what our television talking heads don't dare speak. Occupy was not a Democrat versus Republican, or a left versus right thing. On the contrary, it was both sides of the political spectrum joining hands.

Most mainstream media depicted the Occupiers as disorderly, unorganized, and without any clear agenda. However, none of these points was true.

The protesters were very orderly and had their own rules of conduct, even to the point of telling Occupiers not to drink in Zuccotti Park, as it could get them kicked out. They organized young volunteers to clean the park, picking up garbage by hand. One young man, probably a student, wearing a dark blue sock hat, blue sweatshirt, and jeans, was picking up garbage. He had a small earring. A middle-aged couple visiting the protests wanted to throw out some scrap. He picked it up right away.

"Thank you," they said, acknowledging his responsiveness.

He smiled, responding with a very soft voice, "Thank you for thanking me."

The whole point of the Occupy Wall Street was that it was a movement experimenting with new forms of representation and values, including one that our politicians lack: respect.

Their action in creating a mini-government as a form of protest was a pantomime that involved disrobing our politicians as dysfunctional and myopic. Everything Occupy did was intentionally free from the constraints of the current American political system, mimicking its societal norms and economic mechanisms. By efficiently running a government of Zuccotti Park that was transparent, open, tolerant, and that exuded positivity, they were showing that America was capable of achieving on a small scale what government organizations and politicians continually failed to do on a national level.

ANATOMY OF A FAILED PEACEFUL REVOLUTION

Occupy organizers were intelligent people. They knew what they were doing, but failed to take the movement to the next stage. The Occupy movement, at its critical third to fourth week, could have formed a political party and used its manpower to collect signatures to put that party on the ballot of each state. The momentum was such that this decision—if taken—could have pushed Occupy from street protest to organized party in a meaningful way. This, however, was not the vision of those in the street.

There was such euphoria and thrill to have what seemed like a mass movement embracing all of America, that they did not want to do what they thought might slow the movement's momentum. Because there were so many diverse groups in the street, potentially antagonistic toward each other, the organizers feared putting forward a specific agenda.

There were tactical errors as well. Initially, they protested on Wall Street itself, which carried powerful significance. The police cleverly got the protesters away from the New York Stock Exchange, moving them to Zuccotti Park. But what counted was occupying the sacred New York Stock Exchange space! Unless the means of capital could be prevented from functioning, the power brokers would not have to compromise on anything. So Occupy just became a waiting game.

Occupy was a cacophony of spontaneous speak-ins. I often stood on the Broadway side of the park across from those towering offices of Brown Brothers and Harriman, telling gathering pedestrians about the four animals in Tibet—the elephant, monkey, rabbit, and bird, and how they all have a relationship with each other and the tree. It seemed amazing how this simple story about the interconnection of our biodiversity and the power of giving rather than taking could cross cultures from the Himalayas to Wall Street and be understood so clearly.

The issue is not just activists against big business and banks. The truth is, corporations and hedge funds are not going to disappear. But we can change their way of thinking. Multistakeholders must be involved and work together to achieve positive change. The question is how we can restructure governing policies and proceed to change the direction of our lives, not destroy each other.

Egyptian activists from Tahrir Square joined us one afternoon. Everyone felt a rich irony when they raised the Egyptian flag. Speaking in Zuccotti Park, they told how Washington spent $1.3 billion each year to support Mubarak's military that repressed those very Egyptian protesters themselves. That kind of money could be spent in America to upgrade infrastructure and create jobs. Moreover, the Tahrir protestors revealed that the key turning point in their revolution was when Egypt's economically squeezed middle class joined hands with youth activists to fight Mubarak's regime.

The Egyptian protesters advised the Occupy movement to demand something. This was Occupy's key failure. Already there were signs that both the public cheering the protesters, and many of those out in the street themselves were becoming frustrated with the game and the inability of Occupy to deliver a clear agenda or at least a negotiable demand. The Egyptian activists explained that in demanding Mubarak's resignation, it was only a step in the process toward change, not an end in itself. But they had to win that first crucial step in order to take the next. Some Occupy protesters then called for the resignation of Fed Chairman Ben Bernanke.

Regardless of the substance of such a move, this would have at least been an articulated position, something to negotiate for. As a matter of tactics, in a situation like this the protesters have to put a demand on the table that they can potentially win. It almost does not matter what that demand is. If they can win it, this gains credibility and with it strength behind the movement. Then they can move on to the next demand with greater force and achieve a broader strategic objective through attrition of issues. But Occupy did not adopt such strategy. The approach was too free-for-all. In fact, the GA did not want to articulate any position at all.

This was the same problem with the once widespread antiglobalization movement. Attending the World Social Forum in Dakar, I listened to many speeches condemning the global order, but they failed to present a viable alternative, which is what everyone is looking for. The audience is there, but the performers are only speaking to the converted. Observation: a blueprint (script) is needed for a new economic paradigm that can be the foundation for a "new global consensus" (positive and constructive) rather than an "antiglobalization movement" (negative and deconstructive). Otherwise, the speeches and protests only catch a media sound bite but fail to articulate a clear direction for change, which is what people are looking for and need.

Many people wanted to turn Occupy into a real movement for change, but were then turned away from Occupy by the very facilitators who were trying to grow the movement. In the end, maybe it had to do with layered prejudice within our own society, huge generational distrust, and just pure clique tribalism. Ironically, that is why our current political system is dysfunctional.

The broader Occupy movement was a constellation of smaller movements that actually did not want to work with each other. There was a firm intolerance within the narrower rather than broader Occupy movement for taking ideas and putting them into policy and trying to get the system in Washington to move to the next stage. This made Occupy very different from an organization like Greenpeace or 350.org, which actually aim at specific issues, protest and lobby to achieve a goal, and then move on to the next one. Occupy did not want to get specific on anything. It was all about process and not actual agendas, so the movement started to dissipate. The protests succeeded in occupying the mind of Americans by putting problems in people's faces on Facebook and YouTube, but could not take the next step in figuring out how to really solve problems.

A middle-aged African American woman named Valerie had a masters' degree, kids, and no work. After a speech, she joined me in attending working committee meetings and then the GA. Finally she said, "This is OK for students who have lots of time and parents paying for their education. But I have to feed kids. I need real change in the system. Actually, I need to go get a job."

REAWAKENING THE AMERICAN SPIRIT

The demonstrators' anger focused on a range of seemingly disconnected issues, from the current mismanaged regulation of capital markets, to unemployment, to the bulldozing of local culture, to the loss of community and ethnic identity, to environmental degradation.

But actually, each of the issues was finely interlinked with other aspects of our global economic system and the prevailing financial architecture.

Boiling it down, there were several points of similarity among protesters in the Occupy movement as it spread virally across America. "Occupy Everywhere" might agree to the following:

1) *Our global economy is not sustainable as it is being run*. The global economic and financial system concentrates wealth among a few and impoverishes many. Diminishing the middle-class buffer between rich and poor leads to class war. Accepted notions of economics are not working anymore.
2) *The financial architecture is outdated and must change*. Overreliance on capital markets, currency, and debt trading has made a few rich and disempowered multitudes. The anticipated trickle-down effect has not occurred. There is a call for balance, from globalization to localization. Neither extreme is good. We need both. Balance requires financial and banking systems that can provide for community development and entrepreneurship for small and medium-sized businesses. We need to develop green business and green financing. Micro-finance should be creatively adapted. We must be open to alternative economy movements that seek other means of trading goods and services at the community level.
3) *Climate change is the single biggest security threat to our planet*. The cost of natural disasters is obvious. Continued environmental degradation and global warming will herald food and water security threats. Environmental militancy will arise. This is not a question of beliefs, but survival. Mitigation of greenhouse gases is a global priority that is delayed at our expense. Enter

environmental economics: a reprioritization of stimulus packages, from supporting financial houses to investment in renewable energy infrastructure to converting grids from fossil fuels to clean energy. It may not be what oil company lobbying interests like, but it will create jobs and sustain our planet. The technology is there. This is the real New Deal. Politicians need to wake up or get kicked out.

4) *Military expansion fails to make our planet a peaceful, prosperous place.* In fact, recent military campaigns have created more suffering, leading to increased instability, insecurity, and terrorism. Funds that support military buildups should be used to empower people with the skills and small finance they need to run their own business and generate local prosperity. Sustainable economics requires infrastructure upgrades, education, health care, and skill transfer. Funding these needs will do more for peace and security than military might.

5) *Our current political systems are dysfunctional.* People are no longer fooled by politicians, who are increasingly seen as avatars for commercial and lobbying interests. The problems are systemic. Electing a new face solves nothing. The system has to change. Ultimately, this may mean fresh systems for direct popular voting in America and an end to the Electoral College, a mechanism that should be obsolete. We need electoral reform in our own system, and the introduction of a third party or multiparties to break the dysfunctional deadlock of the two entrenched political parties we have. After this happens, we can talk to the world about democracy. Let's solve our own problems first.

6) *The Media are not independent and reflect corporate-government sponsored opinion.* Mainstream news media is slanted and narrow in its reporting. Controlled by corporate and political interests, the media don't want us to talk. We have no choice but to go to the streets, or we can level the playing field with social media and the Internet. Enter online news streaming and guerrilla television.

7) *Peaceful civil disobedience has become the response to political inertia.* When the protesters shut down the means of capital flow, the politicians and media will finally sit down with them and talk about what needs to change. Only when the tap of capital is cut off will they wake up.

The Occupy movement was about occupying space so that it can occupy minds. That is what these protests were all about.

The media managed to stigmatize the movement, but they have not suppressed the American people's feelings of frustration or being ripped off. The media's 24/7 coverage of ignoramuses in election battles belittles Americans by making them think their vote counts. Occupy should have taken over CNN and Fox studios with a demand: stop treating us as if we are stupid!

On November 15, 2011, in a nationally coordinated sweep, police in riot gear forced protesters to evacuate the public spaces they had been occupying for nearly two months. America's Homeland Security apparatus had good intelligence on Occupy. They knew the movement had no leadership, no agenda. With leadership, a movement that is suppressed can go into exile, and its leaders can become symbols of a continuing struggle. With an agenda, people know what they are fighting for and can continue to support it. These things are difficult for authority to take away because people associated with a movement can move, go underground, and continue to apply pressure simply by existing.

But with the altruistic idea of occupying space, the movement made a fatal mistake. The authorities realized that cracking the movement could be accomplished by simply taking away the space they occupied. That is exactly what they did. It occurred in one night.

Coordinated police action went down in all cities at the same time. The mainstream American media—so quick to criticize the suppression of protest in any other developing country in the world—reported the entire repression as a neat and orderly event. As the crackdown got underway, on the other side of the world, President Barack Obama spoke to the Australian parliament in Canberra, reading a long drawn-out speech about upholding freedoms as a universal value. Meanwhile, the largest coordinated police repression of American freedom of expression since the Civil Rights movement was taking place at home.

Was it the end of the new global consensus, or maybe just the beginning?

On the one hand, the Occupy movement may have failed to transform itself from mass expression of dissatisfaction into a real political movement or party. On the other hand, it succeeded by grabbing the attention of Americans. Taking the pulse of the people, it showed them that something is very wrong with our system, and it needs to change fast. And something might be out there that is better, or at least offers other ways of looking at things. It challenged the establishment by throwing everything into Wall Street's face.

Maybe the mainstream American media did not get the message clearly. Actually, they must have. They just did not want to deliver it to the American people.

As a peaceful revolution, Occupy failed to evolve from an outraged street movement into a political force with a clear agenda and goals. Because common people demanding real change were able to observe this, its momentum dissipated.

But its tremendous spontaneity inspired us all. The greatest success of Occupy is that it occupied our minds. Nonviolent and peaceful, it reawakened the American spirit. It threatened our politicians enough that they had to shut it down abruptly. Today, any group applying for a rally using the Occupy name cannot get a permit to legally protest. That smacks right against the very freedoms our ancestors fought for. As a peaceful people's movement, Occupy scared the authorities that much! This means, in the end, what we did out there on the street must have been pretty damn good.

CHAPTER 11

"RE-PIONEERING" AMERICA:
Revitalizing Communities and Environmental Economics

SOLAR AS NEW SECURITY: DECENTRALIZE THE GRID

Honolulu, 2011. It was early morning. The sun had just risen, when the plane touched down at Honolulu airport. It felt so strange coming back to Hawaii where I had gone to school, coming full circle around the globe back to an America struggling with itself, desperately in search of a new idea.

Taking the airport shuttle into Waikiki, I was shocked by the changes since my student days. The old family inns that dotted the narrow streets along the lagoon were all gone. Even the charming jungle-overgrown Tahitian Lanai Inn with its carved tiki statues had been replaced by new cement developments and luxury brand chain stores.

Trump Tower loomed over it all.

On arriving at the hotel, I met one of the staff, who was a student from the University of Hawaii. He lived just off campus, at a crossroads known as Puck's Alley, where I had lived as a student. The old neighborhood once had thriving Japanese family stores, Hawaiian lei flower shops, and local communal vegetable markets. Was it the same, or "Trumped" over like this new part of old Waikiki?

I had been invited to speak at the Asian Pacific Securities Studies Center, a branch of the US military located at Fort DeRussy, which is in Waikiki, of all places. Assembled in the room were generals from countries across Asia: Afghanistan, Nepal, Mongolia, Indonesia, Thailand, Cambodia, and Vietnam.

But why was I there?

Were these generals really interested in empowering people as a means of preventing violence and addressing terrorism at its root? To my surprise, most of the generals sitting in the room agreed that we need a new framework as the old one is not working anymore.

Jim Hirai, the acting executive director of the center, had invited me to the meeting. "After running all the scenarios, including water and food security issues, we find that the Himalayan Consensus may be the way forward in preventing conflict in Asia," he explained. The whole approach was about avoiding violence rather than reacting to it. Core were resource management, which is the result of development policies, which in turn are tied to values.

I met one-on-one with Dan Leaf, the general who commanded the center, and formerly the second in command of the entire Pacific operation of the US armed forces. He asked my opinion about North Korea.

It is entirely predictable that China will invest across its border, establishing special economic zones in North Korea and outsourcing cheap production. Costs of labor in China are rising, and college graduates don't want to work in factories. The bottom line is China will capitalize its aid. Chinese enterprises will then operate factories in the zones, and life there will gradually improve as it did in China over the past three decades. North Korea will undergo a similar transition and reform as China and Vietnam have done. The pattern seemed clear. Meanwhile, American soldiers are bunkered up behind barbed wire on the demilitarized zone. Few of them speak Korean, and locals in South Korea find their presence uncomfortable, irritating, but a necessity given the continued tensions that a warlike state of mind carries. Looking way beyond the conflict, we see that China is South Korea's biggest trading partner and that universities in Seoul are packed with Chinese learning Korean to bolster business ties. China business will ultimately buy stability on the Korean Peninsula, with money.

The general seemed shocked at these comments, his second in command and the aides busy taking notes.

I then asked him if the building we were sitting in used solar energy panels. Everyone in the room was silent and thought about it. No, of course not. "Then your energy comes from the grid, which means oil fired, right? Hawaii spends about $6 billion a year just to import oil (and a little coal, by the way) for its electric grid. It is entirely fossil fuel dependent."

They must have thought the conversation was way off-base, because the general asked, "Why is this relevant?"

I explained, "If there was another Pearl Harbor, say, you were being attacked, why should they bother bombing the ships? They just need one rocket on the power plant and everything shuts down. Knock out the grid, and the game is over. You don't steer boats anymore or even planes. It is all click-click on your computer. If an attack shuts down the grid, the armed forces are impotent. But if you have solar panels on this roof baking in the sun all day long, then you have decentralized your power. Every military base on this island could have its own autonomous power sources separate from the grid, making each function independently even if the power source is cut. My point is that renewable energy is not about hugging trees. It is about national security interests."

They just stared at me.

AFRICAN STUDENTS CAN TEACH US ENVIRONMENTAL ECONOMICS

Following Occupy Wall Street, I attended the United Nations Framework Convention on Climate Change (UNFCCC) talks (Cop 17) in Durban, South Africa, as an NGO observer.[1] Together with Didier Awadi, we convened negotiators from India, China, Brazil, Singapore, and several African countries in an attempt to build consensus on the sidelines of the UN talks.

All agreed that the survival of our planet depends on the total reduction of carbon dioxide (CO_2) emissions and that this requires government investment in infrastructure to convert grids from fossil fuel fired- to renewable energy. Fiscal policies and rebates would be needed to encourage corporate investment in renewable energy to make it commercially viable. All agreed that subsidies on fossil fuels should be withdrawn and that the three stakeholders—government, civil society, and business—must sit down at the table, working together for an achievable solution. In Durban, China announced a huge financial commitment under its five-year plan that would accelerate this process. India seconded similar plans.

But the truth is that at current trajectories, there is no hope. While slowing or stopping climate change is on the agenda of the UNFCCC talks, it is not what really happens in the meeting room. Three countries—America, Canada, and Saudi Arabia—driven by the power of their oil corporate interests, block the process on every front. It frustrates the G77 nations, which represent the new global consensus and which are developing nations that will either face massive desertification in the years to come or coastal flooding. In the case of island states, many will simply disappear. For them, the effects of climate change are real.

When the American negotiator, Todd Stern, addressed the assembly, an American female activist stood up from the floor and shouted that through his inaction on climate change, he had forfeited his right to represent the American people at the UNFCCC talks. Security hustled her out immediately. No pluralism on this issue.

Just to put all that in perspective, the first decision of Barack Obama upon taking his oath in 2008 and being sworn in as president of the United States was to order the closure of Guantanamo Bay prison, which he deemed a violation of international human rights and a shame for America as a nation. Stern was assigned to carry out the closure. Four years later, as Obama took his second oath upon reelection, Guantanamo Bay was still not closed, and Stern was handling climate change negotiations.

More encouraging news, however, continued coming from the sidelines. Kumi Naidoo, the executive director of Greenpeace and a celebrity activist in his own right, was being courted by all the corporate CEOs attending as observers. Now that might sound strange, but the word in the corridors was that multinational CEOs would rather be dining with Naidoo than any of the government officials there. Actually, these CEOs were terrified that their corporations might be singled out by Greenpeace activists.

That June, under Naidoo's leadership, Greenpeace launched a campaign to stop American toy manufacturer Mattel from using paper packaging materials supplied from Asia Pulp and Paper, a company infamous for destroying Indonesian rain forests and the habitat of endangered Sumatran tigers. The campaign was built around the idea that Mattel's classic Barbie doll was suffering from a breakup with her doll boyfriend, Ken (another Mattel classic) over rain forest destruction. The doll couple argument was staged on Twitter, and it spelled out the immorality of using packaging that destroyed rain forests and tigers. Images appeared online of the internationally recognized Barbie doll with a chainsaw, which were soon followed by over 500,000 emails that were sent to Mattel. The big American multinational (that once sued Swedish pop group Abba over the use of the names Barbie and Ken in song lyrics) crumbled before Greenpeace and dropped all packaging suppliers connected to deforestation. As the largest toy manufacturer in the world, their humbling sent a huge message to other multinational corporations about what corporate responsibility really means.

Meanwhile, inside the cavernous meeting room, the entire UNFCCC process was degrading into a show, a tragic soap opera of global proportions. Developing nations will not make progress on anything because a few nations whose politicians have their election campaigns paid for by the oil lobby call the shots. So the UN is just providing a theater for a few countries to pretend that they are seriously going to negotiate something for our planet, when they are actually working consistently to achieve its demise.

In the end, I just walked out of the UNFCCC talks and joined the African protesters outside. But they could not make a difference either. Security kept them so far from the meetings that whatever they said or did, it had no effect on the proceedings or theater within. Their voices could not be heard due to the rings of "Darth Vader"-outfitted security that kept them from the deliberations inside.

African women protesters shouted in unison, "We want to have the right to grow our own food." The impact of climate change in Africa was already that bad. In 1969, the rains in Chad and Darfur failed and never came back. A cycle of conflict has followed, often between great powers competing for oil. But at the grassroots, herders and farmers kill each other for grazing and other natural resources that have become scarce. It is a sign portending the future.

During the protests a young African told me that an "alternative COP 17" meeting was being held by activists at a nearby university and gave me the address.

This was the most inspiring conference I had attended throughout the entire UNFCCC. The topic was "Green Capitalism Is about Making Profits from Climate Change." The participants were all young African students, except for one fellow protester from Occupy who had found his way there. Everything else going on that day was based on the ideas of these African students themselves. The theme was "One Million Climate Change Jobs" for South Africa, calling for "a just transition to a low carbon economy to combat unemployment and climate change."

The conference concluded that there are about 27 percent more jobs in renewable power stations than in conventional energy (coal and nuclear). The quality of jobs in renewable energy would be better. They would also be decentralized and closer to where energy services are demanded, which would mean less loss in transmission and greater reliability.

The conference also noted that South Africa suffered from a 25 percent unemployment rate. To put this in perspective, in the 1930s, 25 percent unemployment in America was called the Great Depression. In South Africa, when beggars, subsistence crop growers, and survivalist self-employed are actually included in the unemployment statistics, then the rate is closer to 40 percent. Ask yourself why violent crime is such a serious problem in South Africa.

But these students wanted to change all of this. They had a very clear written agenda that they presented at their self-made conference:

> First we need work. South Africa has one of the highest levels of unemployment in the world, and this underpins a more generalized social crisis of extreme poverty, hunger, crime, substance abuse, and domestic violence. It in turn affects our health and education system, with women and children bearing the heaviest burden. Our second starting point is that we have to slow down climate change...[it] will exacerbate poverty in our country because, at the very least it will reduce water availability.

All of this made such total sense.

Using their own research, the students spelled out a road map of how to create three million new jobs in South Africa. They presented a clear blueprint for infrastructure conversion, job opportunities, and their actual effect on reducing carbon emissions

The "One Million Climate Jobs Campaign" brainstormed by these South African students was comprehensive, clear, very pragmatic, and entirely realizable. It contained none of the UN wishy-washy, convoluted development lingo and multilateral institution gibberish. It was straightforward, something that any person in the street could understand and vote for, if given the chance. The blueprint spelled out the following:

1) *Produce our electricity from wind and solar power.* With a target of producing 50 percent of electricity with renewable energy in ten

years we will create 150,000 jobs and reduce our emissions by 20 percent.
2) *Reduce energy use through energy efficiency in industries.* If we implemented a 20 percent energy efficiency target by 2025, at least 27,000 new jobs would be created.
3) *Reduce energy use in homes and buildings* by constructing new buildings to be energy efficient and retrofitting existing buildings. Just by retrofitting old buildings and houses alone, we could create 120,000 jobs.
4) *Expand public transport.* Reduce our use of oil in transport by improving and expanding our public transport system. A commitment to shift 10 percent of private car commuters to public transport would create about 70,000 jobs and reduce emissions by 24 million tons of carbon dioxide (CO_2). There is potential for even greater job creation and emissions cuts if we commit to more ambitious targets and actions. Overall, our proposals for expanding public transport would result in the creation of 460,000 new jobs.
5) *Produce our food through organic small-scale agro ecology.* Small-scale family farmers and peasants use farming techniques that protect natural resources, are more labor intensive and more productive per hectare. It is possible to create nearly 500,000 new jobs in local food production in urban areas.
6) *Protect our water, soil and biodiversity resources.* Up to 400,000 jobs can be created if ecosystem restoration projects are increased. Ecosystem restoration has a range of benefits, including improving water quality, improving carrying capacity for wildlife and livestock, conservation of topsoil, and recharging groundwater.
7) *Move to zero waste.* If we adopt zero waste principles, we can create at least 400,000 jobs in the current economy and reduce our CO_2 equivalent emissions by 35 million tons. Zero waste is a cheap and effective strategy to combat climate change.

While the official UNFCCC negotiators were locked in a room trying to articulate gobbledygook lingo, debating points that everyone present in the room knew could never be concluded, these South African students were basically writing a real new deal using climate change infrastructure overhaul to revitalize our global economy. They were thinking way ahead of the curve, with a vision surpassing our economists, the UN negotiators, and certainly the American congress.

I walked away thinking to myself, how much America—and the rest of the world—could learn from these South African students.

PUCK'S ALLEY AND NEIGHBORHOOD RENEWAL

When I returned to the East-West Center, it was like a time warp. Not much had changed since the early 1980s, while Asia had undergone a mega-transformation. It felt like dying and being reincarnated back to the same place.

I started visiting old student haunts like the nearby Puck's Alley. Now the time warp sensation really sunk in. I remembered Puck's Alley as a quiet neighborhood that once had a lot of local Japanese shops. Kids got out of school and went there to buy *mochi* rice cakes. There were Chinese shops selling fried won ton, a Chinese organic grocery where fresh vegetables came from someone's garden, and a lot of lei shops where women gathered in the morning and strung garlands of flowers. The smell of flowers filled the street, together with the laughter of Hawaiian women busy with their creations. On the upper floors were karate and kung fu schools.

Puck's Alley had a feeling of community. Even though many different ethnic groups lived beside each other, they each had their unique culture to give and yet at the same time they were a part of the fabric that is Hawaii.

Then one day, Star Market came into the neighborhood. Soon it was followed by Burger King and 7-Eleven, all offering fast food cheaper than the old Japanese mom-and-pop shops or the Chinese organic grocery. One by one they closed. And the lei shops became fewer. By the time I graduated and left for Asia, globalized brands had taken over, and the old neighborhood was something I could only be thankful that I had experienced passing through. The global impact of monobrand culture was upon us. It had smothered America, even breaking the social fabric in this little neighborhood in Hawaii.

Now back at Puck's Alley, I found that to my surprise some lei flower shops were back in business. And my once favorite Japanese mom-and-pop store was now an organic food co-op. In fact, there were quite a few of these in the neighborhood, a Down to Earth organic shop where produce was locally grown, a Peace Café and bakery, a shop selling worms for organic composting, a modern Japanese grocery. There were new creative enterprises like Da Spot, a garage converted into a kitchen, where fresh Thai, Malay, and Egyptian curry was dished up every night. No surprise, the owner was Egyptian American and his wife mixed Asian. The place rocked on Tuesdays as many local musicians just came and jammed without any particular program. In one evening there was everything from Sufi drums to Hindu chanting, rap, and rock.

The neighborhood was back!

But Star Supermarket was gone. Why? One possibility is that the price of imported food was the same if not more than organically grown local produce. But the islands were importing pineapple from the Philippines when Hawaii has the richest volcanic soil in the world. It now only produces pineapple for tourists who visit the Dole farm as if it were a museum, kind of a Disney thing. Dole felt labor costs are too high. But then why are there so many homeless in Honolulu, sleeping in the parks and on the beaches of North Shore?

America's economics just did not seem to add up. At the national level, it is debt-financed wars and political spectacle, and at the personal level, debt-financed conspicuous consumption. The unsustainability of it all is so obvious. But the media won't say this.

People notice. Clearly a shift was underway in the neighborhoods and streets. People were looking for a sense of community and identity not found in plush shopping malls and in luxury brands. They were finding it in reviving a community, working to see that happen, consuming less and living healthier lives. They were creating a community identity. Life around Puck's Alley was a celebration of diversity among people, and everyone seemed to bask in that, while feeling a part of a greater community. In Hawaiian, they call it *o'hana*.

In this little neighborhood of Puck's Alley, I saw another microcosm of America trying to find its way back to itself.

The fact is that there are many Puck's Alley neighborhoods across America, each community trying to return to what it originally was. Neighborhood revival, social programs, food co-ops, community culture, and a spectrum of interesting, diverse, and creative businesses are driving this process. And behind it are people in the community itself, not banks, hedge funds, or politicians.

Whether through alternative economic movements in Seattle or community revival programs in Detroit, the rebuilding or "re-pioneering" of America is happening. The challenge for all of them is the same as those faced by pioneering social entrepreneurs in the

Himalayas and Africa—finding capital, because the financial system works against those who are small and community based.

To re-pioneer America, we must reengineer our financial system.

Through the East West Center's philanthropy program run by Carol Fox, I met Spencer Kim, a Korean American business philanthropist and social entrepreneur. Soft-spoken Kim does not talk about charity, but rather about using business to empower marginalized Americans to rebuild communities. This man is moving mountains.

Kim runs the world's largest aerospace depot, producing aerospace technology, parts, and products. Located in poor neglected towns, his factories provide vocational skills training and empower local business development. Employees become shareholders, and a sense of community is fostered in towns that were once industrially and commercially abandoned. His business ventures embrace the rich diversity of America, with 26 different ethnic groups and 16 languages spoken between the six factories he established across the Midwest. These factories are local, but their product sales are global in reach. "Anyone in aerospace can come to us and get almost everything they need," Kim explained. "It is not about globalization versus localization. You need both!"

Kim is not only bringing capital to these forsaken towns but, equally important, he is bringing back a sense of community. That is what diversified localization is about: community businesses exporting products globally. Adopting a business model such as his, we can re-pioneer America.

Puck's Alley could be a neighborhood in the Bronx, in Detroit, in Oakland, or in Seattle. Kim's six factories could be in any state. Both are not the story of Wall Street, but the story of real America today, rediscovering itself.

BLUE PLANET AND HENK ROGERS'S RANCH

When I met Henk Rogers, he was driving Hawaii's first electric car, a sports convertible that looked like a racing car. It had quite a pickup, and as we sped down Highway One to Chinatown for a late night drink, I thought to myself that Rogers made environmental consciousness seem really quite cool. Imagine an entire industry in electric cars revitalizing Detroit.

Henk B. Rogers was born in the Netherlands of Dutch-Indonesian descent, and lived in New York City from the age of 11 before studying at the University of Hawaii. Dropping out of school, he ran off to Japan, chasing a pretty Japanese girl who is now his wife. While in Japan, he produced the nation's first role-playing video game, *The Black Onyx*, and then founded Tetris, which has sold over 70 million copies as boxed products, 130 million copies as downloads on mobile phones, and is fast approaching 20 million games played per day on Facebook.

Today, Rogers is the fifth-richest person in Hawaii, after the likes of Pierre Omidyar, the founder of eBay, and Steve Case, founder of AOL, but you would not know it. Despite his wealth, Rogers always wears a black T-shirt, a Bhutanese-style Asian open shirt, and carries his cell phone in a Nepalese cloth sack over his shoulder. "Even when he met the Princess of Japan, he dressed like that," commented one administrator at the East-West Center.

Rogers is not just rich. He is Hawaii's most progressive social entrepreneur, who pioneers renewable energy solutions and promotes environmental awareness through his Blue Planet Foundation. One of his life's missions is to end the use of carbon-based fuel. He started with one simple goal: weaning Hawaii away from it first.

"Hawaii has the highest energy prices and the most potential availability of alternative energy in the country. We now spend over $6 billion dollars on oil every single year. It's the reason we can't affordably grow food here. It's the reason our jobs pay less than those on the mainland. It's the reason we have so many homeless people," Rogers said. "The world will change drastically unless we do something now. I am working on it, but it is going to take everyone to wake up. So that's why I started the Blue Planet Foundation to work on this mission."

A few days later, I was on "Big Island," the local way of saying Hawaii Island (the largest in the Hawaiian chain),[2] spending the weekend with Rogers at his ranch in the mountains that overlook the sea. There he showed me his laboratory and the specialists working to achieve his vision. Outside the lab building are nearly a dozen different solar panels, and the laboratory is measuring the efficiency of each in comparison.

The ranch is over a hundred years old, and the area is one of the highest biodiversity spots on the island. It was here that Joseph Rock learned to be a botanist before moving to China, where he explored the area from Li Jiang to Zhongdian and wrote reports for *National Geographic Magazine*. Those reports inspired James Hilton to write *Lost Horizon*, from which the term "Shangri-la" (a misspelling of Shambhala) came into being. It all started here on Rogers's ranch. For me there was an eerily strange connection between this ranch that was pioneering solar solutions and Shangri-la County in Yunnan, where I found inspiration for the whole notion of the Himalayan Consensus

We sat by the fireside in his ranch house, a restored rustic home full of Hawaiian history. We talked a lot about the Himalayan Consensus. Rogers reflected on a recent visit to Bhutan, "I had the pleasure of visiting a little country in Asia called Bhutan. So, 75 of us from 25 countries went to Bhutan to attend a conference to 'teach' the 'backward' Bhutanese how to modernize in a sustainable way. You know, teach them how to be more like us. We spent two days learning about Bhutan and two days demonstrating sustainable technologies."

"At the end of the conference, all of us left Bhutan in a daze. We had all come to the realization that it was not about them becoming more like us. But rather the opposite: it was about us becoming more like them. Their parliament works pretty much like our congress would if congress was not mostly dysfunctional. The difference is that, thanks to Gross National Happiness, they can't do anything that adversely affects the culture and environment, does not make fiduciary sense, is not good governance. I can tell you this. They are the youngest democracy in the world, and we, the most powerful democracy in the history of the world. And it feels like we can't teach them a damn thing."

When we stepped out on the balcony, Rogers pointed toward the ocean and explained, "Scientists have determined that due to ocean acidification, all the coral in the world would die by the end of this century. Acidification is caused by oceanic carbon dioxide absorption. That would be carbon dioxide made by combustion of what once was organic matter. Humans (that would include us) send two hundred years of sequestered carbon (forests turned into coal and sea-life turned into oil) into the atmosphere (that would be the stuff we breathe) every single year. There is something really wrong with this. The problem is bigger than the disappearing coral. The problem is climate change, violent hurricanes, water shortages, food shortages, sea level rising, disappearing island nations, disappearing glaciers."

"Most people could say, but what does that have to do it me? Okay, I'll tell you. Let's start with Hawaii. Ninety-six percent of the energy we use in Hawaii comes from burning fossil fuel. We only have on average 22 days of fuel at any given time. Imagine if the tankers stopped coming for some reason. No jet planes. No cars. No ships. No electricity. No food. No television. No cell phones."

He pointed out that Hawaii imports nearly $6 billion worth of fossil fuels to fire the electricity grid. These funds could be saved and put to use constructively to improve the economy and upgrade social services. Rogers' vision is to achieve this through decentralization of energy. Each home becomes its own source of energy through solar. Another approach he is developing on his ranch is a solar center to generate energy that will be provided to other ranches in the valley at rates cheaper than Hawaiian Electric can provide.

One step at a time, he is determined to prove that homeowners themselves can decentralize energy, and that the island can thrive with renewable sources. The trade winds and sun are Hawaii's natural resources. His idea is to demonstrate what can be done in Hawaii, for the rest of the United States and the planet.

But at the time of writing, the state government of Hawaii was taxing those families who produce renewable energy. This action effectively penalizes people for leaving the fossil fuel-consuming state grid and choosing renewable energy. Instead of giving tax breaks to people who get off the grid, the state is taxing them. This is incredible! But there it is. Our greed-based system that supports corporate monopoly or oligarchy is working against not only our social entrepreneurs but against you and me, our children, and our planet!

THE GEOTHERMAL DOLLAR: MORE GREEN ENERGY = MORE DOLLARS

At the rim of the Kilauea volcano, sulfur steams from vents. It feels as if one has stepped back into the Neolithic age. The power comes from the earth. It is the source of all things.

At night, the red glow of Kilauea can be seen with fumes rising up in a warming glow that warns us the forces of nature are far greater than what we humans think we are capable of. There is a sense of eternity here, which makes us feel as tiny as a fraction of nothingness in the context of the universe.

Kilauea—considered by Hawaiians as the goddess Pele—has a way of reminding us to put things into perspective. Here I am, standing at the edge of the volcano to give offering to the volcano goddess Pele. Her fury and power can take various forms. Sometimes tentacles of lava pour like rivers, obliterating everything in her path. Sometimes she appears illusionary, as a lovely young girl with the allure of a princess.

I am wrapping a bottle of Russian vodka in a *ti* leaf. *Ti* leaf is considered sacred by Hawaiians because it can ward off negativity, and is used in offerings to the gods. (It is even waved by fans at football games). Pele is known among Hawaiians to like offerings of vodka, and sometimes gin. Holding the *ti* leaf aloft, I toss the bottle of vodka into the mouth of Pele.

Back in Honolulu, I meet with Henry Noa and Luka, leaders of one of the many branches of the Hawaiian sovereignty movement. "It is not about sovereignty," they declare. "It is about independence. The Kingdom of Hawaii has been reinstated. The US Federal government has no legal claim over our lands."

Historically, Hawaii was once an independent nation, with a king and queen recognized by the monarchs of Europe and the emperors of China and Japan. Queen Liliuokalani was overthrown in a coup led by American and other businessmen backed—at least implicitly—by US marines. It was not about oil, but sugar cane, then a key commodity. In short order, the then-forty thousand Hawaiians who comprised four-fifths of the population of the islands had their lands and rights effectively confiscated in one fell swoop. Even under United States law, federal claims over the islands can be challenged, and Native Hawaiian groups actively invoke these claims. This makes federal authorities nervous, even jittery, when the subject comes up. President Bill Clinton acknowledged the national sovereignty of Hawaii, but did not take it any further to give real power back to Hawaiians. Henry Noa and Luka have helped put the whole issue back on the table by reinstating the kingdom, with a full-blown constitution and a legislature running as a parallel authority to the state's. They are even giving out driver's licenses and national identity cards, although these tend to get thrown out of court when violations occur.

"It is not about sovereignty. We need to establish our authority," Noa explains energetically, his white beard giving him the persona of Hawaiian royalty.

"Aside from a standing army, I can think of only one other thing which gives a people both sovereignty and authority," I observe. "It is having your own currency. What the Hawaiian government needs is its own currency and a central bank."[3]

Noa's eyes widen. "And how do we do that?"

"Geothermal energy. Kilauea, or Mother Pele, has the power. And only Hawaiians who can communicate with Pele through the *kahunas*, or spiritual high priests, can access her benevolence. Hawaii has so much natural geothermal energy. To switch the grid over from gas to geo will require an investment of $2 billion. However, Hawaii imports $6 billion every year to buy oil to fire the grid. So $2 billion that will create climate jobs is a rational investment with immediate savings and return. Imagine putting that $6 billion back into the Hawaiian economy each year.

"What Hawaii wants to do is calculate the value of geothermal energy and the potential of that value out by about one hundred years. Then issue a currency that is attached to the value. The currency does not need to be used outside of the islands. As long as it is accepted tender within the islands, anyone who comes here to do business must convert. When leaving, they convert again. Of course the buy/sell rate is different. Given the state of the US economy, national deficit, trade deficit, and continued pilfering by Wall Street, I would imagine on a one-to-one issue, the Hawaiian geothermal dollar would appreciate against the US dollar over time."

As far-fetched as it sounds, there is an underlying logic to local and alternative currencies.

The US dollar was taken off of the gold standard in 1972. The gold standard was a rational and stabilizing peg with international acceptance. The free float is now based on nothing at all except the full faith and credit of the US government, because it is the world's biggest economic and military power. But that's all based on debt spending. It is just about perceptions. America's coffers have been drained fighting imperial wars from the Middle East to Central Asia. The fact is, the nation is bankrupt. China buys our treasury bonds, so technically they own our government.

So we may have to find a creative way of converting our debt to equity and refinancing the dollar by pegging it to commodities with real value and not just a virtual value.

The way our Fed and Treasury are operating, we might as well peg the dollar to Facebook.

The demand for diversified localization rather than monolithic globalization is spreading across America as communities seek to re-pioneer themselves. Fed up with a financial system that supports only those companies seeking capital market listing rather than smaller businesses that are stakeholders in their communities, the communities themselves are taking the means of finance into their own hands. Nowhere is this articulated better than in Berkshire, Massachusetts, where the Berkshire Buck was launched as a local currency in 2006.

Pioneered by the progressive E. F. Schumacher Society, it has become popular, with $2.7 million circulated and accepted by over 400 businesses, with a total of thirteen branches among four different banks accepting Berkshire Bucks.

To date, Berkshire Bucks have appreciated against the US dollar as local banks exchange 105 Berkshire for every 100 dollars. That in turn encourages people to spend their money locally, giving local consumers a five percent discount. Community loan programs in Berkshire have evolved. Like the Green America Exchange, this represents another way of creating a bottom-up local economy that is sustainable.

A dollar bill says, "In God We Trust." That must be true. God is the only entity we can trust because the politicians, investment banks, and their fund managers are just pulling a walnut-and-pea scam on the rest of us. There is nothing backing that currency except what the media says. And do you really want to rely on them? When people catch on, they will seek alternatives.

The same goes for Europe. Bristol, England's sixth most populous city, launched its own currency called the "Bristol Pound." It can only be used by member businesses in the city. Although it will not be legal tender and must be exchanged back to sterling with a 3 percent charge, it has attracted over one hundred businesses to sign on as member users. The vision is to keep local wealth in the community, driven by the realities of the recession, especially at a time when people have lost confidence in Britain's own banks and when the euro currency is facing a potential crack-up.

Enter the Bitcoin, a virtual encrypted currency. Unassociated with any government and unattached to any place, by 2014 this transnational currency gained so much acceptance that it scared governments. China banned it. Russia banned all alternate currencies. US Federal authorities launched an aggressive crackdown on Bitcoin entrepreneurs, arresting the founder of the Bitcoin Foundation. Empowering people with their own currency takes authority away from government. For most people fed up with government, that is the entire idea.

So for Hawaii, a geothermal dollar is not entirely irrational. In South Dakota, a wind-based currency could also make sense. Imagine the Federal Reserve issuing dollars against a basket of regional currencies across America that are based on renewable energy sources as the underlying value rather than debt, which is what is happening today.

This idea is not so crazy if we think about the history of money. During the Ming Dynasty in China, soy and vinegar producers in

Shaanxi Province issued letters of credit for commodities that were traded across the country. For nearly half a millennium (which is a lot longer than our country has been in existence), Pingyao, a tiny town where about a dozen families controlled soy and vinegar production, was the banking capital of the Middle Kingdom.

So if we get back to basics, issuing a currency that is based on a solid commodity such as energy is a real possibility. If America could put our creativity to use, turn our research and development technology into something other than iPad games, we could rapidly evolve renewable energy as a key commodity and use it as a base for a relaunch of the US dollar from the community level upwards. It is all about re-pioneering America from the community first, and that will require new currencies when the old one is worthless or owned by someone else. It is not about "In God We Trust" or trusting your elected politician or the president of the United States. It is better to trust a commodity in future high demand such as renewable energy.

Like water, renewable energy may one day be worth more than gold.

OCCUPY GREEN: DEMAND 13 MILLION GREEN JOBS NOW!

Joshua Cooper is an American, but is Hawaiian in spirit. Middle-aged, hair tied back in a ponytail, he teaches at the University of Hawaii and flies around the globe attending United Nations meetings and working with indigenous people.

He arrives at my office in the East-West Center and looks around. African canes are leaning against the wall in a corner; climate change literature is piled on the shelves and tables; I am drinking Hawaiian coffee out of a tin coffee cup that has been decorated with colorful beadwork by Zulu women. "Hey, this room looks like a mini Durban," Cooper laughs. "I was at Cop 17 too!"

Cooper explains his participation at the UNFCCC negotiations. "We convened a meeting with all the indigenous constituency of the United Nations at the Durban stadium where the 2010 World Cup took place two years before. The stadium had already become a site for tourists, offering thrill sports. So people on one side of the stadium discussed how the Pacific islands will disappear as the Arctic ice breaks up, and how many Africans cannot grow food due to climate change, while on the other Western tourists were having a good time bungee jumping off the upper balcony and hanging there. It was surreal.

People of the G77 are worried about the survival of the human race as we run smack against climate change caused by our own doing. And the folks from the G7 are busy trying to seek frivolous thrills because they have money and time to blow. But as they hang upside down by their feet giggling, they do not realize both the money and the time are running out."

Together with Joshua, we get to work on a proposal for a virtual national campaign. We called it "13 Million Green Jobs Now!" or "Occupy Green."

The message is simple: we are demanding stimulus for the creation of green jobs to regenerate America. Post-2008 crash, stimulus packages were used to bail out the bankers who used tax money to give bonuses to each other. They should instead have been used for infrastructure upgrades and to create jobs. But the politicians had to pay off their supporters. The US government is perfectly capable of achieving green-generated growth. It just requires funding spent in the right places.

Stimulus must be used intelligently, to upgrade our nations' infrastructure with clean investments: grid conversion from fossil fuels to renewable energy, adoption of energy efficiency standards, and fiscal policy to encourage energy savings. This will create jobs, new growth, technology innovation, meaningful education, and employable vocational skills for youth. New energy infrastructure and technology can be made in America.

The idea would be to put forward something that both political parties could take ownership of and use to their own advantage. American politics has become irrationally polarized, making the government dysfunctional. The idea of creating green growth and jobs should not be construed as either left or right. It is forward thinking about an America that can create careers for its citizens, and revive the economy and ecology for future generations. There is no conflict between going green and business profitability. We want business to profit through green to be the next engine of growth.

If we don't do this, China will. In fact, China is already shifting in this direction (see chapter 15). While Henk Rogers is driving a lone electric car in Honolulu to raise awareness that alternative environmentally friendly options exist, China is now producing electric cars in mass, and the government is providing hefty subsidies to push the industry. China is already planning to have twenty million electric car plug-in charging stations across the nation by 2020. It is now offering citizens over $9,000 in rebates if they buy an electric car. In America, Congress is still debating whether climate change is a scientific reality or not. Amazing!

Why should America be left behind? Why should China pioneer the new green technology and sell it to us? This spells business opportunity and a time for America to regain its competitive edge and lead the world on green growth. Moreover, green technology and resources can become a means of refinancing America. But can America's politicians see this? Can they act?

America needs a new agenda. It is not about left or right, Democrat or Republican. People on both sides of the political spectrum have lost jobs. Therefore, it is about recreating jobs. We need to do it through a new real deal: green infrastructure growth and the regeneration of communities. That is where America began, and that is where it needs to go back to get its strength. We need to re-pioneer America.

DON'T CUT DOWN THAT LAST TREE: TRADITIONAL VALUES ARE STRONG AND GOING GLOBAL

The East-West Center is a museum of Asian and Pacific culture. Artifacts from expeditions and gifts presented by visiting delegations are presented in glass display cases in brightly lit corridors draped with tapa cloth and batik. One whole floor exudes Pacific culture, with masks, shields, and decorative canoe paddles from across Oceania hung upon the walls. It was here that I heard a story of how the people of Rapa Nui, the mysterious Easter Island, had engineered their own demise.

Sometime in the seventeenth century, there was a massive boom in carving of *moai*, the huge humanoid statues that have given the island its fame. One could understand the story in the context of a stimulus package (from agricultural output) being spent on redundant construction (GDP growth model) that in turn devastated the environment. Once-ubiquitous palm trees were felled to be used as rollers to move the statues. Cleared lands became agricultural, fueling a population boom.

But with the trees all felled, the art of canoe making was forgotten, and the people could no longer fish. Soon deforestation from overconstruction and population pressures eroded the soil. Yam, taro, and banana yields crashed. A famine led to civil war in 1680, and cannibalism arose. Rapa Nui's residents, who welcome tourists today, are feeble survivors of this ecocide history. Through oral tradition and song they recollect a story of how the last tree was felled by a man who knew that his act would mark the end of their civilization. The tale reminds us how human ego and selfishness can override common sense and destroy the very ecosystem upon which our existence depends.

It was here at the East-West Center that Victor Li, author of *Law without Lawyers*, taught students how to look at any single issue—economy, law, politics or business—from a multiple set of different cultural and geographic coordinates at once.

But he was no longer there.

After quite a search, I finally located Li's contact. We met at the Pacific Club in an airy dining room where ceiling fans turned gracefully and birds flew in from the lanai (veranda) outside, snatching crumbs from the rugs and fleeting out again before the waiters could bother to even notice.

Victor Li appeared a little frail in body, but his mind was sharp. After recalling some of the nicer times in China, lunch with Deng Xiaoping, and visits during the early reform years accompanied by ministers, he picked up where our last conversation had left off. "I am no longer interested in how China will transform Asia by its sheer economic weight over the next decade, but rather how it will transform the world," he said.

He was frustrated with where the American economy was going. Yes, sure those at the very top of the pyramid would be all right. But it is everybody else who will miss out. "The people of this state are so kind. I really care about them," he said. "But the majority, the next generation, I am so afraid where our economy is going right now, they just won't make it."

From here the conversation turned to the Himalayan Consensus, how it evolved into an African Consensus, and the need to re-pioneer America. Yes, outside of Planet Washington DC, there is a New Earth Consensus. It is shared across America as well as everywhere.

Li reflected for a moment. Then he leaned over and asked a single question. "Have you written all this down?

CHAPTER 12

THE WORLD IS NOT FLAT:
Back to Basics, Local Diversity, and Community Capital Regeneration

THE BARCELONA CONSENSUS

Barcelona, 2012. "When you were at Occupy Wall Street, I was out here on Catalonia Square," Martí Olivella, founder of the Barcelona Consensus, laughed. He pointed out the window at the square. "Can you see? I was sleeping right there."

Throngs of pigeons stopped for a few seconds to pick up seeds being tossed from the benches. It was a beautiful summer day. Tourists photographed each other before the resplendent fountains. Clearly it was not the scene of tent-encamped protesters barricaded by police that had sparked global revolt—transitioning the Arab Spring to the European Summer—just a year before.

Olivella explained the origin of the protests. "The M-15 movement sought to transform through nonviolence. It was named for May 15th, the day we first occupied the square. We were the spark that inspired Occupy." He looked out the window again. "So Occupy Wall Street really began in Catalonia Square. Ironically, the European financial crisis began in Wall Street."

In many ways, M-15 as a movement grew very much as Occupy did—a hydra with many heads pulling in different directions. M-15, or what would become known as the "Indignants," spawned from locally formed organizations, many quite small, which congregated together out of common outrage. When the movement was born on Catalonia Square, the Barcelona Consensus was deeply engaged as a participant.

However, since that time Barcelona Consensus has evolved, pioneering regeneration rather than leading protest. Olivella explained how he prefers to focus on constructively building a new economic paradigm rather than just venting outrage. Being in the street, creating civil disobedience is only one part of the equation. Without actively constructing the foundations for a new economic system, venting outrage at the existing system will not alone accomplish the goals for which outrage is being expressed.

Olivella and I first met on the dusty grounds of Cheik Antiop University in Dakar, during the World Social Forum. There, amid heady euphoria, global activists rallied, seeing a cusp of change as the Jasmine Revolution erupted across North Africa. Olivella thought pensively, undistracted by the immensity of whirling energy around us. "Revolution to overthrow the old order is not enough," he observed. "The question is how to construct a new order. When social movements get stuck repeating the same criticisms, they often fail to turn ideals into action."

COMMUNITY CAPITAL REGENERATION

Back in Barcelona, Olivella was determined to achieve this in a systematic way. He convened a drafting convention and, with input from thinkers and progressive movements across Europe, they produced the Barcelona Consensus Declaration. It was all about consensus. The document called for a new global economic and financial order, recognizing the power of community, the need to get capital to people running real businesses, the importance of protecting our environment, and values of humanism.

"The whole problem is we need a monetary system that keeps the value of goods equal to the value of money," explained Olivella. "The Breton Woods system is about creating endless money in the stratosphere, legitimized by the IMF and Washington Consensus. But the problem is this money does not go into productivity, agriculture or communities. It does not create more jobs and businesses. It goes to 60,000 people who control global wealth. Money invested in unproductive financial instruments that create more paper money is just putting money in a black hole. We are not getting productivity out of our money. Never before in history has there been such inequality, with the rich becoming richer and the poor, even poorer. In Roman times, this did not happen."

Many Europeans feel cheated by their governments and angered by the huge charade that has been played out in the Western media for two decades—yes, everyone will benefit from a "flat" planet. But people have not benefitted. Moreover, people are not stupid, and they have finally caught on to the game.

Olivella observed, "The government feels they represent people and can choose a direction to keep things together and get back on the neoliberal track. So they bail out banks, impose austerity cuts, and try to keep the euro as a currency from breaking up." He shook his head. "But it is not working. Now we have a big monetary mess. People cannot eat, people are expelled from their homes, and businesses must close. Meanwhile, governments want to use stimulus to increase consumption. But did any of these institutional economists figure out people cannot buy things because they do not have jobs with which to earn money? Productivity is not increasing. Instead, what increases is unemployment."

He pointed out his window as if indicating both Catalonia Square and Zuccotti Park with one sweeping gesture. "We are all seeking different solutions. They are arising in community financing, local currencies, and the whole idea that small is better."

"Actually, the local response is something that is just natural for Europe," said Rahel Aschwanden, the international relations coordinator for the Barcelona Consensus. Sitting beside Olivella, she had been taking notes the whole time "The truth is, different ways already exist," Aschwanden added, noting that she was neither Catalonian nor Spanish. "I am from Switzerland," she explained. "For centuries, our Swiss canons—local township governments—have been issuing their own currencies, keeping business in the community. There is nothing new to us in Europe about taking this approach."

"Fresh alternative approaches to redefine our future economy are springing up across Europe," Aschwanden explained with enthusiasm. "Even in crisis—mainly because of the crisis—Europe is regenerating and finding itself again in the power of community rather than in transnational capital flow. It is about community capital regeneration." She gave some examples.

The Triodos Bank in the Netherlands and Belgium, which are pioneers in social enterprise lending. They finance everything from organic food and farming businesses, fair trade, renewable energy, recycling, and nature conservation. As a "social bank," Triodos seeks to finance social businesses to improve and enrich lives, while building strong, green communities in the process.[1]

Christian Felbur in Austria pioneered a "Common Welfare Matrix" to measure corporate stakeholder rather than shareholder value. The matrix coordinates include ecological sustainability, social justice, transparency, and democratic codetermination. The matrix evaluates not only a company's management principles and employment relations but also whether the practices of their suppliers are environmentally sustainable.

Turning back to Spain, the Mondragon cooperative, a collective of 250 companies and organizations, turned an entire town into a cooperative to boost productivity and reduce unemployment. Every employee is a shareholder in the company. Major decisions are made at a shareholder's assembly of the employees. Everyone gets one vote. Daily decisions are made by a governing committee elected by employees. Management salaries are capped, and cannot exceed six times that of a worker. The Mondragon cooperative engages in "real business"—production of machine and auto parts—and exports to North and South America, China, and Brazil. While its management ideals may be built upon the deep egalitarian culture of the Basque area, it is already expanding with projects as far afield as Kazakhstan and Lithuania.

The rise of cooperatives as an alternative economic model is not only happening in Europe but across America as well. But because the term "cooperative" is not politically correct (in a McCarthy-era paranoia carryover), the mainstream media hardly dare report it. Today, there are nearly 30,000 cooperatives in the United States operating at seventy-three thousand locations. This should not be dismissed as "alternative economics." It is becoming a new mainstream. The cooperative sector owns $3 trillion in assets, generates half a trillion dollars a year in revenue, and pays 856,000 people $25 billion in annual wages. Their multiplier impact on the economy supports more than two million jobs nationally.[2] Imagine, if the word "cooperative" were as politically correct as "technology," or if cooperatives just called themselves "social media networks," then investment banks could package and list them, and hedge funds might trade their stocks.

While Spain was one of the worst victims of the euro crisis, it also had become one of the most creative and regenerative, in many ways pioneering, progressive economies, with local movements emerging across the country, coming up with their own solutions in the vacuum of government response. Local communities were even issuing their own currencies. In the Catalonian fishing town of Vilanova I la Geltru, residents were experimenting with local currency worth more than the euro at neighborhood stores; the city of Malaga established a special website allowing individuals to earn money and buy products via virtual currency.

Only a few months later, Olivella was issuing (through the Barcelona Consensus) its own Catalonian currency called the "Ecosol." He began with vouchers that would soon become an online tool. The "Ecosol" is based on a cooperative or union of enterprises. One euro is equal to one Ecosol.

These community efforts give a new face to the idea of diversified localization, by introducing local monetary policy. At least 20 different local currencies have been issued across Spain since the 2008 financial crisis. Individual communities have been applying their own denominations and value.

Globally, over 70 local currencies have been issued in response to the crisis. "Time Dollars" (effectively trading services against a time denomination) are used in 200 communities spread among 30 states in America, and in localities in England and Japan. Core to it all is the idea of community capital regeneration: finding practical alternatives to keep money in the community and revitalize local business.

The key original principle of Adam Smith is to invest in the community. Remember, that was the original meaning of the "invisible hand" of self-interest.

THE EURO: A POLITICAL PROJECT THROUGH ECONOMIC MEANS

Now, in the vacuum of leadership, individual communities across Europe are creating their own local economies, and even currencies. Interestingly, this is also happening in North America. While these "alternative economy" or progressive movements may still seem marginal, at a certain tipping point of convergence, they could represent a new mainstream. These communities are adopting individualistic economic approaches out of self-interest. It is not about economic ideology, but survival of the community because politicians have no answers, are corrupt, or are just incapable. So a kind of community go-it-alone attitude is on the rise.

But doesn't this run absolutely counter to what the European Union is trying to accomplish with the single euro currency? Of course, every reaction has a counterreaction. After decades of the neoliberal model of globalization (the one-size-fits-all, cookie cutter approach) being pushed on Europe, now there is a backlash.

In the wake of the financial crisis and continuing recession, opinion polls in Europe reflect that people emotionally are less convinced that Europe needs a single currency or centralized governance of European finance for that matter. There is a shifting mood back toward more local or national orientation. So while the European Union and certain governments such as Germany under Chancellor Angela Merkel are fast-tracking toward greater federalism, people and localities are going in a different direction, especially because they fear losing control over their own economic policies. America's sequestration (budget cuts) fight in Congress and the European debate over austerity both represent similar reactions to similar problems created by similar people.

"We are at a historical crossroads in Europe," explained Robert Bergqvist, Chief Economist of SEB (Skandinaviska Enskilda Banken AB), "We have the one currency, monetary policy and central bank. They have come to the conclusion that we have to stabilize the euro. But to get there we need to create four building blocks: banking union, common economic policy framework, unified fiscal system, political union."

SEB is a powerful Nordic financial institution that is controlled by Sweden's influential Wallenberg family. (The Wallenbergs' industrial, commercial, and financial empire stretches to include such household names as Ericsson, ABB Group, Saab Group, SAS Group, Electrolux, Investor AB, and the ritzy Grand Hotel of Stockholm) You cannot get any more 1 percent than that. Regardless, Bergqvist foresees the euro's inevitable break up, with the reissuing of national currencies as "something in-between," a middle-road course. Sweden and Denmark did not adopt the euro and kept their own national currencies. In many ways these Scandinavian countries feel that they were better off doing so.

Bergqvist sighed, "The difference in outlook between Germany and Greece is so big. If you have countries that have these kinds of differences and push them together, it will only create tensions and imbalances in the system. It is not a problem if the German and Greek economies are similar, but if you have such wide differences, then one monetary policy for 17 countries is not good."

"It only works if you can reduce differences between countries. And this could take a long time. The last ten years of globalization has been impressive. But you still have lots of differences. A German and a Greek will earn money and spend it differently. Cultural values and behavioral patterns still and always will differ vastly in the eurozone. Meanwhile, the World Bank and IMF want to create solutions that fit all. But that simply does not work."

ART IS POLITICAL DIXIT PICASSO

Overlooking Catalonia Square from his office balustrade, Olivella pointed into the distance. "To the right, over there, is the Miró Museum. To the left is the Picasso Museum." Pigeons flew past. "Picasso and Miró both offered a crucial vision of society. After they died, the commercial value of their collectible items skyrocketed, and only the very rich, bankers and investment bankers, could afford to buy them. As soon as it is in a frame, it becomes a commodity, because it can be transferred."

The works of Pablo Picasso and Joan Miró were not just breakthroughs in color juxtaposition but also geopolitical economics. They tore up classical tradition. It was not about art for the sake of aesthetics. It was part of a rebellion going on in Europe against the rise of fascism and its severe classification of ideas. Through their art, Picasso and Miró were symbolically tearing apart the political ideals that Francisco Franco was trying to impose. Decades later, these artists inspired another generation in New York, led by Andy Warhol, whose pop art was attacking a new form of conformity, the products of multinational corporations, extreme commercialism that puts everything into a soup can.

Today rich investment bankers buy the works of Picasso, Miró, and Warhol, and hang them in their living rooms. Purchasing global sophistication comes with being part of the 1 percent. But do they understand the underlying meaning of the art they choose to hang on their walls? This art calls for the overthrow of their establishment.

Olivella sat down again. With a pensive look, he took a pen and a blank piece of paper and began drawing circles big and small connected with lines. At first I thought he was trying to knock-off a Miró by drawing Zen-like circles and squares. Then he explained it was a map of the global progressive movements and how they need to work together with governments.

"We are influenced by three different experiences, in three different ways." He pointed enthusiastically with his pen to the three big circles on the paper. "The first is utopia—we have cooperatives for work or consumption, social currencies, transitional towns, alternative monetary systems. These utopias all express a different set of values through a complementary economic reality."

He pointed to another circle and shaded it with his pen. "Second, are nonviolent strategies, of which outright civil disobedience is just one form of expression. There is another more quiet approach." He pointed again to the first circle with his pen. "The systems in utopia are all functioning without cooperation with the mainstream system. So when they grow in scale, it is also a form of civil disobedience. If we are not cooperative with the structures in which we live, then those structures will have to change. Our structures can actually be changed at any time if we believe it is time."

Olivella then pointed to the third circle. "This is where government must come in. Make laws and grant the progressive economy reciprocity. But in some cases, government will make laws to stop them." He shook his head. "Believe me, this creates reaction! The whole point lies in the third circle." He tapped it incessantly with his pen. "Government needs to be influenced. Either you elect people to help and make the change you want, or you have to change the government with nonviolent action that keeps government accountable to the people. Otherwise, the government will have to face the people in the street."

On September 21, 2012, protests in Madrid became violent. Activists from across the country organized and arrived to demonstrate before the parliament building. Police were determined to stop them from getting there. Obviously, youth became frustrated and then offensive toward the police, who in turn became violent against the protesters. In Spain, youth face 50 percent unemployment. So, of course, they are furious and demand that the system change. With that kind of mess, obviously something is not working.

Authoritarian crackdown is a sign of insecurity and, moreover, the fragility of a political system. If a government feels secure in its position, it will not use authoritarian measures to crack down on protest or dissent. If it feels insecure, it will.

Since the Spanish government is turning to the European Central Bank and IMF for loans to support those bankers who bankroll the government, officials in both Madrid and Washington do not want to see these protests spread and their comfortable debt refinancing arrangements disrupted.

Actually, the protesters are quite transparent and democratic. Think for a moment. It takes weeks to prepare a demonstration, which is entirely organized using social media tools. Organizers publicize when, where, and how they plan to have their demonstration. Moreover, the meetings are open to anyone who wants to participate. Of course, authorities can follow because social media is totally transparent. They know what will happen and when, and they can send plainclothes police to attend. Yes, they too are welcome to attend the meetings because the demonstrators have nothing to hide. They are protesting within the constitutional framework of their country's freedoms. The demonstrators feel they are being transparent, democratic, and playing by the rules.

So when our democratically elected institutions—that are supposed to be transparent—begin repressing the demonstrators, then they are upping the game and pushing it into a totally different realm. Maybe they want the rules of the game to change?

Maybe the authorities want peaceful protest to turn violent so that they have unbarred access to all of the weapons in their arsenal of repression to wipe the protesters and their organizations off the game board.

RISE OF THE INDIGNANTS

On the other side of Catalonia Square, I found an alleyway that ran somewhat parallel to the Ramblas, that energizing eclectic boulevard that never sleeps. With its bustling restaurants, clamorous shops, lively artists, and spontaneous pantomime, it is a 24/7 living street performance.

A world a part from the Ramblas, this tiny narrow lane of old buildings was quiet, almost deserted. Disconcerted, I found the entrance to the building address I had been given and took an old rickety elevator to the office of Arcadia Oliveres, Spain's legendary activist and the father of the "Indignant Movement."

Oliveres exuded a humbleness that was disarming. Jovial and relaxed, a fatherly figure stroking his beard, this soft-spoken gentleman was actually Spain's firebrand. Since the outbreak of the euro crisis, he had been constantly making speeches across Europe at rallies and protests, calling people to the street en masse, undauntedly challenging economic systems and confronting inert politicians.

He twisted his eyebrows in consternation. "The politicians fear a sea of insurrection," he exclaimed. "Today people in the street are against the euro. It is not in the interest of Greece, Portugal, or Spain. It is in the interests of Germany, big banks, and multinational corporations, but not the countries of Europe. Why? The reason is that we have compromised our most important national right—monetary policy. The right to make monetary policy for Greece, Portugal, and Spain is not in our own capitals, but is in the hands of the central bank of the European Union. And today that central bank is located in Frankfurt."

Relaxing behind his sparse wooden desk, he told how the "Indignation" movement arose (in Spain called *Indignados*). People did not agree with the government's decision to bail out banks at cost of people. With political systems dysfunctional and duly elected representatives unable to represent those who elected them, people just took to the street expressing their outrage or indignation. That is how the movement began and why it spread across continents.

In fact, the real origin of the Indignation movement began with a book published in 2011 called *Time for Outrage: Indignez-Vous!*, authored by Stéphane Hessel. Born in 1917, Hessel was a former French Resistance fighter and concentration camp survivor, a celebrated human rights advocate, and one of the original editors of the 1948 Universal Declaration of Human Rights. *Time for Outrage* immediately became a French bestseller, was soon translated into 30 languages, spreading as a bestseller across Europe and other continents. In many ways it was the real spark of the 2011 protests that spread from North Africa to Europe, later becoming the Occupy movement. *Time for Outrage* screams out against our current global system as hypocritical, unfair, perpetuating greater gaps between rich and poor, desecrating the environment for future generations. The book calls for people to take action themselves through nonviolent insurrection, basically a peaceful people's revolution. Hessel wrote,

> The wealthy have installed their slaves in the highest spheres of the state. The banks are privately owned. They are concerned

solely with profits. They have no interest in the common good. The gap between rich and poor is the widest it's ever been; the pursuit of riches and the spirit of competition are encouraged and celebrated.... We therefore maintain our call for a "rebellion—peaceful and resolute—against the instruments of mass media that offer our young people a worldview defined by the temptations of mass consumption, a disdain for the weak, and a contempt for culture, historical amnesia, and the relentless competition of all against all.³

The Spanish term *Indignados* (the outraged) came right from the title of Hessel's book. Just as with Occupy, when the Indignants movement started, the reaction of the Spanish right was to dismiss it. They called occupiers on the street *perroflautas*, a derogatory term meaning "young beggar with a dog." As in America, the mainstream media in Spain chose to depict the movement as derelict or hippie. But just the same as with Occupy, the movement was not about just the poor. So to counter this image in Spain, a fresh movement called *iaioflautas* arose, led by affluent and socially respected Spaniards—with a conscience—who stood up and joined the protesters. Because just as with Occupy, it was as much a middle-class revolution, as both poor and upper-middle-class people were getting kicked out of their homes by the banks. With respected, well-heeled professionals occupying public space, it sent a clear message to members of the hard-line establishment that M-15 and the Indignants as converged movements were not just young, lost derelicts begging, but rather a consensus representing a broad social and income spectrum, fed up with a system that no longer works.

Oliveres, while a firebrand of the Indignant movement, also fell into the same camp with Olivella. On one hand, protesters and activists are taking to the street across Europe demanding sweeping change. That is necessary to get the message across to politicians that they need to come up with pragmatic solutions or get out of their cushy seats. On the other hand, these same activists realize they need to take the reins into their own hands, affecting change on specific issues often in small ways that are collectively transformational. Both approaches are needed together.

Take the example of credit. In Spain, the home as an asset is only a guarantee of an individual's personal credit. So if a home is worth EUR 100,000 at the time of purchase, but depreciates to a value of EUR

70,000 at the time of the borrower's default, then the bank not only takes back the asset but also chases after the borrower for a lost value of EUR 30,000. This differs sharply from America where, if somebody defaults on their home mortgage, the banks take the home.

This draconian notion of credit is embedded in Spain's constitution, requiring a referendum to amend it. Protest in the street may catch media attention, but will not change the problem. Another parallel action is required. Instead of protesting, Oliveres had them pool people for signatures calling for a constitutional amendment to change this core concept of credit.

"The world is not flat!" Oliveres exclaimed, placing his fist square upon the table as he stood up to make me another cup of coffee. "International neoliberalism says it is necessary to make a free market everywhere. But this market is not free," he pointed to the cup. "Columbia sells coffee, but is in no position to negotiate the price as the big coffee companies are buying. So power is not the same. Columbia as a nation does not have the same power as Nestle, a multinational corporation. In commercial trade, when Columbia buys photocopy machines, they are not for Columbians but for big corporations who have offices in Columbia. So commerce and international trade cannot be equal under the system, the way it is being run. That is why the world is not flat."

Oliveres was referring to Thomas Friedman's *The World is Flat: A Brief History of the Twenty-First Century*. As the title indicates, the book is a simplification of the globalization process. It envisions technology as a quick fix that is creating an "an even playing field" and heaps praise on Walmart. Diversity is dismissed as something the world should be delivered from by American monoculture that brought to everyone through the liberating force of broadband. The book reflects "our model" as the cookie-cutter approach to carve up the rest of the planet, shaping it to look just like America, a naïve notion, but one that certainly epitomized the ideology of America's neoliberal establishment over the past decades. The inequalities of our global financial and trading system that make this planet not so flat are left out of Friedman's equation.

Hessel's *Time for Outrage* (29 pages) is without question the antithesis of Friedman's *The World is Flat* (659 pages).

Oliveres explained his outrage at the "flatist" view. By following the neoliberal globalization model, economics in Europe became distorted. "Only one-fourth of wealth is created by real businesses run by real people, while three-fourths is created by theoretical instruments being traded on the capital market by only a few people." He acknowledged that communities, which were once the backbone of Europe's own economic model, had been forgotten in the process of trading leveraged debt instruments into infinity.

Oliveres sighed again and stroked his beard. "Yes, 40 years ago a real company went to the stock market with a real business that had real production that needed new machines to raise real productivity, and they had to raise the capital to do it. Those were the days when work equaled capital. Today, real work is only one-fourth the value of capital. The other three-fourths are just speculation."

Looking out the window of his simple, almost austere office, he stared up at passing clouds as if they were listed web pages. "Now people go to stock market not to raise money for production. The end objective is not products and production, but pure speculation. There are many financial products trading for a future that may not even exist. That is good for hedge funds but not for people. More than 80 percent of stock market is not even legitimate if you put it to a hard test. Capital is not going to the economy, but benefitting only a few people. And we the people are expected to pay for their losses. That is why people are on the street protesting against austerity."

There is distorted view in America as to why there is a "euro crisis," and adamant denial that Europe's financial woes may somehow be connected to America's or that one crisis created another. It would be heresy to even suggest that the export of the "flatist" view, the reliance on capital markets to create wealth and pushing deregulation to get there, could in any way have been a factor behind creating the whole mess.

The view from America is that austerity is the IMF remedy, that bitter medicine that Europe has to swallow because it practiced socialism and the people don't want to work hard. That is the neoclassic view—no free lunch. "It is not about people not working." Oliveres shot down this "no-free-lunch" notion with that same fury with which he can rally thousands. "It is about people having to work to support the banks. The European bailout is for banks, not people. For instance, look at the situation here in Spain. Our external debt is 400 percent of GDP. Of that 400 percent, only 80 percent actually comes from state costs—that is the cost of state provinces and municipalities running services from transport, medical, and education. The other 320 percent is debt that the government must service to the banks. But the banks do not use the money they are receiving to lend money to the people who will run real businesses for local community growth."

He shook his head and stood up to make a cup of coffee, handing me a mug. "So, of course, under the austerity plan people resent having to underwrite excesses of the bankers. The situation we face is that the middle class are joining the poor, while the poor are getting poorer, and the rich are getting much richer. We call for nonviolent revolution to change this conundrum. However, if things continue on this trajectory, the revolution will become violent." He looked up again and pointed in the direction of the window, somewhere toward Seville. "Look at what happened in Seville just recently. Poor people went to the market to just take food right out of the grocery store. Trade unions are organizing to do the same on behalf of the poor. It is a sign of things to come, that is, if they don't change."

Oliveres berated the hypocrisy of it all, why policymakers in America just could not get it through their heads why people across Europe are protesting against austerity. "In America, they are only theoretically in favor of free market, but they don't practice it."

The twisted irony is that Washington points the finger at Europe for not adopting austerity to solve its problems. Yet by 2013, the United States government was technically bankrupt and facing much the same problem. Almost immediately after President Barack Obama was sworn into his second term, a vicious blame game erupted in Washington between Democrat and Republican parties over who actually brainstormed the "sequester," America's own version of austerity, something which congressmen on both sides of the aisle were able to agree is a "dumb" idea. So why should austerity be good for Europe? Nobody bothered to ask this in America's mainstream press.

In Washington, theatrics have become politically more convenient than actually addressing any real problems. Theatrics have also become convenient for the media, which are in need of seasonal hype for corporate advertisers and hedge fund managers trading on market fluctuations (after a while, this stuff is so predictable) as America lurches from one crisis to another with all of that pizzazz. Unfortunately, the people on the bottom suffer.

The point that Oliveres drove home—on behalf of the Indignants and Occupy—is knowledge that is shared by so many but that cannot be broadcast because it is so politically incorrect. Capital markets are the source of wealth creation for a select few. But the emphasis is not in trading shares of solid companies—what most Asian and European analysts call "real businesses"—but of those wonderful fuzzy websites we call "social media" or "tech stocks." Actually, most involve relatively low-level Internet technology. There are no breakthroughs, just numbers of eyeballs looking at the sites to create value. It is all about hype, selling and buying shares as they fluctuate with the hype, and trading them again, something like soybean futures options (the trader will never see who gets stuck with the product in the end).

Profit is irrelevant. It is all about potential, that wonderful infinity factor. The dot.com boom of the late 1990s was all about burning money on unprofitable websites. Most disappeared because the investment bankers had just a casino mentality. However, four companies became big enough with users and eyeballs to dominate the "tech stock" story: Facebook, Twitter, Yahoo, and YouTube. As an example of the game, Facebook shares started trading on May 18, 2012, with a market capitalization of US$104 billion. Within a fortnight, it had lost US$28 billion in market value. Disclosure problems over its lack of revenue model were swept under the carpet by regulators. Today, Wall Street analysts continue talking gaga about Facebook. Most analysts in Asia consider it another ponzi scheme, because they know that younger generations have already created newer social media sites that kids are switching to—many based in different nations using other languages. So could Facebook possibly be the next American subprime that is incubating?

From the perspective of Oliveres, financial reform needs to refocus capital in either the form of lending or investment into the hands of real businesses, more often at the community level, that is, among people who are providing actual goods and services that can be profitable. Technology innovation is one particular area where Europe can easily excel, but it also has to be real technology, not just a website for chatting. The current environmental crisis calls for technology innovation in areas of renewable and efficient energy and water conservancy, with application for all industries, services, and households. But capital needs to get to those who are able to create real things. $104 billion being thrown at Facebook (with over a quarter of that disappearing into a black hole a week later) tells you something is seriously distorted in our system's very inefficient use of capital.

"In Spain now, 23 percent of our population is unemployed. Among youth, the number is even higher, hovering at 51 percent. We need to prepare to take care of the old, and the ill need help. We need to protect our environment. We need innovation," Oliveres declared. "All of this can create jobs and business opportunity. But it must come back to the community. That means we need real finance to real business at the community level. But we cannot achieve this if the government money is all going to the banks to pay for the losses of those who are speculating with the people's money. The problem is, we do not need more speculation. What we need is real innovation, real productivity, and real growth."

SISTER ACT

Without question, Sister Teresa is the coolest nun I have ever hung out with. We met late one morning in a simple coffee shop where breakfast runs into lunch, on a quiet alleyway. Not surprisingly, it is a short walk from Catalonia Square.

Disarmingly soft and exuding compassion, she was no ordinary cloistered nun. Sister Teresa, like Oliveres is another firebrand, one of Spain's most outspoken progressive activists. Sister Teresa had become a living icon of local activist culture in Catalonia, a region that vociferously considers itself separate from Spain.

We were having late morning coffee because she had just gotten off the plane from Venezuela the night before, and the first thought on her mind was food security. Why were the mainstream Western media uninterested in this? She noted that, while Hugo Chavez was characterized by his extreme politics, the Venezuelan government had set aside 4000 million acres for self-supportive agriculture, and she emphasized the importance of sovereign control over the sources of food.

"Sovereignty over food and water are key to ethnic civil and human rights." She pointed out that Bolivia's president, Evo Morales, gained one of his earliest political victories over the question of water. "The local government privatized water supplies, giving a monopoly to an American company named Veri. They soon had control over distribution of all local water conveniently sealed in plastic bottles." She explained the dilemma in Bolivia. "When local poor began collecting rainwater to drink, the government made it illegal. Morales fought this."

Teresa recalled her early confrontations with the "globalization of everything" idea. "In 1992, I went to America and realized food there looks beautiful. But tastes bad because it is genetically modified. They think it is necessary to standardize everything! In Spain, we have 200 types of pear, but each grows best in its own place. Some types of pear are different from village to village, distances of only a few kilometers away. If you standardize the seed, you lose connection with the earth."

"A flat earth will divide because nothing holds it together except capital flows, which do not unite us. Rather, in the end it separates us, because capital flowing freely goes right into the weapons trade. This is not by chance, is it? We have a system that prioritizes war because, unfortunately, many nations build their identity by projecting others as their enemy. We must recognize that in the end, we don't have a flat earth but instead an organic one. Our world can function better if we recognize and cherish its diversity. If you look at it that way, a more complex earth that celebrates its human diversity will be more united."

In Seville, there is a hall where the king of Spain once held court, and the Spanish Armada pondered the question of retaining global authority through force of arms over the trade of goods and the flow of capital (then gold). Moreover, they pondered how to expand their monopolistic control over the flow of gold (capital) under terms they thought could be dictated to the world through the military power of their Armada.

Today, the hall remains a museum where tourists gawk at the solemn crests of each admiral of the Spanish Armada, hanging over the chairs upon which they once presided and deliberated over the global trading and financial system of that time. There, before them, an explorer without name recognition, sometimes criticized as a daydreamer and at other times as outright crazy, dared to express a vision. His name was Christopher Columbus. Standing before the conceited establishment of his day he made a statement that would transform the economic geography of our planet: "the world is not flat."

This page intentionally left blank

CHAPTER 13

FROM RUSSIA WITH FUSION ECONOMICS:
The National Response, The BRICS, and the Changing World Order

ALL NATIONS ARE NOT CREATED EQUAL

Moscow, 2012. I stood at the lectern before the Duma and wondered what I was doing there. Nobody in Washington had ever asked me to testify before my own nation's congress on China, Vietnam, Nepal, on development policy, or fusion economics for that matter. But here I was before Russia's parliament—the Duma—presenting my views on the World Trade Organization (WTO).

It had taken 19 years of negotiations for Russia to enter WTO, although formal entry was still pending parliamentary approval. Many in Russia did not agree that WTO would benefit the country, particularly its vast rural population and agricultural sector. Activists were convinced that WTO entry would hurt Russian farmers and manufacturers, while feeding those interests controlling the oil and gas industry and their distribution monopolies over Western luxury goods.

Inside Russia's parliament a debate raged over whether Russia should enter WTO or not. While the Western media criticized President Vladimir Putin for not moving fast enough, the activists claim it was his negotiators who had hastily hammered out a last minute deal in the interest of the Russian wealthy, disregarding 19 years of preceding talks. The irony of it all was that Russian protesters saw Putin as playing to Russia's money elite and the interests of Western multinationals with whom they were allied. Regardless, after 19 years Duma ratification was the final step.

Russian activists had invited me to address the Duma, believing a last ditch effort was needed to protect domestic agriculture and industry. I took a deep breath and started my address to the Duma.

"All nations are not created equal," I explained as the interpreter beside me translated my words into Russian. "Each nation has evolved and must develop under different circumstances. Geography, population, resources, culture, religion, community structure are all part of each nation's heritage and the collective unconscious of its people. Therefore, economic development for each nation will be different. One formula cannot be forced upon all nations equally. WTO establishes a universal set of trading and investment rules for all nations to follow equally. But the problem is that all nations are not equal. So the starting point of each must be different."

Why was I here addressing the Duma?

It all began when I met a young Russian activist named Ian Vodin on the dusty grounds of Cheik Antiop University in Dakar, Senegal, a year earlier, when the African Consensus was declared. "I want to take these ideas back to Russia." Vodin suggested, "We can build a Russian Consensus and then invite you to speak there as well."

A few months later we met in Paris, at the offices of Attac, a vigilant antiglobalization activist group based there. Their office in a Paris alleyway was piled with leaflets advocating street action and buzzing with plans for protests across Europe.

But we have to think beyond the next clash with police and evolve from ranting against our global system to systematically reforming it. Radicalism and vigilance get media attention. The mainstream media will otherwise ignore these views unless they are shoved in their face. But such action alone is not going to bring about positive transformation. This will require more quiet, and frankly tedious, retooling of financial, banking, and monetary systems to meet the changing needs of our resource-exhausted planet. In the end, government must sit at the table together with financial leaders and civil society to achieve this.

Fusion economics is all about finding a middle way, and pragmatism to achieve an ideal.

At the core of our global system is the financial architecture, and those who manipulate it. It is easy to scream the usual antiglobalization slogans "Down with the World Bank" and "Destroy the IMF," but these entities, like Coke, Pepsi, and Goldman Sachs, are not going to just go away, even if we burn money in the street and throw the ashes in their face. The central banks will just print more money.

Ultimately, if we really want change to occur, then multiple stakeholders need to be cut in on the arrangement. Revolution cannot be about revolt just for the sake of it. Wearing a Che Guevara T-shirt may be cool, but revolution has to be for a purpose. When the Cuban revolution kicked the Batista dictatorship out of power, Che became Cuba's first central bank governor. As charismatic and inspiring as he might have been, Che knew where the real work had to get done. Everything is connected to the flow of capital.

WATER SECURITY IS DICTATED BY THE PRICE OF PEPSI AND COKE

The day after my address to the Duma, Vodin met me at my hotel, a funky modernist building shadowed by vast Stalinist architecture along the Moscow River. We walked through the streets of Moscow. Blue and yellow old buildings were being renovated everywhere, community restoration embracing traditions within a new context. I thought about the nearly two decades that had passed of my heritage restoration and community work in Beijing and Lhasa.

Vodin, when not leading activist rallies through the streets of Moscow, is a martial artist who has mastered several styles, from karate and kendo to tai qi, and is a Formula 1 race car driver. He looks like a younger version of Daniel Craig. We strode through Red Square and past the twisting turreted St. Basil Church with its Byzantine staircases and labyrinthine passages between chapels that seemed to twist and turn in directionless convolution that always led back to the same point.

He led me through the winding streets, up the narrow staircase of an old high-ceilinged building, and into a simple meeting room. Russian ginger cookies and whole meal cakes were sprawled all over the conference table.

A gently speaking, slightly bearded man entered the room and sat before us. He was Boris Kagarlitsky, a well-regarded activist, formerly a Soviet dissident.

Kagarlitsky then spoke with the definition and confidence of an activist with years of street cred trod under his feet. "We need a new economic model. That is what this is all about." He put it in a Russian context by telling a simple almost folk-like story. "Russian farmers growing apples cannot make money. They are so cheap in the market, because big monopoly distributors control all the apple distribution. Agricultural production is fractured and localized. Mafia then takes over at the local level, because there is no way for capital to get to communities."

From this example he explained how approximately 100 billionaire families in Russia are tightly tied to Putin's administration. Through their massive gas and aluminum exports, they effectively control Russia's foreign exchange reserves. In turn, they monopolize imports and the distribution networks. WTO would benefit them. "These families are raping the country and could not care less about its future development since they themselves don't think it has a future," explained Kagarlitsky. "Their children are all going to school in London." To some extent, Putin has reconstructed a tsar-like court, squeezing wealth out of the country the way the old elites did, but with multinational corporate buy-in. Boris looked forlorn. He shrugged, "So Russia is a horizontally integrated corporation, not a nation."

"Russia can offer the world food," he explained with a more positive inflection to his voice. "Our agriculture is rich. Once, in an earlier time, we were Europe's breadbasket. Now China's soil is depleted. They face imminent food security problems and will at some point have to import food." He then offered me a cookie. "Here try this." Then, pondering for a moment, he smiled. "We can become a global breadbasket again, but we must revitalize agriculture and solve distribution. We have lush rivers from Arctic melt-off nourishing our water, but we cannot become a global water supplier without resolving our own distribution issues. Even our own water security is now dictated by the price of Pepsi and Coke."

In a way, Kagarlitsky was making the same argument as Sister Teresa did in Barcelona about food and water security. Their concern was that such an important state security and environmental issue was not being determined by national considerations, but by multinational corporations. In the summer of 2012, activists groups rallied against Putin not because they saw him as an individual oligarch, but because he represented an oligarchy of vested interests held by the wealthy elite of Russia. In turn, their concerns were tied to the multinational oil interests as well as the consumer goods corporations. With the wealth from oil, gas, and aluminum exports these families could control the distribution channels of imports from commercial to luxury consumer goods. And that was what people in the street were turning against.

"A crisis of unprecedented proportions is upon us. Russian people know it very well. We have been living with it for decades." He saw a pattern over the past decades. He was looking at it from that kind of long perspective that can still be found in a Russian intellectual. Kagarlitsky feared that dismantling financial regulation (originally put in place to prevent another Great Depression and a world war) could lead us back into an economic depression and with it the danger of war, something Europeans and Russians alike understood all too well. "Now, because of the reaction of market extremists, the planet is left with huge social and economic disproportion. Politics becomes fighting for power, ultimately the control of wealth and resources." Kagarlitsky warned, "But at the same time we should not go into Marxist study circles as Lenin did a century ago."

VOICES OF DISSENT JUST WANT A BETTER FUTURE

Kagarlitsky convened a press conference, "What Is the Future of Russia in the WTO?", held at the Gorbachev Foundation. Three economists spoke.

"There will be war for water," declared Vasi Levskiy of Moscow's Trade Union of Works for Life Support. "Pepsi and Coke can have access to global markets, but people cannot have access to water."

"WTO was largely forced down Kyrgyzstan's throat as conditionality from the IMF and World Bank," explained Cyril Lutsyuk, editor of the media site "Vesti.kg," who was from Kyrgyzstan. "Following entry, Kyrgyzstan's textile industry crashed, destroying what was essentially the national product. Some 800,000 people were unemployed. Today, Kyrgyzstan's economy depends on some small trade, buying cheap goods from China and reselling to Russia, or buying cheap textiles from China to make clothes for Russia. Since entering WTO, Kyrgyzstan has had two revolutions."

"After entering WTO, the World Bank said that Greeks must cut down all their fruit trees so they can have industry," Vasiliy Koltashov, a Russian economist living in Greece, explained. "Today in Greece we cannot get Greek oranges, but can buy ones from Florida. We survive on tourism because agriculture has diminished. Teenagers cannot find future work and only have unemployment to look forward to."

Following this conference, I was invited to the office of one parliamentarian, Nikolaj Kolomejtsev, leader of the Committee on Labor and Social Affairs of the State Duma. "WTO will destroy Russian agriculture and what is left of our own domestic industry." The idea of a BRICS development bank and alternative trade system was appealing. But this he warned might be halted when those powers that be finally understand what is happening. It is one thing to protest against the Washington Consensus, but it is another thing to construct a parallel system.

"It is a necessary, but possibly too vigilant a move, especially when they start adopting alternative currencies based on baskets of yuan, ruble, rupee and pesos," he suggested. Kolomejtsev warned almost as an afterthought, "Remember, they killed Gaddafi and Hussein when they stopped denominating oil sales in dollars. Actually, this is the main issue."

THE NEOLIBERAL DEVIL WEARS PRADA

Across from Red Square stands the Gum, an atrium arcade built a century ago. Once a bazaar crammed with Russian goods, scents, and rhythms, today the place has been completely renovated into an upscale shopping mall. The goods are imported through the same channels and distribution networks that export gas and aluminum. These networks control the import of luxury goods, Coke, Pepsi, and even apples for that matter. They are the same group who support Putin, the takeover of local business by multinational corporations, and police brutality against anyone who wishes to question this arrangement to keep it from becoming too politicized.

Across from the Gum, Vodin waits at a coffee shop with rustic brick walls, wrought iron fixtures, a massive painting of a cat wearing high heals and a purple hat, and where a girl with tattoos covering both arms greets me with a nod.

Vodin pulls an Indonesian Kretek cigarette from his jacket pocket with cool abruptness. "Protest alone does not work," he sighed. Vodin had already been arrested once and detained several times in the street fighting that had erupted over the previous months. He lit his cigarette. "The protests of this past year are beginning to die down, mainly because they did not provide an answer. Fusion economics can become a nexus for a new economy here. Young people want something different and will be inspired if a new economic system can be built from the grassroots. Grass-roots movements and NGOs can be social enterprises in the making. We need this approach in Russia, particularly to build agriculture and local industry across our vast interior. But we need guidelines on how to develop a good social enterprise."

Some, but not all, aspects of the China experience and fusion economics could be applied to Russia. Russia's lack of population and massive land mass are its assets, not a liability. China's success story, built on cheap labor, will ultimately be broken by its own population as inflation drives up labor costs, as technology and robotics outpace manpower, and as China's national health-care and pension system creaks under the weight of a massive aging population that must be taken care of. Communalism under socialism (1950s–1970s) and massive real estate developments under capitalism (1990s–2010s) either depleted or stripped China of its agricultural fertility. Chemical pollution contaminated water supplies, and industry's vomiting of carbon already has melted much of the Himalayan glacial water source. Russia's southern neighbor faces catastrophic food and water shortages in the future.

"Development of agriculture and water resources can make Russia a net exporter of food and water to China," Vodin remarked, "possibly one day reversing the flow of trade. But fusion economics will be needed to prepare for that future."

This vision will require government investments into the transport systems to bring agricultural products and water to China's border for export. Free-trade agricultural and water supply zones may be established on their shared border. Certainly with the $500 billion in foreign exchange reserves that is growing from gas sales, Russia has the capital to easily lay this infrastructure. Such national infrastructure transport grid policies will need to be coupled with diversified localization. Credit policies are needed that can provide finance to small agricultural producers. Local government will need to organize community business cooperation to build critical mass. Badly needed fiscal policy should encourage Russian businesses to keep their money in Russia, reinvesting in these sectors domestically rather than sending their cash to London.

"We need to build a social movement that can take us out from corrupt oligarchy into a modern world," sighed Vodin as he rammed the kindling butt of his Kretek cigarette into the art deco ashtray before us. "Fusion economics will be an attractive answer for youth here, because historically Russia looks to the outside for answers. Just as Marxism was an old import, fusion economics can be a new import. In Russia, nobody believes in socialism, but at the same time nobody believes in the market either. So fusion economics is the only way to go."

He then remarked, "Russia once had a great economy, built around individual agricultural communities. Then we had industry and technology. Somehow it was all lost. We had three huge disastrous economic experiments in Russian history. One was collectivization under Stalin. The other was the shock therapy of Jeffrey Sachs. The other maybe, Ivan the Terrible."

"BACK IN THE USSR"

Six months later, I am back in Moscow. It is blanketed in snow. I thought Beijing was cold, but Moscow is freezing. The towering Stalinist red-star crested buildings that loom over Moscow's gridlocked traffic are lit like Christmas trees. Plush shopping malls are packed. Consumption in Russia has been going through the roof. To avoid the traffic, I moved around the city on its mammoth subway system, each station stop dominated by murals or larger-than-life melodramatic statues of workers, farmers, soldiers, and scientists erected during Joseph Stalin's era. Regardless of how Russians might feel today about the policies of that era—they would all agree Stalin contributed the coolest and most kitschy public space art imaginable.

Stepping from the vastness of Moscow's stylized subway system onto the street, I found Boris Kagarlitsky in an outlying hotel of stark 1980s vintage, highlighted by blue neon lights. Kagarlitsky was convening a meeting of South.gov.net, a network of activists and academics determined to do something to change the global economic system. The subject of his conference was the BRICS (Brazil, Russia, India, China, and South Africa) and how they were making this change possible.

Barri Gills, professor of Global Politics at Newcastle University in the United Kingdom, was speaking. "Collective rationality crisis means we repeat the same behavior with obvious negative consequences, a kind of mental disorder. What we need is comprehensive radical system change, not just quantitative easing stimulus. Money and debt instruments should be created that go directly to people to create jobs. You must do this, not just lower interest rates and bail out banks."

He was highlighting the fact that America's economy is effectively on life support. The quantitative easing program of the Federal Reserve that began during the administration of George W. Bush has continued unabated throughout the administration of Barack Obama. It comes down to the government's printing money with which to purchase back its debt in order to issue more money supply. The effect has been to pump American banks full of cash. The banks nevertheless have not increased lending, but instead have increased management bonuses. The program has not stimulated the economy, but has stimulated the wallets of the one percent.

Andrey Kolganov, a senior researcher of the Economic Faculty at Moscow State University, explained, "The financial sector became a fake sector that creates artificial demand. Every crisis reveals the reverse side of this fake prosperity. It tells us the whole modern model is endangered. It depends on high doses of drugs injected. If they try to administer the same drug in the next crisis, it may lead to collapse of the modern financial system. They want to reform the financial sector, but based on what they offer, it's just cosmetic. In Russia, it is similar as in the West."

In the vacuum of global leadership on financial restructuring from America and Europe, new players will arise.

The global recession had its roots in Reagan economics, even going back to Richard Nixon's decoupling the dollar from gold reserves, and then flipping on the printing press. Deregulation was the game changer. During the Clinton administration, intoxication with globalization led to the outsourcing of production from America. Europe followed. Both became dependent upon capital market and debt instrument trading for wealth generation. Real stuff was made in China and India. Brazil, South Africa, and Russia led the resource supply chain, fueling their industrial growth. All five nations benefitted and became the power centers of their respective regions. Now five regional power centers have emerged to take their place in global policymaking.

While all this happened, America printed more money on the back of military muscle that was exhausted by President Bush's distant desert wars. He was chasing the resources—oil. Or maybe it was all about promoting an American Empire ideology. Some $6 trillion later, both America's hard cash and political capital were exhausted. From Bush onward, it was not about the globalization of American ideology, but rather the globalization of America's self-created financial crisis.

Barack Obama was elected president—oh, change feels so good! But not much changed. The dollar depreciated when more money was printed to cover debt and deficit under the continued policies of quantitative easing. Bankers got their big bonuses, and the rest of those greenbacks went into the capital markets of emerging economies where real business has happening, in turn fueling their growth, which rocketed.

Effectively, such voodoo economics unintentionally created the BRICS that successfully rose out of this mess.

THE BRICS GO SOLO

Fast forwarding, in July 2014, at their sixth summit in Brazil, the BRICS announced their own development bank established with an initial capital of US$50 billion accompanied by a new bailout fund—their own IMF.[1] As an effective alternative to the IMF, the crisis reserve allocation was capitalized at US$100 billion. This move will enhance the stature of the BRICS not only as regional power centers of the developing world but as a force for pulling their neighbors out from underdevelopment.

Clearly, the BRICS countries are dissatisfied by Western-dominated institutions such as the World Bank and IMF. Throughout the European debt crisis, the BRICS countries pushed for more influence at the IMF. Their influence is limited to only a combined 11 percent of the IMF's voting shares. By way of comparison, the United States holds a 16.75 percent voting share. That means the US can technically veto any major IMF decision (which requires an 85 percent supermajority). The United Kingdom and France both have larger voting shares than any of the BRICS countries individually.

Of all the BRICS, China has been the most frustrated. For some time, it has sought an evolutionary globalization of its currency. China, in a steady yet subtle manner, has been lobbying for the yuan to join the basket of currencies that comprise the Special Drawing Rights (SDR), the IMF's reserve asset, but these efforts have been thwarted. In 2010, China rose from the sixth to the third position of all nations contributing to the IMF. Regardless, on November 4, 2010, the IMF board only agreed to raise China's voting rights from 4 percent (the amount that China has held since 1980, when its position to the IMF was restored and its foreign exchange reserves were zero) to 6.39 percent. This was a true wake-up call.

Up until then, China felt that money could buy influence over the IMF. But in 2010, China realized the IMF's existing institutional parameters offer no elasticity for new policy frameworks. The core reasons are ideological and historical, dating back to Bretton Woods, a time when China and the other BRICS had little say. So instead of trying to influence the old consensus, there is now a push within the BRICS to forge their own alternative to Bretton Woods, to create a new global consensus.

On March 20, 2012, leaders of the BRICS nations, which were meeting in India, issued a Delhi Declaration calling for a new financial architecture:

> The build-up of sovereign debt and concerns over medium to long-term fiscal adjustment in advanced countries are creating an uncertain environment for global growth. Further, excessive liquidity from the aggressive policy actions taken by central banks to stabilize their domestic economies have been spilling over into emerging market economies, fostering excessive volatility in capital flows and commodity prices. (Article 5)[2]

The Delhi Declaration established the principle that an alternative financial architecture is necessary to parallel the old one—in short, the democratization of our global financial system.

> We therefore call for a more representative international financial architecture, with an increase in the voice and representation of developing countries and the establishment and improvement of a just international monetary system that can serve the interests of all countries and support the development of emerging and developing economies. Moreover, these economies having experienced broad-based growth are now significant contributors to global recovery. (Article 8)

For years, the World Bank's policies have been characterized by attaching political conditions to its low-interest loans, a practice detested in developing countries and viewed by many among them as "neocolonial" or "neoimperialist." As a fresh alternative, the BRICS development bank may be expected to offer nonconditional loans, but at a higher interest rate—a more business-like approach. A BRICS bank may also fund projects in industries that the World Bank does not, such as biofuels and nuclear power plants, thereby challenging the World Bank.

Just months later, in March 2013, China's new president, Xi Jinping, took his first state visit to Russia, where he and Putin signed some 30 agreements. Immediately after leaving Russia, he traveled to several African countries en route to South Africa to attend the fifth BRICS Summit on March 26–27. There a clear road map was laid for a BRICS development bank as an alternative to the World Bank, with the BRICS Business Council to function as a smaller scale WTO and a de facto administrative body should a free trade zone be established under the BRICS mechanism. One year later at their sixth summit in Brazil it was announced that the BRICS Development Bank would be established and headquartered in Shanghai. The next obvious steps may call for a new global reserve currency as an alternate to the US dollar.

The leaders of the BRICS nations have adopted the idea of conducting trade between the five BRICS nations in their own currencies. This idea has wide acceptance among other emerging market nations. Two agreements, signed among the development banks of Brazil, Russia, India, China, and South Africa, say that local currency loans will be made available for trade between these countries. Easy cross-country convertibility among the five will offer an alternative to dollars as settlement currency, and moreover shield their economies from dislocations in the West.

This will evolve into a BRICS intercurrency trading market. In time, it will further reduce dollar dependence. The emergence of a special reserve BRICS currency (based on a basket of all five) could rival the IMF's SDRs. A BRICS currency stabilization fund could effectively replace the IMF as lender of last resort to the developing world.

And with these developments, the post-Bretton Woods arrangement that we have all come to know and accept haplessly will have changed forever.

JUST ANOTHER BRIC IN THE WALL

The term "BRICS" was not coined by an activist or economist from the developing world. In fact, it was entirely a Wall Street concoction.

The novel thought was that of Jim O'Neill, chairman of Goldman Sachs Asset Management. He first espoused the "BRIC" acronym in

"Building Better Global Economic BRICs," an article published in 2001. The idea stuck. It soon symbolized the global economic power shift from the developed G7 toward the developing south. Ironically, O'Neill is not a spokesperson for the developing world. Actually, he is a leader of the 1 percent!

Why did O'Neill choose these countries?

Kagarlitsky suggested, "What brings all five countries together is that their policies are not orthodox from the perspective of Washington Consensus or neoliberal theory. It is more about the need to try and define something because it seems opposite to what you have. They realized there are five huge countries with different models, with high growth rates of anywhere from 6–11 percent per annum. The structure and root of growth of each country was so different that the neoliberal thinkers could not fit them into any single box. It was easier to just draw the conclusion that these five countries must be similar because they are so different from America. This is an artificial construct." Kagarlitsky added, "From the neoliberal perspective these countries all pursue economic policy in a nonorthodox way. This is the only thing that binds them."

Vaniak Ashin, a political science professor from the University of Delhi, noted, "Each [BRICS] is the dominant power in its own region. Once the idea of these BRICS as a bloc was established and accepted, these countries suddenly found it better to work together. Because together they can gain more entry into the international framework."

The entire magic of O'Neill's acronym is that by simply stating it in 2001, people accepted it, talked about it, and eight years later these nations started to meet together as a real bloc. The first formal BRIC summit was held in Yekaterinburg, Russia's fourth-largest city, on June 16, 2009. The first items on their agenda was reforming the global financial system and creating a global reserve currency. South Africa joined a year later, and they became the BRICS. And it all happened because an investment banker stated the obvious, something that others had observed, but preferred not to say. And then everybody said it.

Never underestimate the power of a single idea.

This page intentionally left blank

CHAPTER 14

WE WANT A FUTURE:
To Save Our Planet, We Need New Leaders

A QUANTUM SHIFT IN VALUES

Rio de Janeiro, 2012. "My car runs on biofuel," explained Marcel as he picked me up from Rio Gealano International airport. It was mid-June, and immigration was packed with delegations from all over the world arriving to attend Rio+20.[1]

As we drove through the streets of Rio, a light summer rain began to fall, permeating the air with the scent of inland jungle mixed with ocean salt. Marcel explained proudly, "You see, we don't need to use any fossil fuels for our cars here. Sugar cane and natural gas are the ingredients in biofuel."

We whizzed down another street onto the Copacabana beach drive with its gracious hotels, rhythmic juice bar music, and winding back streets jammed with evening revelers. "In Rio we have terrible traffic jams, but at least they are sustainable ones," Marcel laughed through his white beard, raising his eyebrows. He then gave me a quick rundown on the economics of it all. "In Brazil biofuel is cheap. It encourages drivers to use inexpensively produced engines of our own domestic-made cars. In the end it is cost effective for everyone in the economic supply chain."

"But how did Brazil get to this stage?" I pried.

"That requires government policy," Marcel explained. "Under our former president, Luiz Inácio Lula da Silva, government policies prioritized the environment.[2] But it was not just about carbon reduction but how to stimulate our economy, cut costs, and create jobs through carbon reduction. So industrial, fiscal, and financial policy got behind the biofuel idea to make it work commercially. Eventually everyone bought in. For us drivers stuck in traffic most of the day, it was an easy choice. Biofuel is clean and cheap."

Marcel dropped me off at a Copacabana hotel where the prime minister of Bhutan, Lyonpo Jigmi Y. Thinley, had summoned some two dozen scholars in the room. Earlier in the year, on April 2, 2012, this group had brought a GNH proposal before the United Nations General Assembly in New York requesting that a new measurement of development be adopted.

The tiny kingdom of Bhutan was challenging assumptions underlying our global financial architecture, by questioning the materialist growth matrix as the measurement of success. Thinley said in his address, "Economics equals poverty alleviation. Sustainability equals survival." He then called for "redesigning economics from bottom-up."

Our glitz media feeds into the minds of adults and youth alike that consumption and material accumulation are measurements of success. And our entire economic structure is built around this notion. The reality is, however, we cannot afford it. Individuals and nations are running on debt. Moreover, we are borrowing too many resources and clean air from the planet that cannot be paid back. By globalizing GNH, Thinley was essentially calling for a value paradigm shift.

Just two days later during a side meeting at Rio+20, Helen Clark, then Secretary-General of the UNDP and former prime minister of New Zealand, introduced over half a dozen new matrixes to measure growth.[3] Surprisingly, the research she presented came from the world's most developed nations and from those very universities that once incubated neoliberal theories like shock therapy.[4] That signals a nascent awakening in the West that it is time to rethink the old model. As Clark reviewed these alternate approaches, she explained that now the "UNDP believes that the Human Development Index could also be a starting point for designing a more comprehensive measure of sustainable development."[5]

Ironically, at Rio+20, it was the major industrialized countries that blocked progress toward a meaningful agreement to reaffirm principles of global sustainability. Oil and corporate interests remained puppet masters in the process. But on the sidelines of Rio, among youth groups, NGO activists, and many government delegations, a new global consensus was being formed. Economic sustainability is not about profit aggrandizement for just a few individuals. It is about the survival of this planet.

"Many movements are coming together right now across the world. They are calling for an alternative to the GDP approach." Thinley thought pensively for a moment, and then called it "a tipping point of human society." He smiled knowing that the catalyst was the Kingdom of Bhutan.

WHAT RIO+20 WAS SUPPOSED TO ACHIEVE AND WHY IT DIDN'T

In 1992, the first Earth Summit (known officially as the UN Conference on Environment and Development) was held in Rio de Janeiro and is considered historic. It articulated the concept of "sustainable development" and forged the UN Framework Convention on Climate Change and Convention on Biological Diversity. That framework has been the basis upon which UN Climate Change negotiations have been held each year, ever since.

"Sustainable development" became an internationally accepted notion that views environmental problems in the context of development needs. The broad-brush Rio Principles, adopted after marathon negotiating sessions in 1992, were all about environment, development, and equity. Key notions included "the polluter pays," "development as a right," and "common but differentiated responsibilities."[6]

Twenty years on, there has been little in the way of substantive progress on climate change, the resulting water and food security crisis, or the very question of our global financial system, now in chaos. That very financial system has increased the gap between rich and poor, and left our planet's environment unsustainable.

Failure to address these issues is due to the weak and evasive political will of our global leaders, many of whom are strangled by the financial grip that multinational oil corporations hold over certain governments.

Meanwhile, glaciers melt, deserts widen, and seas rise around us, with environmental catastrophe affecting vast numbers of people.

Rio+20 was intended to reaffirm political commitments made during the Earth Summit of 1992, and to frame a road map of principles to address climate change, food and water security, and the global financial crisis. This was to be expressed in an outcome document entitled "The Future We Want." However, after a year of prenegotiations, the document fell far short of any and all expectations.

Within one day, over a thousand organizations signed a petition called "The Future We Don't Want," negating the text and even demanding that the words "in full participation with civil society" be removed. Nick Meynen of the Brussels-based NGO Northern Alliance for Sustainability circulated another petition stating, "We urge world leaders to reopen negotiations to raise the ambition level. We did NOT elect you to come here, make a political statement, and then head to Copacabana beach."

The highlight of the protest was when Leida Rijnhout of the Northern Alliance for Sustainability addressed the plenary:

> It feels amazing to be sitting in this room among all the world leaders, and feeling all this power around me that can shape the World.
>
> We all know the threat that is facing us, and I do not need to repeat the urgency. Science is very clear. If we do not change the way our societies function within the coming five to ten years, we will be threatening the survival of future generations and all other species on the planet.
>
> Nevertheless, you sitting here in this room have the power to reverse all of this. What you can do here is the dream of each one of us: to have the opportunity to be the saviors of the planet. It is all up to you.
>
> And yet we stand on the brink of Rio+20 being another failed attempt, with governments only trying to protect their narrow interests instead of inspiring the World and giving all of us back the faith in humanity that we need. If this happens, it would be a big waste of power, and a big waste of leadership.
>
> You cannot have a document titled "The Future We Want" without any mention of planetary boundaries, tipping points, or the Earth's carrying capacity. The text as it stands is completely out of touch with reality. If you adopt the text in its current form, you will fail to secure a future for the coming generations, including your own children.
>
> We see countries using the economic crisis as an excuse, while at the same time spending 100s of billions of dollars subsidizing the fossil fuel industry, the most profitable industry in the world. The first thing you can do is eliminate the existing harmful subsidies, especially fossil fuel subsidies, which was voted as the number one issue during the civil society dialogue.

The next morning, a pervasive feeling of frustration emanated through the corridors and vast open spaces of RioCentro where the meetings were being held. At pavilion T-3, where "major groups" recognized as stakeholder observers by the UN—NGOs, indigenous peoples, and women—held their side meetings, representatives of women's groups expressed outrage at the document.

There was a magnetizing feeling that emanates (and can inspire) in moments of total outrage when everybody feels an injustice has been committed. It was a compelling moment.

Anita Nayan, representing the NGO Dawn, was among the most dynamic, "What we are seeing in the Rio+20 process and text is ridiculous," stated Nayan. "There is no recognition that the problems are caused by the interrelation of issues. The Rio+20 text is unbalanced, little attention to inequalities. The economic pillar does not address systemic issues of our monetary and financial systems. In the environmental pillar the so-called green economy prioritizes economy over ecology."

Women's representatives from across the planet stood up one after another to take the microphone and express their fury and frustration at how the entire Rio+20 had become a hoax as the UN stood by haplessly while a few nations and their corporate interests manipulated the process while so easily disorienting the media, which they owned anyway.

ANATOMY OF (ANOTHER) UN FAILURE

Rio+20 was a vast tragedy in the making. While the UN outcome document heaped self-praise on a long list of past UN actions, it conspicuously dropped from the text any reference to the 2009 UN Conference on the Impact of the Financial and Economic Crisis on Development. The United States negotiators objected vociferously to even the slightest reference, as this strikes at the heart of America's debt-based stimulus bailout that protects the financial interests of the one percent.

Also conspicuously missing were the leaders associated with the crisis. With over 100 state leaders attending the summit, everyone was disappointed that key G7 individuals such as US President Barack Obama, UK Prime Minister David Cameron, and Chancellor Angela Merkel of Germany shied away altogether. That says a lot about the agendas of each, and why there was such a sharp divide.

Ironically much of the mainstream Western media either did not bother covering this historic summit or simply played the whole thing down, as they had done with Occupy. By 2012, the idea that the "one percent" is calling all the shots had become a cliché. But at Rio+20, it was the problem.

At Rio+20, most agreed that our current patterns and trajectories of consumption are not sustainable. If we are to keep going like this, then we will need seven planets to live on! Sadly, the divide between Washington's position and that of the rest of the planet was brought into sharp focus during the negotiations.

The US negotiators rejected the concept of *"changing unsustainable patterns of consumption and production"* that was proposed by the European Union, the G77, and China. Instead, the US negotiating team called for yet even more consumption by proposing the wording "promoting sustainable patterns..."

While enshrining the right to overconsumption, the US negotiating team contested the right to development. However, eventually, they had to drop this issue. The right to development has been such a long-standing UN principle that there was really nothing to debate.

Nevertheless, the US negotiators then refused to accept "the right to food." Instead they proposed "the right to an adequate standard of living, including food." Presumably that refers to a golf and country club lifestyle where fine food is served to members only. When developing countries offered a compromise, proposing the "right to adequate food," the United States rejected it outright.

The whole point is that the American negotiators wanted to enshrine the right to overconsumption, but not the right to adequate food for people.

The most intense debate came over the principle of *"common but differentiated responsibilities"* in Section II, "Renewing Political Commitment."[7] The G77 repeatedly stated that together with *"equity,"* these principles are essential for global cooperation on sustainable development. According to sources, a heated exchange broke out between India and the United States on this issue. The discussion ran into the early morning hours of June 18, but went nowhere after that.

The G77 proposed affirmation in the outcome document of *"the continued need for increased voice and full and effective participation of all countries, in particular developing countries, in global decision-making."*[8]

> The United Stated demanded the deletion of the term *"increased voice."*

In some ways, that explains everything.

THE FUTURE WE DON'T WANT!

At Rio, the UN "green washed" a process whereby governments avoided core issues concerning our planet's survival in order to protect immediate political interests, which are financed by oil interests. After months of wasteful negotiation and bickering, the summit produced a so-called outcome document titled "The Future We Want," a text completely out of touch with reality, unbalanced, and with little attention to inequalities. There was no attempt to address systemic issues concerning the failures of our monetary systems and financial architecture. Moreover, it failed to chart any road map for our planet's survival.

Rio+20 was a UN orchestrated theater that aimed at giving people hope that global leaders could construct a framework to assure our planet's future. For those on the ground, it was just the opposite, however, underscoring the political inability and lack of will to address financial crisis, poverty, a widening income gap, food and water security, and imminent disasters related to unmitigated climate change.

While the summit billed itself as embracing all stakeholders in a global process, it broke down into a three-ring circus. Government negotiators locked in plenary sessions, amounted to political speech grandstanding. Business leaders lounging in ritzy beachside hotels thrashed out their own deals. Meanwhile, civil society was divided between indigenous activists protesting through the streets of Rio, while accredited NGOs held their own sideline meetings outside the sealed government negotiation room. Contrary to the image that was intended, it was an elitist, manipulated show. But in a surprise to the UN, this time civil society refused to buy into the game.

"It's difficult to describe Rio+20 as anything other than a tragedy," reported ETC Group, an environmental watchdog, having tracked the negotiation process from 2010. "Despite years of preparation and months of negotiations, nothing said or done in Rio can cover up not just the 20 lost years since the original 1992 Earth Summit." ETC Group's Neth Daño noted, "Many delegations are genuinely embarrassed by the title of their outcome document, 'The Future We Want,' which sets sights on a future that can't be achieved by the haplessly short-sighted initiatives proposed."

The truth is, at Rio+20 those major leaders of the dominant nations on this planet, who have the power to bring about meaningful change, failed us. Their own personal, monetary, and narrow short-term political interests overshadowed concerns about the long-term sustainability of our planet. However, their inaction underscored both the political ineptitude of our leaders and the dysfunctions of a post-Bretton Woods order.

Civil society as a transnational force cries out for change and a new economic paradigm. If Rio+20 served a purpose, it was to make this point perfectly clear to not only the people protesting in the street, or UN stakeholder groups—NGOs, women's groups, environmentalists and indigenous peoples—but to the negotiators in the main plenary room itself. Everyone in and outside the room was clear that certain systems, together with interest groups, have had their time—and that that time is now over.

A new economic model was being thrashed out in the corridors outside the negotiation room and in the street among protesters. A clear and resounding collective voice of civil society called for new values. Youth activists openly stated that their generation is willing to sacrifice GDP for the environment. It is not all about greed and unbridled profit. For today's aspiring youth, success can no longer be measured by abject material wealth adhered to by older generations, but rather by the well-being of people and our planet, which will be inherited by future generations.

In the corridors and the streets, activists and youth recognized that the problems of our planet are not in trying to create more consumption, but rather in overconsumption. They called for reorienting global finance to reach communities and empower people with real business, not just to support capital markets trading leveraged financial instruments. Instead, they envisioned a world of diversified localization with holistic approaches to economic decision-making.

These voices represent a new global consensus of youth who want to shape their own future.

In a dramatic moment, youth protesters dressed in red, caught security staff off guard. They held hands and surrounded that negotiating room packed with state leaders inside. The youth message to world leaders was: don't cross that red line. In the corridors outside the negotiation room, there was a burning feeling. While those old men in the room might have authority and power, they do not have the right to negotiate away the future of this planet. That future belongs to our youth.

CHAPTER 15

ENVIRONMENTAL ECONOMICS:
Cutting Semantics, Creating Genuine Green Growth for Survival

THE "GREEN ECONOMY" DEFINITION CONUNDRUM

Beijing, 2012. At Rio+20, by far the most critical—and for me most unnerving—debate erupted over the definition of a "green economy." In the Outcome Document, the definition was left vague and open to interpretation by industry, governments, and international financial institutions. Activists and NGOs deplored what they called the "financialization of nature"—"the notion that every watershed and water lily will be priced and pigeonholed as part of nature's 'environmental services'."

This all goes back to the Wall Street game of turning everything into a debt-leveraged commodity to be bought, sold, listed, traded, and squandered. Essentially, activists were angry that investment bankers were reducing the planet and its natural resources to the status of websites.

At Rio+20, government, industry, and activists alike were stuck on semantics. Frankly, it seemed that positions were locked in vitriol, and most people around the table did not actually know what they were talking about.

The bottom line was how to reduce total carbon emissions, while placating corporate interests and maintaining sufficient economic growth to alleviate poverty. It might seem like an impossible balancing act. Now think about the fresh and creative ideas of South African students during the UNFCCC talks in Durban.

Back in Beijing, Sun Yiting of the World Wildlife Fund (WWF) was lobbying China to reduce its carbon footprint, meeting regularly with financial institutions and regulatory authorities and brainstorming how to create financial mechanisms that would encourage businesses to become genuinely green.

"Green economy consists of two things," Sun said with clarity. "First, is the 'economy' itself. Logically it must grow, which means an increase in GDP with businesses that are profitable. Charity is nice, but should not be confused with economy. The economy is all about industry, trade, and finance. Second is 'green,' which means in hard terms reducing the carbon footprint. That calls for a total reduction of carbon and waste. So putting the two together, how do we facilitate a boost in production and ecological conservation at the same time? This is what the green economy should be all about. Using the tools of a real economy to preserve natural resources contributing to overall growth. That will involve technical changes to productivity and finance."

We should call this "environmental economics" to be clear and stop debating the term "green" and its many shades of use.

Sun then explained the anger among activists over "green washing." "Carbon trading and other financial instruments are labeled green and used as an offset for carbon emissions. Carbon trading is not part of green economy. We have to view the planet as a whole. Carbon trading is only an offset. This is a game of the rich countries and financial institutions. I am rich and generate carbon. So what? A poor country that does not have industry can sell its clean airspace to me. Then I can continue polluting, business as usual. This is a financial hoax. Carbon trading must be ended altogether. We need a total reduction of carbon emissions instead."

"Total reduction of carbon will only occur through either renewable or efficient energy." Sun drove home his point, "It is about real businesses reducing carbon and waste, not an accounting game on the corporate books."

This can only be achieved through environmental economics. That is, infrastructure stimulus for grid conversion (the government's investment), combined with credit and fiscal policy that drives businesses to adopt renewable and efficient energy for their own bottom line. Back to the fusion drawing board.

China and America represent the biggest and second-biggest emitters of carbon into our planet. Sad to think, to have any positive impact on climate change, it might be more possible to get leverage through China—despite all of its problems and convoluted nasty politics—rather than America. Today, the political constipation in Planet America regrettably makes it impossible to get anything done on such an issue; whereas, China's leaders are ruthlessly pragmatic and if something is presented in their self-interest, they may do it, and can act fast if they want.

The strategy: convince China's State Council to undertake major economic measures to reduce the nation's carbon footprint, and then embarrass America's Congress into doing the same (or at least try to catch up with China).

I dusted off former Premier Zhu Rongji's "16 Measures on Macro-Economic Control," the founding document of Fusion Economics. Then I placed beside it the proposal for creating "One Million Green Jobs Now" that the South African students had suggested for their own country. The question was, how they could be merged?

FUSION ECONOMICS FOR GENUINE GREEN GROWTH

China is the biggest carbon-emitting nation in the world. According to the PBL Netherlands Environmental Assessment Agency, in 2006 China had already surpassed America as the largest CO_2 polluter by 8 percent emissions. To date, some 70 percent of China's energy comes from coal. Hydropower and nuclear account for most of the remaining output, while renewable energy—mostly solar and wind—is a remarkably low 0.7 percent. That is not even 1 percent of the total!

In China, coal is cheap. Solar and wind capacity remains small. And there are issues to be solved over the quality of energy output and scale. On the other hand, none of those obstacles are anything more than a simple technical or technological issue that can be addressed through finance and investment. In fact, all of the obstacles to the mass adoption of renewable energy as a nation-wide priority can be viewed as industrial opportunities.

While in America, research and development are struggling to get costs down, in China the sheer volume of production is achieving this because everything there occurs on a massive scale.

Charles Gay, president of Applied Solar, a subsidiary of the American industrial giant Applied Materials, believes "The learning curve for solar is actually accelerating, as cumulative scale has grown and connections between the individual process steps have evolved. When the solar panel reaches a cost of about $0.50/kilowatt, the total system cost will be about $1.00/kilowatt, which is about the same capital cost as coal, oil, or natural gas power plants. This 'learning curve' has had a historical ratio with costs dropping by 20 percent with every cumulative doubling of installed PV panels."

Here fusion kicks in with macro-policy guidance, which needed to make solar work as a national energy source. In China, political will is everything. Economic policy and business opportunity follow. Moreover, as China's former premier Zhu Rongji so clearly pointed out, "the social psychology effect on a herd of sheep" is key to the success of any economic policy. China can shift to renewable and efficient energy to drop total carbon outputs, that is, if China's leadership has the political willpower to make this happen.

The future of renewable energy in China is a question of the politics of transition. China's leadership for the past decade has judged everything based on GDP. Therefore, each province invests in redundant infrastructure to meet targets.

But in the summer and autumn of 2012, an almost silent tension incubated across the country, as the leadership was about to change. Historically, while each regime expresses continuity, in the end they actually want to do their own thing. Leadership in China has become generational.

As a result, the blind growth model of China's former leaders Hu Jintao and Wen Jiabao may have to change in the decade ahead in which Xi Jinping and Li Keqiang are the new leaders.

For China, environmental economics is not about idealistic tree hugging. It is about the very survival of China's Communist Party and its own Darwinist self-interest, because the China "economic miracle" has become an ecological disaster. And people are angry. Ten years ago, the Chinese government itself estimated some 80,000 riots each year throughout the country, mostly over local land grabs, police abuse and corruption. Today there are some 150,000 riots a year, a conservative estimate. The number has almost doubled. Chief among the causes is environmental desecration.

Throughout 2013–2014, Beijing and most major cities in China were smothered in the worst pollution levels in history, to such an extent that China's government, usually prone to cover up anything negative, came out and simply warned people not to step outside. The toxic skies seem to come straight from a science fiction end-of-the-world movie. But it is real. Meanwhile, China's urban rich have to import their food because they know the soil is toxic. Sixty percent of China's underground water sources are polluted, and 70 percent of its river systems are deemed too polluted for human contact. So the future of China's new leadership has taken a twist. It now depends more on cleaning up the environment than pumping up the growth rates that destroyed it.

The hypergrowth model is at the root of the problem. China's new waves of social unrest and public anger are often aimed at industries supported by local government that need to feed GDP, the standard way of measuring economic success. In 2012, social stability through hypergrowth was the demarcation of economic success for the outgoing leadership of Hu and Wen and their coterie of business cohorts. But people coughing in the street or choked in toxic traffic gridlock were beginning to question the equation.

China's high growth dependency on fixed asset investments has brought with it high energy costs, opening a Pandora's box of inflation, rising costs of production, transport costs, and labor wages, knocking back China's competitive advantage. The very policies of the past decade have threatened to roll back the earlier economic achievements of Zhu Rongji, which characterized the China economic miracle. Moreover, the social cost of a teetering medical-pension system and popular outrage over environmental destruction and its impact on human physical and mental health across the country represents the call of China's people upon its new leadership to rethink this hypergrowth model in favor of something more holistic. That means getting back to Zhu basics on one hand, and reexamining China's social values on the other. In the end, that means redefining what qualifies as success. Maybe China's leaders will have to look across the Himalayas to Bhutan for an answer as to what happiness means. So back to the Himalayan Consensus.

For a decade, Wen Jiabao and his team rolled back Zhu Rongji's policies, eliminating the macro-coordinating economic ministries. They ceased his reforestation policies and instead contributed to forest desecration by issuing a torrent of indiscriminate mining licenses. They crushed the private sector in favor of heavy state industry, and distorted

Zhu's model of stimulus for infrastructure growth into becoming redundant fixed asset investments—growth for the sake of growth—but not for the purpose of economic efficiency. This was exactly what Zhu warned against. He called it "blind economic growth" and the disease of "money worship."

The need for a fresh dose of fusion economics was made clear when, on October 24, 2012, former premier Zhu Rongji held a meeting with his old cabinet at Diao Yutai State Guest House in Beijing. Unseen in public for many years, the old former premier who was the father of China's economic reforms suddenly appeared at a high-profile venue, a mere two weeks before the opening of the Chinese Communist Party's big baton handoff between one generation of leaders and the next.

There seemed to be an eerie echo of the past. Many problems that China is now facing are a distorted shadow of those same problems Zhu had to combat 20 years ago, with one big difference: in the mid-1990s, China's reforms were driven by its leadership, now they are demanded by the people.

THE FIRST EMPEROR OF CHINA INVENTED KEYNESIAN ECONOMICS

I returned to my studio located beside the Great Wall, and began drafting a single policy proposal that merged principles of fusion economics with those ideas of the South African students for creating jobs to combat climate change. With a leadership transition in China, they might be open to new ideas. What the hell. It was worth a try.

The Great Wall with its looming ghostly towers is a kind of DaVinci Code revealing China's economic history. In the minds of most people, it was a great feudal castle or defense bulwark against Mongolian and Manchurian invaders. But from a fusion economics perspective, it is the world's largest nonperforming asset.[1]

The Great Wall represented massive fiscal stimulus for infrastructure investment, using fixed assets to fuel economic growth and assure jobs. The Great Wall was a failure as a defense system, but it was a remarkable and sophisticated national telecommunications program at that time. Whether by horse relay messenger (the Wall was built wide enough for horses to run on it) or bonfire signal, one end of China's vast empire could communicate news to the other within almost real time, relative to the day. China's two-thousand-year-old telecommunications project was government fiscal funded and slated as part of the military expenditure budget of the time. This was not so different from many of our technology communication undertakings today. It provided jobs for everyone from Confucian scholarly engineers, to blustering commanding generals, right down to the masses of Chinese workers who built it. While one son in every family across the empire was conscripted to work on the Wall—a cruel undertaking—this practice also assured that each family received a Keynesian cash injection to boost local spending power. Arguably the first emperor of China invented Keynesian economics. The Wall's greatest construction periods usually coincided at times when Chinese exports surged together with its foreign exchange reserves. But each dynasty's overextension of construction coupled with a depletion of resources, led to its own collapse. Remember the lesson of Rapa Nui from Easter Island?

China's new economic stimulus would have to be different to avoid a tragic collapse. A continuation of the existing policies of hyper-growth would deplete the planet's resources while accelerating its already dangerous carbon footprint. China's use of water to wash coal alone to fire its own national grid would deplete its own water supply in 15 years. With the glaciers of the Himalayas melting and vanishing, water and food security not only for China but South Asia and peninsular Southeast Asia, whose populations collectively constitute half of our world's humanity, is a disastrous tragedy in process. It is not about keeping social stability by encouraging people to buy more cars and stuff their homes with luxury brands. It is about whether people will have water to drink and food to eat. (At the time of this writing, parched Beijing is putting up another golf course under the Jack Nicklaus franchise). This is not a question of the right to carry out development, but the right to exist. It spells regional war over a precious resource—not oil—but water.

CAN THE "GREAT GREEN GRID" BE SEEN FROM THE MOON?

Fusion economics for renewable energy and efficient energy means rather than building roads and docks to get goods to market, converting China's national energy grid from fossil fuel to solar and wind. The Great Green Grid proposal offers a sequence of three core parallel policy reforms.

First, China will need to undertake massive state investments into the conversion of China's grid from fossil fuel-based to renewable. This will need to be funded by new green bond issues.[2] It will create new waves of jobs from the most senior engineers to blue-collar workers. The political challenge will come from the coal industry. About 70 percent of China's coal comes from Inner Mongolia, and the remaining 30 percent from Shannxi Province. Sequencing will need to kick in for a pragmatic transition to cleaner coal derivatives such as methane to phase down the industry, while making massive investments into wind energy (which Inner Mongolia has a lot of).

Interestingly, China is already the second-largest owner of wind production assets in America (through acquisition of Portugal's global wind farms following the 2008 financial crisis, when China bought real businesses in Europe rather than bad debt).

Second, industrial economic policies—tax incentives and rebates—must encourage a new growth cycle in developing and manufacturing products that are energy efficient for consumers. In 2012, China was already giving rebates encouraging consumers to purchase energy-saving television sets. In this policy lay a potential repeat act of China's export surge in the 1990s, now with energy efficient exports.

Third, the banking system and financial sector must lead through "green credit" for low-carbon developments in the property sector and for companies investing in renewable or energy efficient products. The capital market regulatory authorities could favor the listing of energy-efficient or renewable energy-driven companies. Policy guidance of the market could introduce new standards of stakeholder value.

The truth is, with a global recession that is teetering on depression, China needs a new economic stimulus. But with all of China's redundant roads and cement blocks, what is there left to invest in? The answer is not another mortar and brick Great Wall, but the Great Green Grid.

Here is the twisted irony and potential business opportunity: at the time of this writing, renewable energy accounts for less than 1 percent of China's energy needs, while China now leads the world in both investment in renewable energy and production of renewable- and energy-efficient systems. For the communist government, cleaning up the environment and reducing the carbon footprint is in its self-interest. For the rest of capitalist China, it is a business opportunity. That's where fusion economics comes in.

The ultimate power to reduce absolute carbon in China lies with its leadership.

The tools to achieve this lie with the banking regulatory and fiscal levers.

China's banking sector fully senses that a massive green financing opportunity is sitting right in front of them, waiting to be grabbed. But it is not yet clear to them how? Government policies await decision. But what the market wants is clear. Chinese banks are not just interested in carbon trading, but rather how to finance low-carbon buildings.[3]

The idea of low-carbon city financing mechanisms is real, and China is courting the most cutting-edge European technology to get there. The challenge for China's banking sector now lies in how to establish financing products and services for a host of interconnected urban services—both public and privately managed—from green energy transport buildings, to waste treatment, to a plethora of related products needed to make a city work. Imagine entire buildings in which the glass windows are actually solar panels—buildings that produce energy rather than consume it! As futuristic it might sound, this is something China could accomplish. The technology exists. China can scale it.

Pilot programs are already underway. The Ministry of Construction and Urbanization selected several test cities including Suzhou, Hangzhou and even Baoding (of coal-pollution-drenched Hebei Province) to become trial green cities during the coming five-year plan. Many experiments are incubating at once. Government officials and financiers know they must do something, and although they are not exactly sure what to do, at least a frenzied brainstorming process has begun.

For those outside the system, the edifice of China's growth and short-term profit seems invincible. For those inside, however, it is clear China's economy has become very fragile. In many ways China is facing the same problems as it did a decade ago in the 1990s. It desperately needs financial and industrial reforms, sparked by new products for each, and massive stimulus to drive the economy. Environmental economics offers a roadmap. It is therefore necessary to go back to fusion economics, this time for green growth.

"ECOLOGICAL CIVILIZATON" AND GREEN GROWTH

With the help of Zhu Rongji's daughter, Zhu Yanlai, we together drafted a document the "Sixteen Measures on Green Macro-Control

Policy" to mirror Zhu Rongji's famous "Sixteen Measures on Macro-Control Policy," the founding stone of fusion economics. The reason for presenting the policy brief as 16 articles was symbolic precedent. Many of Zhu's protégés came back into positions of power under the new administration of President Xi Jinping and Premier Li Keqiang. Every economist in China would know immediately what "16 Measures" signals.

The document was submitted to China's Ministry of Environmental Protection and also to Li Wei, former personal secretary to Zhu. Li was now the minister heading the State Council Economic Development Research Center, the foremost economic think tank of the premier. I was soon appointed senior adviser to the Ministry of Environmental Protection and simultaneously to the European Union's Environmental Director General on China's green growth policies under a China-EU Dialogues framework agreement.

Working with the ministry, we condensed the Sixteen Measures into a five-pillar framework defining "ecological civilization," a term freshly coined by China's president Xi Jinping. The five pillars include 1) state infrastructure investment into renewables (the Great Green Grid), 2) fiscal and credit policy to guide businesses in adopting renewable and efficient energy, 3) replacing GDP with a broader, more inclusive, set of measures, 4) a macro-coordinating policy body to promote genuine green growth among ministries,[4] 5) education to transition values toward conservation. Core to the success of this policy transition would be creating a fresh awareness among Chinese people that all things are connected and that we need new measures of success and pride other than material ones. In a nutshell, this is what "ecological civilization" would have to be about to succeed.

At the Ministry of Finance, one official commented quite frankly. "China should use economic crisis as opportunity and get rid of outdated enterprises and push green." Referring to the previous generation of leaders, Hu and Wen, he observed, "They did not have the political will. They had built their careers on stagnant stability, not on principles of reform and progress."

He then added, "The current generation of government officials know that this needs to be done. The Great Green Grid is a bigger challenge than the reforms of '80s and '90s. Back then we did not know what capitalism was, but now we know. Today, each department of government and every sector of the economy, guard their own interests. Whether at the central or local level, it is all about controlling and profiting from resources. So this reform will be challenging because we are not entering an unknown area. It is about people giving up what is already known."

Without carefully guided state policy, nothing will happen in China. This requires political willpower. As a managed market, ultimately a political decision is required to put in place the right policies that can guide market forces to make wind and solar power competitive with fossil fuels. However, the policy document we put forward would also need to be penned by other Chinese economists in order to achieve buy-in, build consensus, and advance up the rungs of decision-making. In short, it had to have total Chinese ownership.

As a foreigner, my role had to change tactfully. I could openly acknowledge and support the ideas in the document, but it could not be seen as coming from me. These policies had to become Chinese, in order to work in China.

CAN KUNG FU PANDA AS "DRAGON WARRIOR" SAVE THE PLANET?

China is not unlike Kung Fu Panda in the contrast between its clumsiness and overweight, and at the same time, its ability to get things done when it wants to. Regardless whether it was Mao Zedong, Deng Xiaoping, or Jiang Zemin, those three generations of leaders oversaw gargantuan and in many ways convulsive reforms. At each separate time, tumultuous changes were necessary in order for China to step away from its creeping stagnation, the sheer weight of its past, and the mass population, and somehow push a creaking edifice into forward lurch. But for some reason, that process skipped one generation of leaders—Hu and Wen. Time and circumstance will not allow it to skip another. Both drought and flooding across China signal that time is running out. So do the blackened skies.

By 2013, China's new president, Xi Jinping, had officially pronounced the concept of "ecological civilization" and called for quality rather than quantity growth. The Chinese government suddenly seemed to buy into some ideas of the Himalayan Consensus. They wanted to project a nontheory-based pragmatic set of alternatives, presenting many paths of development rather than one.

So maybe when China's green growth policy is on track, it will be time for me to return to America to work with activists and social entrepreneurs and push for a similar program of national environmental economics. Yes, join Joshua Cooper, organize, and demand 13 million green jobs now!

When Rob Parenteau, an independent financial adviser based in San Francisco, heard of the green growth policy proposals underway for China, he wrote the following: "Yes, and with the banking system essentially an extension of their fiscal policy, they [China] have the capacity to drive down the unit costs of production and push out the technological frontier on green tech. Done right, they could end up owning the 21st century industries while correcting their own growth path toward one more sustainable than the current suicidal one. Meanwhile, in the US, we will be debating whether we can afford to saddle future generations with the horrible curse of public debt…which is actually an asset held by households…that can help finance the construction and implementation of public assets…that improve the profitability and prospects for the business sector as well as lower future cost trajectories. Solarize all public buildings in the southern half of the US and insulate all government buildings in the northern half, as an opening Green New Deal. Create jobs, teach skills, and scale up demand to drive down unit costs. Or wait until the Chinese own the whole thing."

Whether in North America or Europe, Asia or Africa, a plethora of renewable energy and energy saving industries will need to replace our old existing systems. With the potential to roll out a spectrum of new employment opportunities for both white and blue collar, in sectors ranging from finance, engineering, environmental science, transportation, and infrastructure.

In 2010, global investment in renewable energy jumped 32 percent to a record $211 billion. The new driver for growth will have to be green energy. China may lead it, if its own domestic corruption and political paranoia don't derail the process before it begins. India could follow as a leader too. Actually, America has the potential to lead all of these efforts. It has the technology, and is ahead of both countries in research and development. But does it have the political will?

Does America want real change? Does it want to evolve and lead renewable and efficient energy as a mega trend and the next driver of global growth? Or will America sit back and let others take the lead as its economy declines further because it is fossilized in old ways and ideological debates?

The problem is that America is locked in a political stalemate that defies rationality. The politics have become like the economics, ideological, not pragmatic, only black and white, without any room for grey. Regardless of which side you take, Democrat or Republican, the result is that views are stagnant and entrenched—one side votes opposite the other just for the sake of it. It is no longer logical politics, but that kind of vindictiveness that comes about when nobody has an answer but everyone wants somebody to blame. So the strategy is to blame the other side. It has just become an knee-jerk reaction, which means that any form of logic—like, let's try to avoid a crisis rather than just react to another one—is off the game board altogether. Even Niccolò Machiavelli, if he could see this mess, would throw up his hands and tell the Prince to call it a day. There is just nothing you can do with these guys.

WEAVE TIGER RUGS THE WAY GANDHI SPUN COTTON

The bottom line is adaptation, or economic Darwinism, that is, the ability to change and survive.[5] This brings us back to our group of women artisans weaving tiger rugs in Lhasa. As small as that little cottage craft project may be, it represents a powerful idea. When the British Raj bounty hunters decimated tigers, an ecological cycle of balance was broken. Meanwhile, Tibetans adapted and wove tiger rugs. The tiger rug became a revolutionary replacement product, the way biofuel and solar should become in our world today.

Those tiger rugs portend a message for future generations about the importance of product replacement in adapting to the crisis of sudden environmental change, and the necessity of making it economically work. At Rio+20, heads of state failed to express clearly what a green economy is. Maybe in those simple tiger rugs they would have found the definition.

Once upon a time, not such a long time ago, we all hoped for change. But change does not occur with one person. It occurs when many people come together with a shared vision and a determination to make that vision work. That is what consensus is all about. Negativity only creates inane debate and stagnant antagonism that goes nowhere. True change is about magnetism that arises from collective purpose, and positive intention that eventually turns into a self-propelling energy of its own.

Yes, there is a positive energy bank out there. It offers hope. You can draw down positive energy if you use it for a transformational purpose, and pay it back through good constructive action. I often think about the philosophy of a mercurial monk on the top of the world, who remains my teacher.

And there is the simple Tibetan story that I often told at Zuccotti Park during Occupy Wall Street teach-ins. Four animals, an elephant, a monkey, a rabbit, and a bird once argued over who was closest to a tree. The elephant declared that he bathed in the tree's shadow each day, so he was closest. The monkey giggled and explained he ate the tree's fruit each day. The rabbit snickered that he was nibbling at the tree's root and was closer than the rest. In fact, they were all taking from the tree. Finally, the tiny bird spoke humbly, suggesting that he was closest to the tree. All the other animals laughed at him. Then the tiny bird politely explained he had brought the seed to plant the tree. The story reminds us of the environmental interconnectivity of all things, and of the importance of giving more than taking.

Every Tibetan child across the Himalayas knows this story, even those who can barely scratch out a primary education. One day, if this story is taught in the curriculum of Harvard Business School, we will know that change has happened.

CONCLUSION

THE POST OCCUPY WORLD:
Imagine an Economy Without Greed

"First they will laugh at you; then they will threaten you; and then they will follow you."

—Gandhi

ORACLES OF A REVOLUTION

We are in the midst of a revolution. And it is global. Yet those sitting in government offices, multi-lateral institutions, think tanks and the financial institutions that link them together—all running on debt that cannot be paid—do not seem to realize this.

At least they won't tell you.

The mainstream media focuses our attention on things like rich starlet breakdowns, or the daily insipid personality attacks on comic-book-politicians (imagine, these people actually run a country). Lurching from one self-made crisis to another; airtime dedicated to inane frivolous programming and golf. Paid for, courtesy of advertisers who are running on debt as well.

It is the politics of public distraction.

Certainly, they do not want us to connect the dots.

It would shatter all of the assumptions and beliefs that have propelled the world economy and financial system for half a century. But deep down inside, we all know that these systems are antiquated and need to be replaced.

Just imagine a planet without water, people without food. Where unemployed youth riot endlessly in the streets until they take over government offices themselves setting up ad hoc committees in the once pristine cities of Europe and the now decaying ones across North America. Money collapses and we fall into regional barter systems. Are we really headed toward that?

They tell us not to worry. The listing of Facebook promised to save us. It has already become the opiate of America, which drifts on from crisis to crisis listlessly in its own dream.

And the Fed will print more money to purchase more debt with which to print more money, while Congress cuts healthcare, education, infrastructure, and congratulates Europe on its austerity programs.

Now, look out of your window into the street.

Ask those who have protested peacefully in New York, Tunis, Cairo, or who rioted in London, Madrid, Athens. Somehow the mainstream media forgot to interview them. Why aren't they on the talk shows? These people in the street are the oracles of our decade.

Oracles? How could they read the tea leaves of our future?

The oracles of our age are not well-endowed think tanks inside bureaucratic institutions where badly made coffee is served. Nor are they the tight-suited high-paid analysts on Wall Street, or the arrogant Ivy-league university economists sitting in stuffy library offices uptown. They are not the talking heads appearing daily on the morning show.

No, the soothsayers cannot pay their bills, or their school loans either, because they do not have jobs awaiting them.

But they have dared to speak out against a global system that has pushed itself to its own brink. They are tired of wars that are fought out of old ideologies, when the governments waging them are in deficit, running on debt. They ask why their governments continue to use drones to bomb schools in distant lands when they cannot afford to build schools in their own.

Meanwhile, the leaders of the G8 slap themselves on their backs over champagne, self-congratulating their globalized economic order as they discuss another war and raise more debt to finance it. (What's next, Iran?). Don't worry the oil companies will have their cut when the invasion is finished so they will be able to fund advertising for another political campaign. Benefits will be chopped for the soldiers returning from those wars (sorry sequester or austerity), because those who actually fight are never from the one percent. They are what the one percent call, "those other people."

And the oligarchy of oil will ensure no measures are taken to address climate change, as the world faces desperate water and food shortages, and scores of islands and coastal nations face flooding and disappearance while those on high land watch their farmland become desert. That means the price of oil will remain stabilized, until the price of water catches up.

DO SOMETHING!

At Zuccotti Park the protestors may be disbursed but what they stood for has not. It is still occupying minds, not only in the streets but in boardrooms too. "Liberty Park" was a mirror of our consciousness, a microcosm of global movements and changing patterns occurring in parallel, on different continents, all at once.

Occupy was just a signal of what to expect. They warned us. Who listened? By condemning excesses of corporate and bank greed, the very corporations that Occupy rallied against have been forced to rethink their role in order to survive. It is no longer just a game for profit, shareholder's value or management bonuses.

Can we imagine a future based on principles of *compassionate capital, conscientious consumption* and *stakeholder's value*? Management bonuses will be issued in the form of tradable shares in clean air and units of Gross National Happiness that earn compounded interest.

Are these ideas so far flung? Or are they the next reality already happening?

Countless NGOs, activists, social entrepreneurs and every day people who care about their community and their environment are in the field, on the front lines, fighting poverty and climate change for a better future. They are not dreamers. They are visionaries who apply *pragmatic idealism*. But you do not hear about them on the evening news or in the newspaper. Often they are doing this by creating a business to generate the funds to solve a social problem in their community, or the renewable energy technology that will sustain this planet. It is not just happening in the far-off Himalayas and Africa. It is taking place just around the street corner from us, right there in our neighborhoods.

Go look, find, and join them!

Enter *compassionate capital*. Can you imagine making an investment not only for profit but to improve somebody's life, take away pain, build a school in your own community, save water, grow safe food, or re-grid a neighborhood so that they can get off fossil fuels and go solar? These are all business opportunities.

Enter *stakeholder's value*. Alongside its profitability, a corporation should be valued by what it does for the community, environment, and how it treats employees. All are interconnected. The formula is pragmatic, holistic, and sustainable. It is the future. Start putting it into MBA courses.

Enter *conscientious consumption*. Consumer behavior must change as well. We are not just statistics without responsibility. Consumers have the power to vote with their money, buy or boycott. Changing values will alter consumer demands and force corporations to react and adopt products and services that can assure our planet's sustainability. In turn financial institutions will have to respond to these changes. Actually, it is an opportunity for them too. If they don't get it, organize a boycott in a neighborhood near you or flood their corporate inboxes with emails, and see how fast they wake up.

Enter *environmental economics*. Job creation through technology and innovation to convert national grids from fossil to renewable, with credit and fiscal policy to encourage businesses to become energy efficient is the next business opportunity that is about to become a mega trend. This is not about tree hugging, but basic water and food security (you cannot eat a derivative). It is not about oil for someone's luxury car, but about water to drink. If the glaciers continue to melt, then we should expect nations and communities to fight for water. Either we prepare to reduce the carbon footprint or we prepare for war.

Now gentlemen, after a hard day of fixing stock prices over a good game of golf, let's sit back with a martini and sushi appetizer laced with avocado and mango salsa sauce and think about *fusion economics*. Before people riot, take over your golf course, and set up an organic crop commune under a barter economy, close your eyes for a moment and think. Can you imagine an economy without greed?

A PEACEFUL REVOLUTION GOES GLOBAL

Across our earth, the elderly, looking ahead without benefits or hope, feel ripped off. The youth, strapped with debt to pay for an education that cannot even secure them a job, demand a say in their future that is currently being determined by others, in fact taken away from them.

Ideologically driven wars have bankrupted the nations that started them. Money is being printed on the back of debt that will saddle generations to come in order to pay for it all—and with it the bonuses of those already grossly wealthy investment bankers and politicians who have created all this mess. Yes, those politicians who refuse to recognize the already clear scientific warnings of climate change, because they are beholden to multinational corporations that enrich themselves in the most profitable business of all—fossil fuels. These same politicians wave their finger at the world and talk of the need for governance and transparency, while sending the poor off to fight wars that their children will only play on video games—funded through the global market offering of another junk tech stock that will be traded just like a derivative.

In this decade of protest, people across our earth have responded to the dysfunctional politics by occupying public space, engaging in nonviolent disobedience, and forming transparent ad-hoc governing councils in open areas or locally, where they are creating community economies of their own. Essentially, people are taking the power back!

Protesters across the planet, regardless of background, creed, or birth, have united in a single voice. We have all had enough! It is time to change the rules of the game, the blind belief in greed taken to the extreme, the globalization of everything. It cannot continue because our planet's resources simply cannot sustain it. And the increasing numbers of people falling below the poverty line— and the extreme poverty line—will not tolerate it. So the rules have to change.

These protesters demand more than just a new swap of politicians. They call for reconstructing our global financial architecture. This requires new economic models to replace outdated ones, fundamental policy changes, and a reassessment of underlying assumptions and values that have long been taken for granted without question or consideration.

To change the economics means to change the assumptions, which really means those tiffany twisted values that underlie it all. That is what the peaceful revolution is really all about: a new earth consensus built on principles of compassion, care, and consideration for our fellow man and environment, not predicated on unbridled greed.

It is time for all us to realize that we are all sharing planet earth, a single satellite in the orbit of our vast universe. If the mechanics of this planet fail to work, sustaining glaciers, ocean levels, and arable land mass and forests (yes water-food security and the very lungs of our planet), then we will not have a planet to live on. And we cannot get off of this satellite and land anywhere else (all of NASA's space exploration research funding has been diverted to imperial folly wars). Somehow, we must think above it all, drop our differences, and make our future work.

That will require pragmatism and compassion, planning with vision while sequencing the steps to get us out of this mess and into a new paradigm as a workable framework that can sustain our existence and all of the natural biodiversity that we need to exist together.

We are sharing an increasingly complex and integrated, multi-ethnic planet of rapidly diminishing resources. Ideologically based economics as practiced in the past are no longer relevant for our rapidly transforming multilateral world. Greed-based neoliberalism, market fundamentalism, shock therapy, and monolithic globalization are concepts that had their time in a past era. They are far too simplistic in the broader context of our planet's challenges today. They are being replaced by an entirely new vision that blends pragmatic bottom-up economics, compassionate capital, stakeholder value, diversified localization, and the need for environmental economics.

Governments must reexamine their own responses, too. Stimulus to create rapid consumption does not solve economic hardship because too much consumption is one of the problems. So consumer behavior must change as well. But that does not mean austerity is an answer. It is not a solution. Stimulus funding needs to be invested into communities, education, the upgrading of infrastructure, and power grids that accommodate renewable energy, all of which will create new jobs. Then people will consume, sustainably.

The decisions affecting our planet must be made by a wider set of interests than just one narrow street in New York City, a wide boulevard in Washington DC, and a traffic-clocked roundabout in Brussels. This decade that has begun with global protests is a signal that people are asking for this to change.

The tectonic plates of our global financial and economic systems are shifting with the kind of velocity and force that leave some species extinct and give rise to new ones. Such is the nature of radical change. It can shatter empires and their comfortable political arrangements.

A new economic order is evolving rapidly through multilateral trade and currency swap agreements among the fast-emerging "South." The classic tools of the old Bretton Woods order—the World Bank, the IMF, and the WTO—are quickly losing much of their relevance. The IMF even struggled to solve the financial crisis of a tiny country like Cyprus with a population smaller than any single district in most of China's major cities. How can the IMF's policies be relevant to the developing world that is struggling to rise out of poverty? System credibility is in question.

The global South is calling for new financing mechanisms relevant to them. A new BRICS development bank and currency stabilization fund announced in July 2014 may offer an alternative for developing nations from the World Bank and the IMF. It is really about the *democratization of global finance.* Underdeveloped nations and the poor deserve a choice.

An alternate reserve currency may follow, possibly based on a weighted basket of currencies from the BRICS. It could change the financial architecture of this planet. Certainly, it will shake up all of the assumptions and economic arrangements we have come to take for granted. And the very political alliances that have been long accepted as the status quo will shift with the changing flow of capital.

ENTER THE NEW EARTH CONSENSUS

A new financial architecture is being constructed that does not see free capital flows as necessarily benefitting economies. It does not see extreme market fundamentalism as a panacea for all economic order. It does not see a flat world, but rather one that is round, uneven, and requiring local solutions to local predicaments and also to global ones. It is calling for capital to come back to communities, back to people, back to ways of life that are local. It is calling for an end to a monolithic order envisioned by a few for their own benefit. The response is occurring on multiple levels at the same time in diverse regions. It is happening locally in America too.

Youth are joining hands across continents for their future. They have the know-how to do this. They are linked by technology (that can hack any firewall) and a holistic vision of a planet that can sustain generations to come. Our youth demand a voice in a future that belongs to them, not us. We must look to our youth to break the straight jacketed monopolies on media and news through forming guerrilla television networks and online live news streams. People need information. They need to know the truth.

Across our planet, social movements are forming often spontaneously and out of the chaos of protest and riot. Some of these networks will become organizations that can gain political traction and a voice. Heads of state will have to sit at the table and deal with them. Governments will have to determine policies for a future that belongs to them. Otherwise this current generation of stale leaders will be kicked out of power through youth voting or through people's taking to the streets.

This collection of ideas is only part of a growing matrix of often separate, yet interconnected, movements that are running in parallel, but are coming into an inevitable synergy and convergence that will change the economic architecture of our planet. Some of these innovations come from villages and ghettos, while others are being driven by business and financial leaders who have a vision and want to change what they know is not right.

Civil society is creating grass-roots businesses to support the ideals people wish to achieve (and the social, medical, and renewable energy projects that are essential to our survival). Meanwhile, there are executives in boardrooms who suffer frustration, knowing that this system is not right, and certainly will not assure a future for their children either. So they have to do something too.

Protest in itself is not enough. Yes, civil disobedience in its multiplier forms is absolutely necessary to force key issues into the face of a media that is owned by those same corporate and banking interests that own the politicians to whom they give airtime. However, we must also present rational and constructive frameworks and lay the foundations of new and pragmatic systems so that a new earth consensus arising from the different movements across this planet can parallel and then displace the old consensus that has already had its time. History moves on. We must continue to reinvent ourselves, and our systems, to keep up with the change that we in fact have created.

The shocking and widening gaps between rich and poor, and the apocalyptic crisis of climate change, are outcomes of those systems we have been relying on for decades, which no longer work. It is time to dismantle that old architecture and rebuild systems that are more equitable for all and that can ensure the sustainability of this planet.

A new earth consensus is on the rise. It is pioneered by youth, NGOs, and social entrepreneurs unhindered by national boundaries, race, or religion. As anthropologist Margaret Mead once said, "Never doubt that a small group of thoughtful, committed citizens can change the world; indeed, it's the only thing that ever has."[1]

This is about the democracy of people's economics at work, the voices and action of people in communities across this planet coming together in common purpose, putting idealism to work in a practical way. If we connect the dots and look at these independent grassroots and community efforts as a whole, respecting their differences and diversity, we will realize that all of these progressive economic movements—what the mainstream calls "those alternatives"—have already in fact become a new mainstream. And so dawns a New Earth Consensus. Now go join it!

This page intentionally left blank

NOTES

INTRODUCTION THE WASHINGTON CONSENSUS IS DEAD!

1. "Add 'financial stability' to the Fed's mandate," by Stephen Roach, *Financial Times*, October 28, 2008, p. 11.
2. Ibid.
3. In fact, Adam Smith made only one single tiny reference in his whole life to that "invisible hand" so acclaimed as the core principle of neoliberalist ideology. Smith wrote: "By preferring the support of domestic to that of foreign industry, he intends only his own security, and by directing that industry in such a manner as its produce may be of the greatest value, he intends only his own gain, and he is in this, as in many other cases, led by an invisible hand to promote an end which was no part of his intention."
4. The ten points of the Washington Consensus are intentionally vague, as they were meant to represent a baseline. They include keeping competitive exchange rates within the country; liberalizing foreign investment opportunities; privatizing enterprises run by the state; giving strong legal guarantees for property rights; letting interest rates be handled by the market and remain positive and moderate; moving spending away from subsidies and toward direct investment in infrastructure, health care, and education; reforming the tax system to a broader tax base; having a policy of strong fiscal responsibility; liberalizing trade by removing or lessening restrictions on imports and tariffs; and deregulation that lessens competition, except in the cases of consumer safety, environmental health, and financial institutional stability.
5. Nobel laureate economist Joseph Stiglitz explains in his book *Globalization and its Discontents* (New York: W.W. Norton & Company, 2002): "The Washington Consensus policies...were based on a simplistic model of the market economy, the competitive equilibrium model, in which Adam Smith's invisible hand works and works perfectly.... The theory says that an efficient market economy requires that all of the assumptions be satisfied. In some cases, reforms in one area, without accompanying reforms in others, may actually make matters worse. This is the issue of sequencing. Ideology ignores these matters; it says simply move as quickly to a market economy as you can. But economic theory and history show how disastrous

it can be to ignore sequencing…. The mistakes in trade, capital market liberalization and privatization described earlier represent sequencing errors on a grand scale. The smaller-scale sequencing mistakes are even less noticed in the Western press. They constitute the day-to-day tragedies of IMF policies that affect the already desperately poor in the developing world."

6. "Needed, A Moratorium on Trade Liberalization," by Walden Bello, Guerilla Information Network, Transnational Institute, April 4, 2001,

1 REENGINEERING CHINA:
Ending Ideology and Getting Pragmatic

1. After Mao Zedong's death in 1976, successor Hua Guofeng adopted a hard-line communist position. "Mao thought," could not be changed. It had to be taken literally. When Deng Xiaoping sidelined Hua, taking the reins of power at the Communist Party Plenum in 1978, he began to de-deify Mao and bring common sense into economics, toning down ideology. After three decades of radicalism, getting everyone to think outside of the ideological box was difficult. So the wily Deng introduced market reforms that could be swallowed in dumpling-sized bites, cleverly setting a lower threshold, while pushing the goal posts back. Deng's persuasive logic went like this: Communism is an ideal, but just a goal. So drop the term "communism" and replace it with "socialism," something more realistic, while keeping "communism" as an abstract goal. A decade later at the 1988 Communist Party Plenum, "socialism" became the new goal, and "communism" as a term was then dropped altogether. After his 1992 "southern inspection," Deng injected the term "socialist market economy with Chinese characteristics," an idea open to broad interpretation. In 1997, at the 15th Communist Party Plenum, Jiang Zemin declared "Deng theory" as China's leading ideology, which was understood implicitly as a sanction for extreme state capitalism.

2. During the Cultural Revolution (1966–1976) extreme leftism reigned. Between the early reform years of 1978 to 1992, market initiatives were a confused start-stop-start without any clear breakthrough. Only in 1992, following Deng's "southern inspection" when Deng put Zhu Rongji in charge of economics in 1993, did reforms push forward. This was not easy as then-Premier Li Peng continued protecting the state sector. China's real reforms began in 1998 following Deng's death, when Zhu became premier, introducing a massive five-year transformation that mesmerized the world. Ten years later, Hu Jintao and Wen Jiabao would attempt to roll it all back again.

3. The author came up with the term in a book called *China Inc* (a guide to foreign investors) published by Butterworth-Heinemann in 1996. It is still available from sellers on Amazon. In Washington, this view was politically incorrect at the time. But eventually it was picked up by politicians and journalists alike. Ted Fishman later published an eponymous book called *China Inc.*

NOTES | 237

3 RED GUARDS WITH CREDIT CARDS:
Merge Planning and Market the Fusion Way

1. Deng's 1992 "southern inspection" was considered so challenging to conservatives that it was reported initially in the Hong Kong press, and only later in the Beijing media, which re-reported Deng's statements as secondhand information by cautiously quoting the Hong Kong media.
2. Following Tiananmen in 1989, the leadership feared high growth that could respark an inflation bout, which would bring people into the street protesting. Deng's promotion of Zhu Rongji from mayor of Shanghai to the vice premier of the State Council challenged conservatives. Deng threatened, "Whoever does not want 9 percent growth should step down." Thereafter China became fixated on high growth rates. In 1998, Zhu promised during his press conference at the National People's Congress no less than 8 percent per annum growth during his term that ended in 2005. His successor, Wen Jiabao, oversaw growth rates averaging well above 9 percent. But by that time, it was just blind growth, led mostly by government-driven fixed asset investments, often creating as much disruption to communities and the environment as contributing to the health of China's economy. This approach would come under criticism from Zhu in retirement, explaining in part the long silence of the retired premier until Wen's near retirement in 2012.
3. People (including some Chinese) confuse the word *hutong* with the term "courtyard," or *siheyuan*. In Beijing dialect, *hutong* means "alleyway." Actually, it is a Mongolian word for "water well," dating back to the Yuan Dynasty emperor Kublei Khan (1215–1294), who ordered an Arab architect to blueprint the city of Beijing. A *hutong* alleyway was wide enough for six Mongolian ponies to ride through the street abreast, obviously a security control measure.
4. Zhu kicked the entire banking system into shape, not through manipulating interest rates, but rather by slapping on the banks administrative edicts forbidding redundant lending, particularly on real estate, or the manufacturing of products in oversupply. Zhu aggressively tightened credit across the board to reduce money in circulation. He raised the reserve requirement on banks to control money supply growth. He emphasized pumping up the nation's foreign exchange reserves through aggressive export promotion policies to stabilize its currency, the Yuan.
5. The "16 Measures" included 1) controlling money supply, 2) prohibiting the raising of capital illegally, 3) actively leveraging interest rates, 4) prohibiting "chaotic" fundraising, 5) controlling lending, 6) paying back depositors, 7) strengthening financial reforms, 8) reforming investment and financing structures, 9) addressing national debt issues, 10) refining the management of issuing and trading shares, 11) restructuring the foreign exchange market, 12) strengthening control over the real estate market, 13) tightening tax loopholes, 14) stopping construction projects, 15) using price controls, 16) controlling purchasing power. These represented an unabashed merger of planning and market tools.

6. The effect of the 16 Measures was that by 1995, inflation dropped to 15 percent. A year later, it dropped again to 6.1 percent while growth was successfully maintained at 9.7 percent. In 1997 inflation dropped to 0.8 percent, while growth stayed at 8.8 percent. By 1998, at an international press conference held in Beijing's Great Hall of the People, Premier Zhu Rongji assured that growth was maintained at 8 percent, and inflation contained below 3 percent. This is how the 8 percent growth rate for China became mantra.
7. By 1998, Zhu borrowed from Sweden's debt-to-equity model and America's resolution trust system, combining the two. The result was China's "asset management companies," which were established under each insolvent bank. Sweden was able to simply sell off its companies that had bad debt because the scale was relatively small, and Swedish management quite sophisticated, so it was just a question of refinancing. In contrast, in America the federal government just wrote off the debts, which at that time it could afford to do. Zhu faced a different set of practical problems. In 1998, China lacked the financial resources to clear these debts, and enterprises suffered from management incompetence. Zhu cleverly shifted debt from one entity to another, selling it to Western investment bankers who repackaged the mess, listing it on capital markets.

4 THE TAO OF SHANGRI-LA: *Learning Social Enterprise from Nomads and Monks*

1. Few realize the extent to which ethnic groups from south, central, and north Asia influenced the evolution of what we deem today as Chinese culture. Often these influences came from far-off lands, attesting to the aesthetic tastes of these peoples who ruled China at different times and dynastic cycles. Most of the traditional foods considered "old Beijing cuisine" are either Manchurian or Mongolian, and most bread, noodle, and snack foods are actually Muslim. The city of Beijing was based on a North African medina designed by an Arab architect who was hired by Kublai Khan, Most remaining traditional architecture of the capital is drawn from Mongol or Manchurian styles. Many Buddhist sites were built by Nepalese architects, brought to Beijing during Mongol and Manchu dynasties.
2. Another twist of irony: in late spring 2000, after the North Atlantic Treaty Organization rocketed the Chinese embassy in Yugoslavia, Chinese students participated in government-organized protests. They first lined up at Starbucks, buying iced latte, before heading over to the nearby US Embassy, which they slammed to smithereens, throwing bricks that broke all the windows.

5 THE POSITIVE ENERGY BANK: *Quantum Economics Taught by Lamas and Bodhisattvas*

1. Rinpoche is an honorific used in Tibetan Buddhism. It literally means "precious one," and is used to address or describe Tibetan lamas and other high-ranking or respected teachers.

2. There are a series of concentric circumambulation (*Kora*) routes in Lhasa. They start inside the Jokhang Monastery itself. Two routes are important and followed the most: Barkor, which is the street encircling the Jokhang Monastery, forming the central pilgrims market of old Lhasa; Lingkor is the route for circumambulating the entire historic city, including the Potala Palace. Lhasa literally means "holy place."
3. James Hilton's 1920s classic *Lost Horizon* introduces the Himalayan paradise "Shangri-la." He literally misspelled Shambhala, which is described in Buddhist texts as a "pure land," but which can be understood more broadly as a state of mind bearing a positive outlook that has a transformational effect on others and events. Shambhala teachings influenced many German philosophers and scientists from Friedrich Nietzsche, Sigmund Freud, and Carl Jung. Karl Marx's explanation of a perfect communal world reflects passages directly drawn from the Shambhala Sutra. Albert Einstein's theory of relativity is essentially a Western simplification of the Kalachakara teachings, which are core to the Shambhala ideal.
4. Kali can be described as the Indian goddess of destruction. According to Buddhist astrological predictions, the Kali Yulga, or "Age of Destruction," occurs 2,500 years after the death of the Sakyamuni Buddha. So we are currently in the Age of Kali.
5. A Bodhisattva is a fully enlightened being that chooses not to enter nirvana, but instead returns to help those suffering on earth.
6. The author first introduced the concept of "compassionate capital" in *Manager Magazine*, the business publication of Malaysia's *Edge Magazine*. It presented "compassionate capital" in a cover story interview with the author entitled "The New Face of Capitalism" during his 2009 Southeast Asian speaking tour

6 CREATING SHAMBHALA: Building a Social Enterprise on Top of the World

1. In addition to Jokhang Monastery, there are countless small monasteries and temples tucked away in alleyways devoted to different deities and sects of Tibetan Buddhism. In fact, the whole ancient city is devoted to and built around worship. In Tibetan, *Lha-sa* means "Holy Place." Consequently the Buddhists speak of the "Holy City of Lhasa." The sprawling Chinese quarter sharpens into focus the cultural distinction and continued standoff between both peoples.
2. The first old Tibetan building we acquired had a colorful history. Gathered piecemeal, from older people in the neighborhood who remembered bits and pieces, we came to understand that it was connected with an oracle shrine from the seventh century. The courtyard next to us had a guarded well that historically provided the water for drinking and blessings used by Johkang Monastery. During the time of the Thirteenth Dalai Lama (1876–1933), our building was a home of his agricultural minister, who later turned it into the first secular Tibetan school. When civil war erupted across China, the home was given to the Thirteenth Dalai Lama's general, who died fighting. It was then taken over by the general's son, a notorious

poet, songwriter, and womanizer, who grabbed it from his mother. The Thirteenth Dalai Lama, being compassionate, ordered the home returned to the general's widow.

3. *Empower the Monks as Medics:* Tibetan medicine traditionally came from the monasteries, but became institutionalized in hospitals after the Chinese administered Tibet. We put it back into the monasteries. In rural villages, people do not have access to medical care. They often do not trust doctors, but they do trust monks. When a relative is sick, people will ask the monks to perform medicine Buddha prayers. That is important, as in Western medicine we all too often ignore the power of psychology and holistic care. But it is also important to have medicine and basic medical treatment available. We established four clinics and one mobile clinic (consisting of Jeeps outfitted as ambulances) either located in monasteries or run by monks. By 2012, the Chinese authorities (having observed our approach) adopted policies to establish clinics in monasteries across the Tibetan plateau. It was one case of transformation by example

4. *Let the People See:* In summer 2007, the chairman of the board of SEVA came to visit. SEVA is a nonprofit organization based in Berkeley, California, that specializes in treating blindness (mostly cataract) in underdeveloped countries. But their Tibet operation was at the bottom of the financing chain. He asked me to partner with them and try to raise funds. We committed to 100 eye operations. Using our courtyard restaurant in Beijing as a fundraising vehicle, we raised enough for over 300 operations the first year and over 400 the second. Following the 2008 financial crisis and instability on the Tibetan plateau, SEVA prepared to cut all funding and close its Tibet operation. We arranged financing for another two years of operations with support from New Zealand, insuring 1,000 operations each year. People in the Pacific Islands similarly suffer from ultraviolet rays. For New Zealand, fighting unnecessary blindness is a national priority.

5. *Give the Children a Chance:* With support of donors in Hong Kong and Singapore, the first Montessori school was established in a village about one hour outside Lhasa. Pembala oversaw the construction and administration. I designed the adventure playground and brought the teachers to Beijing for Montessori training. We raised books for the library and teaching materials. Today, 150 children receive free education and lunch in the school. During the opening ceremony, the village head thanked me, noting that each year their village lost so many children to trucks passing on the road, because the children had no place to go.

7 THE DISEMPOWERMENT FACTOR: *Stop Terrorism at Its Root*

1. Despite the heady vitriol, all this revolutionary red flag-waving actually worked against the Nepalese Maoist popularity on the international scene. The George W. Bush administration labeled them "terrorists" for being so red. On the downside, it prevented American diplomats from directly contacting the Maoist leadership. If they had, there probably would have

been a lot of room for dialogue, if not cooperation. The lack of diplomatic contact only distorted Washington's reading of political turbulence in Nepal. But Bush had his own distorted view of the world, and in the end it cost America trillions of dollars and a major loss of global influence.

8 THE HIMALAYAN CONSENSUS: Happiness, Micro-finance, and Community Development

1. 1987 Financial Times article by John Elliott cited in www.sunday-guardian.com/artbeat/the-royal-pleasure-index.
2. Remarks at the University of Kansas, March 18, 1968, Kennedy.Library@nara.gov.
3. While it was Bhutan's fourth king who coined the idea of GNH, it was Bhutan's first democratically elected prime minister who took GNH global. The fourth king had taken the very bold step of establishing a constitutional monarchy and introducing direct elections. He was influenced by both his Indian and British education and the Maoist revolt in neighboring Nepal that overthrew the monarchy there. When I first met Thinley he had been serving as prime minister by royal appointment, but was not yet the elected prime minister. Open elections for parliament took place in 2008, and Thinley was reinstated as prime minister through democratic election. He set about globalizing GNH and even bringing the concept before the United Nations.
4. The word *grameen* means "village" in the Bengali language.
5. Cover story of *The Economist*, March 16, 2013.

9 THE AFRICAN CONSENSUS: Community Empowerment to Prevent Violence

1. This is the same university where US Secretary of State Hilary Clinton would give a speech in 2012 criticizing China for exploiting Africa. The talk went down badly, mainly because Cheik Anta Diop is a very progressive university and a hotbed of anticolonial/imperialist sentiment but also because Senegal has no resources to be extrapolated (their largest export is peanuts), while China provides a lot to Senegal in terms of infrastructure investment, largely because of the political influence of this particular country. It begs the question why Clinton delivered a speech like this. Either she was badly briefed, or the people briefing her were out of touch with the country.
2. The African Union (AU) can be described as a regional United Nations for the continent of Africa, located in Addis Ababa, Ethiopia. The African Commission on Human and People's Rights is an organization under the AU that is located in Banjul, Gambia. Each year it holds an NGO forum, effectively a congress of NGOs from across the continent to provide feedback on human rights practices and call for action through resolutions and declarations that form an effective body of common law used by the AU to enforce human rights in member states.
3. The nature conservancies operate on the basis of three principles: 1) promote a broad vision of environmental sustainability through education of

the conservancy's own staff, guests, and local communities; 2) ensure that ecotourism remains the chosen alternative to mining, agriculture, farming, or hydro schemes; 3) create a profitable ethical and responsible business that others will want to imitate.

4. The effect of the African Consensus Declaration was to push the idea of the African Consensus. Between October 20 and 25, 2011, the Africa Regional Preparatory Conference for the United Nations Conference on Sustainable Development (Rio+20) met in Addis Ababa, Ethiopia, and prepared "The African Consensus Statement to Rio+20," which emphasized "The green economy in the context of sustainable development and poverty eradication" as a core principle. The statement was submitted by the Economic Commission on Africa jointly with the African Union, the African Development Bank, the United Nations Economic and Social Council (UN ECOSOC), the United Nations Development Programme (UNDP), and the United Nations Environment Programme (UNEP) to the Rio+20 conference. Building upon the principles in these documents, an African Consensus Forum has been established in 2014 to convene as an annual event in Dar es Salaam, Tanzania. Initiated by Tanzania's president, Jakaya Kikwete, as an extension of the Helsinki Process, the core principle of the African Consensus Forum is to convene multistakeholders (civil society, business, and government) in addressing global problems. The African Consensus Forum is now spearheaded by the Uongozi Institute (an outcome of the Helsinki Process dedicated to training future leaders from Africa's youth) and the University of Dar es Salaam. Joined by other stakeholders, including Kofi Annan's African Progress Panel, and the World Wildlife Fund Africa, the African Consensus Forum seeks to highlight initiatives of small and community-based groups that are pioneering pragmatic solutions to challenges of agriculture, water security, community finance, renewable energy, and prevention of conflict as pathways to a holistic and organic development approach for Africa.

11 "RE-PIONEERING" AMERICA: *Revitalizing Communities and Environmental Economics*

1. The UNFCCC or FCCC) is an international treaty setting mandatory emission limits to stabilize greenhouse gas concentrations in the atmosphere. The parties to the convention have met annually from 1995 in Conferences of the Parties (COP) to assess progress in dealing with climate change. In 1997, the Kyoto Protocol was concluded, and it established legally binding obligations for developed countries to reduce their greenhouse gas emissions. COP 17 was held in Durban, South Africa, in late 2011.
2. The state (or kingdom depending on who you are talking to) of Hawaii consists of several islands: O'hau, Kauai, Maui, Molokai, Lanai, Ni'ihau, and Hawaii Island, which is the biggest of all the islands. All locals just call Hawaii Island "The Big Island."
3. The Baltimore Green Currency Association (www.baltimoregreencurrency.org) defines "local currency" (also called complementary currency)

as "money that is designed to be used within a community, town, or city." They differentiate "national currencies, like the US Dollar, [which] are now loaned into existence, necessitating their repayment with interest to a bank or financial institution," whereas "local currencies exist solely to facilitate commerce within a community and to preserve and restore the social nature of trade and business. Dollars are universal, but they don't have the same power that local currencies have, to promote and grow a local economy, in ways that benefit the people and not banks."

12 THE WORLD IS NOT FLAT: *Back to Basics, Local Diversity, and Community Capital Regeneration*

1. Global Systemically Important Financial Institutions (GSIFIs) is a study comparing key financial information concerning the world's biggest banks and a group of sustainable banks undertaken over the decade 2002–2011. It reveals some surprising data: Dominant banks lend less, attract fewer deposits, and have a weaker capital base than sustainable banks, which are, in contrast, investing more in a greener, fairer society and performing in a more resilient and robust manner. The Global Alliance of Banking on Values (GABV), an independent network of 20 of the world's leading sustainable banks, believes that the results of the study demonstrate the strength of values-based banks by comparison. The study has been used to call upon politicians and regulators to recognize the sustainable banking model as a means to strengthen banking systems in order to ensure they serve the real economy.
2. Michael Shuman, *Local Dollars, Local Sense.* pp. 45–46. Chelsea Green Publishing, 2012.
3. Stéphane Hessel, *Time for Outrage: Indignez-vous!*, Twelve, 2011.

13 FROM RUSSIA WITH FUSION ECONOMICS: *The National Response, The Brics, and the Changing World Order*

1. The origin of a BRICS development bank and bailout fund can be traced to the Chiang Mai Initiative, which is a multilateral currency swap arrangement among certain Asian nations in response to the 2008 global financial crisis. Drawing on experiences from the earlier 1997 Asian financial crisis, China, (including Hong Kong), together with member nations of ASEAN (the Association of Southeast Asian Nations), joined by Japan and South Korea, responded to the 2008 crisis by pooling an initial $120 billion and launching a jointly managed stabilization fund on March 21, 2010. The fund has since increased to $240 billion, and is seen as an independent regional response without IMF involvement.
2. Reported in the Chinese financial journal *Caijing*: http://english.caijing.com.cn/2012-03-30/111786047.html.

14 WE WANT A FUTURE: *To Save Our Planet, We Need New Leaders*

1. Officially known as the UN Conference on Sustainable Development. It was held in Rio on June 20–22, 2012

2. Brazil built its biofuels policy to reduce carbon footprint, while actually stimulating the already established sugarcane-ethanol industry and emerging biodiesel sector through a fusion economics basket of regulatory incentives such as tax breaks, bank credit, and mandatory blending (an obligatory mixing of biofuels in liquid fossil fuels).
3. UNDP's first Human Development Report was produced in 1990. It recognized the limitations of existing development metrics and introduced the Human Development Index as an alternative to GDP and related income-based barometers of national progress; it captures the key elements of human development, notably education, longevity, and a decent standard of living. While income is a crucial contributor to well-being, it is far from being everything. Human Development Report (HDR), launched by UNDP in 1990, defined human development as a process of enlarging people's freedoms, choices, and capabilities to lead lives they value. UNDP has long since argued accordingly that a measure of progress broader than GDP is needed.
4. The Kingdom of Bhutan and the UNDP are not alone in seeking alternative measures. In recent years, Canada has launched its *Index of Well-Being*; the United Kingdom has been developing a *Happiness index* to measure National Well-Being; France has established the Sen-Stiglitz-Fitoussi Commission to look at "measuring economic performance and social progress" to identify the limits of GDP and consider what additional information and tools could be added to create a more holistic picture.
5. The focus at Rio+20 was on sustainable development. GDP was first challenged as a matrix during the Earth Summit, 20 years ago (*Agenda 21, Information for Decision-making* Article 40.4): "Commonly used indicators such as the gross national product (GNP) and measurements of individual resource or pollution flows do not provide adequate indications of sustainability." Since then, various alternatives to GDP have evolved: *Green national accounting* adjusts GDP to take into account the environmental costs of economic activity. GDP is based on the market value of goods and services, and so takes no account of things that are clearly valuable—like unpolluted air—but that are not bought and sold.

The *Ecological Footprint*, of the Global Footprint Network looks at the natural resources required to maintain current consumption patterns, which are considered unsustainable at the global level and imbalanced regionally.

The *Environmental Performance Index* (EPI), developed by the Yale Center for Environmental Law and Policy (YCELP) and the Center for Earth Information Science Information Network (CIESIN) at Columbia University, ranks countries on 22 performance indicators spanning ten categories, including agriculture, climate change, and energy. It tracks performance and progress on environmental health and ecosystem vitality.

The *Happy Planet Index (HPI)*, developed by the New Economics Foundation, captures the degree to which people are able to live long and happy lives, per unit of environmental impact. It uses life expectancy data from UNDP's Human Development Reports, well-being data from the

Gallup World Poll, and the *ecological footprint* data described above to rank countries according to their ability to promote human well-being, while ensuring that their environmental impact is minimized.

6. The Commission on Sustainable Development was set up to follow through on Rio '92. But it had a design flaw—it meets only two to three weeks in a year, and has too small a Secretariat, making it far too weak institutionally within the UN system to address sustainable development core issues.
7. The United States rejected targeting any single Rio principle. Its position was seconded by Canada, the European Union, Japan, Republic of Korea, and Switzerland.
8. Section II B, paragraph 19 recognized "uneven progress" since 1992, emphasizing "the need to make progress in implementing previous commitments" and "the need to accelerate progress in closing development gaps between developed and developing countries."

15 ENVIRONMENTAL ECONOMICS: *Cutting Semantics, Creating Genuine Green Growth for Survival*

1. Construction of the Great Wall initially started with China's first emperor, Qin Shihuangdi (228 BC), and was rebuilt and reconstructed over other dynasties spanning 2,000 years, with the most recent massive construction carried out during the Ming (1368–1466). The Ming collapsed when a general was bribed to open the gate for invaders.
2. China can undertake with confidence new green bond issues to support the grid conversion that is proposed, since most of its debt is internal, as is the case in Japan. Zhu's infrastructure stimulus during the 1990s was similarly supported through bond issues, most of which were purchased by domestic banks.
3. China's Banking Regulatory Commission first began exploring the concept of green credit in 2007, when the first policy document was issued calling for "energy efficiency measures," encouraged by banking policy. In 2012, a second policy document established "green credit support" for three areas: 1) a green economy, 2) a renewable economy, 3) a low-carbon economy. While these concepts of green credit remain vague, a direction has been set.
4. In the 1990s, premier Zhu Rongji had two key organizations to lead the fusion economic experiment. One was the State Council Office of Reform of Economic Systems (SCRES) that served as a think tank to strategize reforms and coordinate policy. The second was the State Economy and Trade Commission, a superministry that was responsible for dismantling the state-owned enterprise system and the industrial line ministries left over from Soviet-planning times. It had to coordinate all of the industrial and trade policy issues to prevent ministerial turf wars that could stagnate a system (this happens in other countries too). When he became premier in 2003, he cancelled both ministries and merged their powers merged into the State Planning Commission, which was then renamed the National Development Reform Commission.

5. The Kodak case is very telling. In the 1990s, Kodak failed to anticipate changes in technology. It invested heavily, taking over China's film processing chemical industry. Those investments essentially broke the film giant. If it had invested in new digital technology instead of China's debt-ridden chemical industry, then Kodak would not be bankrupt today. Dubai is an example of adaptation. A quiet desert sheikdom discovered oil and became rich, but is now investing aggressively in building itself into a regional financial center and air transport hub. It is investing in a future for Dubai after oil runs out, or is replaced with solar energy.

CONCLUSION   THE POST OCCUPY WORLD:
Imagine an Economy Without Greed

1. Brainy Quotes BookRags Media Network, www.brainyquote.com and Institute of Intercultural Studies cited on www.about.com—women's history.

INDEX

Abercrombie and Fitch, 6
academic shamanism, 4–8
Afghanistan, 8, 90, 95–7, 152
African Commission for Human
    and Peoples Rights, 127, 133–4,
    241n2
African Consensus
    African Consensus Declaration,
        127, 134, 242n4
    craftsmanship and, 130–1
    education and healthcare and, 128–30
    evolution of, 14, 116
    as framework for nonviolence, 133–4
    overview, 119–20
    pragmatic disobedience and, 120–3
    public support for, 123–5
    rap music and, 123–4
    sustainability and, 125–6
    tradition and, 131–3
    water resources and, 126–7, 130–1
African Union, 127, 241n2, 242n4
Aga, Momin, 93–4
agriculture
    Africa and, 132, 155, 242n4
    Barcelona Consensus and, 172
    China and, 195
    community and, 21, 24, 32, 157, 172
    credit and, 40, 111, 174
    economy and, 4, 65, 104, 159
    education and, 126
    environment and, 169, 227, 244n5
    nature conservancies and, 242n3
    Nepal and, 100
    Occupy movement and, 143, 157
    Russia and, 189–90, 192–6
    Venezuela and, 186
    WTO and, 189
AIDS/HIV, 122, 132
anarchy, 135, 140, 143
anger, 94, 122, 131, 143, 147, 212, 215
Anhui Province (China), 22–3, 53
antiglobalization movement, 7, 146, 190
    see also globalization
AOL, 161
Applied Solar, 214
Arab Spring, 133, 171
architecture, 46–8, 80–2, 89–90,
    238n1
art, politics and, 177–9
Aschwanden, Rahel, 173
Ashin, Vaniak, 201
Asia Pulp and Paper, 154
Asian Development Bank (ADB), 27,
    29–30
Asian Financial Crisis, 5, 38
Aslan, Reza, 98–9
Athuraliya Rathana, 114–17
austerity, 10, 136, 173, 176, 183–4,
    226–7
Australia, 149
Avalokitshavra, 75, 94
Awadi, Didier, 123–6, 133–4, 153

Badral, Surin, 34–6
Baker, Ian, 91, 101–2
Ban Ki-moon, 210
Bangladesh, 9, 92, 110, 113, 116, 230
Barcelona Consensus, 171–5, 192
Barshefsky, Charlene, 7
Bayer, 51

begging, 77–9, 113, 181
Beijing Consensus, 103
Benckiser Group, 52
Bergqvist, Robert, 176
Berkshire Bucks, 165–6
Bernanke, Ben, 145
Bhandari, Sanjay, 52
Bhattarai, Bauburam, 102
Bhutan, 91, 104–9, 116, 161–2, 204–5, 215
 see also gross national happiness
biodiversity, 63, 66, 145, 157, 161
"bird-cage theory," 25
Bitcoin, 166
Bloomberg, Michael, 142
Blue Planet Foundation, 160–1
Bodhisattvas, 73–5, 88, 94, 239n5
bottom-up economics, 9, 12–14, 111, 166, 204
Brazil, 10–11, 18, 121, 153, 174, 196–7, 200, 203, 244n2
Bretton-Woods, 1, 7, 13, 106, 199–200, 210, 232
BRICS nations, 11–12, 14, 18, 194, 196, 198–201, 231–2
Brooks Brothers, 6
Brown Brothers and Harriman, 142, 145
Buddha, 44, 57, 72, 91, 107, 239n4, 240n3
Buddhism, 32, 36, 60, 69–70, 73, 82, 86, 92, 98, 106, 114, 240–1
Bush, George W., 197, 240n1

Cambodia, 30, 152
Cameron, David, 207
carbon dioxide (CO_2) emissions, 153, 157, 162
carbon trading, 212, 219
Case, Steve, 161
Catalonia Square, 171–3, 177, 179, 186
Center Bopp community center, 123, 138
Chakpori Medicine Hill, 70
Chavez, Hugo, 186
Chile, 10, 54
China
 Africa and, 119–20, 130
 agriculture, 192
 architecture, 46–9

"bird-cage theory" of economics, 25–7
 Bitcoin and, 166
 BRICS and, 196–200
 Buddhism and, 73
 credit and, 50, 97, 139, 165
 crisis management, 49–51
 direct investment, 55–6
 economy, 10, 17–18
 fusion economics and, 10–14, 43–4, 195
 globalization and, 6, 51–2, 174, 192–3, 232
 green economy and, 168–9, 213–24
 growth, 10, 19–22, 114–15
 Internet and, 8
 Keynesian economics and, 216–17
 Laos and, 30, 37
 Nepal and, 101–3
 nomads and, 65–6
 North Korea and, 152
 Occupy movement and, 139–41
 Pakistan and, 97
 pollution and, 212–13
 poverty and, 18, 101
 pragmatic economics, 45–6
 reforms, 29–30, 52–5, 59–62, 170
 self-responsibility system, 22–5
 shock therapy and, 38–42
 Tibet and, 62, 65–7, 73, 77–80, 82–5, 87, 89–90
 UNFCCC and, 153
 Vietnam and, 38
 water and, 228
 WWF and, 212
Chinese Communist Party (CCP), 25, 27, 37
Chubb, 51
Churchill, Winston, 1
civil disobedience, 102, 122, 148, 172, 178
Clark, Helen, 204
climate change, 9, 15, 84, 92, 127, 136, 147, 153–7, 162, 167–9, 205, 209, 213, 216, 227–9, 232
Clinton, Bill, 164, 197
Clinton, Hillary, 241n1
coal, 43, 153, 156, 162, 213–14, 217–19
Common Welfare Matrix, 174

communalism, 22, 151, 195
community capital regeneration, 172–5
compassionate capital, 13–14, 57, 73–5, 227–8
Confucianism, 44, 47, 60, 92, 217
Congo, 129
conscientious consumption, 13, 57, 227–8
conservancies, 132–3, 185, 231, 241n3
Cooper, Joshua, 167, 222
cooperatives, 86, 174–5, 178
Cote d'Ivoire (Ivory Coast), 127, 134
craftsmanship, 81
credit
  agriculture and, 195
  Asian financial crisis and, 6
  China and, 50, 97, 139, 165, 167
  credit cooperative legislation, 32
  globalization and, 6
  green economy and, 212, 218, 220, 231
  micro-credit, 110–13
  Russia and, 195
  Spain and, 181–2
  U.S. and, 97, 165
Credit Lyonnais, 40–1
Crees, Uttara, 63
Cultural Revolution, 19, 47, 49, 60, 236n2

Dahal, Pushpa Kamal, 100
Dalai Lama, 80, 239n2
Daño, Neth, 209
Darfur, 127, 155
Darwinism, 214, 223
Dawn (NGO), 207
Delhi Declaration, 199
democratization of global finance, 199, 232
Deng Xiaoping, 23, 25–6, 37, 44, 46, 49, 100, 170, 221, 238–9
deregulation, 4–6, 11, 50, 183, 197
Dhondup Lhamo, 87
Doi Moi policy, 30
Donglin Li, 99
dot-com boom, 8, 185
Dou Yan, 62–3, 69
drones, 95–7, 226

E. F. Schumacher Society, 166
Earth Institute, 129
Earth Summit, 205, 209, 244n5
East-West Center, 21–2, 158, 160–1, 167, 169–70
eBay, 161
economic disempowerment, 103
Egypt, 113, 133, 137, 145, 159
energy efficiency, 123, 136, 157, 168, 218, 245n3
Enkhsaikhan, Mendsaikhany, 34
environmental economics
  geothermal energy and, 163–7
  globalization and, 169–70
  neighborhood renewal and, 158–60
  Occupy Green and, 167–9
  One Million Climate Jobs Campaign, 156–7
  Rogers, Henk B. and, 160–3
  solar energy and, 151–3
  UNFCCC and, 153–8
  see also green economy
environmental protection, 13, 107, 116, 220
Ericsson, 51, 176
ETC Group, 209
European Central Bank, 179
European Union (EU), 175–7, 180, 208, 220
exchange rates, 1, 235n4
Exxon-Mobil, 4, 51

Facebook, 13, 112, 120, 124, 146, 161, 165, 185, 226
Felbur, Christian, 174
financial architecture, 6, 14, 98, 112, 135–6, 147, 190, 199, 204, 209, 229
Five Pillars of Islam, 98
Fox, Carol, 160
free trade, 4, 124, 195, 200
  see also globalization
Friedman, Milton, 3
Friedman, Thomas, 182
fusion economics
  beginnings of, 10–11, 21, 27, 41–2, 213, 216
  China and, 10–11, 13, 45–6, 50, 216
  community, 230–1
  explained, 11–12, 17–18

fusion economics—*Continued*
  green economics and, 213–20
  nation, 231
  planet, 231–2
  pragmatism and, 231, 233
  principles, 230–3
  Russia and, 194–6
"Future We Don't Want" petition, 206
"Future We Want," 205–6, 209

Gaddafi, Muammar, 194
Gambia, 127, 133–4, 241n2
Gandhi, Mahatma, 224
Gay, Charles, 214
geothermal energy, 163–7
Germany, 176–7, 180, 207
Ghana, 124
Ghenghis Khan, 35
Gills, Barri, 196
glaciers, 63, 69, 162, 205, 217, 228–30
Glass-Steagall Act (1933), 6
global economic order
  Barcelona Consensus and, 172
  BRICS and, 196, 201
  community, 230–1
  nation, 231
  planet, 231–3
globalization
  Bhutan and, 107
  brands and, 60, 158
  China and, 39, 48, 60, 99, 198
  Clinton, Bill and, 197
  European Union and, 176–7
  Friedman, Thomas and, 182
  G7 and, 226, 230
  GNH and, 107, 109, 204
  Himalayan Consensus and, 112
  localization and, 9, 136, 147, 160, 165
  neoliberalism and, 176, 182
  Nepal and, 104
  Occupy movements and, 7, 146–7
  poverty and, 99, 114
  Smith, Adam and, 4, 6
  Spain and, 187
  U.S. and, 197–8
  WSF and, 121
  see also antiglobalization movement
God of Small Things, The (Roy), 103
Goethe, Johann Wolfgang von, 81

Goldman Sachs, 4, 191, 200
Gong (Chinese ambassador), 119–20
Grameen Bank, 110–11, 113
Great Depression, 2, 6, 140, 156, 193
Great Green Grid, 217–20
Great Leap Forward, 60
Great Wall of China, 216, 218, 245n1
Greece, 11, 176–7, 180, 193
Green America Exchange, 166
green economy
  China and, 216–24
  difficulty in defining, 211–13
  "ecological civilization," 219–21
  fusion economics and, 213–16
  globalization and, 221–3
  Great Green Grid and, 217–20
  tiger rugs and, 223–4
  see also environmental economics
green energy, 219, 222
Green New Deal, 222
green washing, 136, 209, 212
Greenpeace, 154–5
Greenspan, Alan, 2
gross domestic product (GDP), 99, 104, 106, 169, 183, 198, 205, 210, 212, 214–15, 220, 246
gross national happiness (GNH), 105–9, 116, 204, 227, 241n3
  see also Bhutan
gross national product (GNP), 105, 244n5
Group of 7 (G7), 7, 12, 168, 201, 207, 226, 230
Group of 8 (G8), 7
Group of 77 (G77), 12, 18, 154, 168, 208, 231
Guantanamo Bay, 154
Guevara, Che, 126, 191
Gurung, Dasho Meghraj, 106–7
Gyatso, Luntaen, 107

Han society, 60, 65
Hawaii, 11, 21, 151–3, 156, 158–67
heritage hotels, 88, 90
Hessel, Stéphane, 180–2
hidden unemployment, 8
Hilton, James, 61, 71, 161, 239n3
Himalayan Consensus
  African Consensus and, 126, 170

beginnings of, 74, 98, 116–17
China and, 215, 221
development and, 114–15
GNH and, 108–9
holistic economics, 106–7
influence of, 126, 152, 170
measures of success, 105–6
micro-credit and, 110–13
overview, 92–3
poverty and, 110–14
Shangri-la and, 162
Hinduism, 92, 98, 101–2, 159
Hirai, Jim, 152
Ho Chi Minh, 37, 39
Homeland Security, 149
Hong Kong, 23, 25–6, 43, 45, 101, 237n1, 240n5, 243n1
House of Shambhala, 82, 86, 88
Hu Jintao, 214–15, 220–1, 236n2
Hugo, Victor, 110
Hung, Ngyuen Doanh, 38–9
Hussein, Saddam, 194
hydropower, 103, 213
hypergrowth, 10, 44, 48, 215, 217

I Ching, 17
identity, 13–14, 18, 48, 58, 80, 86, 91, 96–8, 101, 103, 116, 124, 126, 134, 136, 141, 147, 159, 164, 187
India, 8, 10–11, 18, 69, 86, 100, 103–4, 153, 196–7, 199–200, 208, 222
Indignants, 171, 179–86
infrastructure, 49, 61, 90, 100, 102–3, 111, 113, 115, 135–6, 138, 141, 145, 148, 153, 156–7, 168–9, 195, 212, 214, 216, 220, 224, 226, 231–2
International Financial Corporation (IFC), 40
International Monetary Fund (IMF), 1, 5–7, 10, 30, 38, 40, 55–6, 101–2, 111–12, 115, 172, 177, 179, 183, 191, 193, 198–200, 236n6, 243n1
Iran, 226
Iraq, 8, 90, 97
irrational consumption, 139
Islam, 92, 95–6, 98–9, 110
Ivy League schools, 5

Jaikahelo Urumiya, 114
Jainism, 92
Jambala, 72–3
Jensen, Jigme, 63–4
Jokhang Monastery, 71–4, 78, 241

Kagarlitsky, Boris, 191–3, 196, 201
kahunas, 164
Kali Yulga (Age of Destruction), 71, 239n4
karma, 18, 72, 108
Kathmandu, 100, 102–3
Kennedy, Robert, 106
Keynes, John Maynard, 1, 216–17
Kilauea volcano, 163–4
Kim, Spencer, 160
King, Jigme Singye Wangchuck, 105, 109
King, Larry, 233
Kodak, 51, 73, 246n5
Kolganov, Andrey, 197
Kolomejsev, Nikolaj, 194
Koltashov, Vasiliy, 193
Korea, 53, 152, 160

Laos, 18, 27, 29–34, 36–8, 41–3
Lashari, Kamrin, 97
Law without Lawyers (Li), 21, 32, 170
Leaf, Dan, 152
Legamex, 41
Levskiy, Vasi, 193
Li, Victor, 21–2, 170
Li Jiang, 54, 161
Li Keqiang, 214, 220
Li Wei, 220
Libya, 133–4
localization
  agriculture and, 192
  diversifying, 91–2, 136, 160, 165, 175, 195, 210
  financing and, 112
  fusion economics and, 14
  globalization and, 9, 147
  Himalayan Consensus and, 98
  Occupy movement and, 147
  overview, 91–2
  Smith, Adam and, 4
  sustainability and, 4
Lost Horizons (Hilton), 61, 71, 161, 239n3

Louis Vuitton, 25
Lutsyuk, Cyril, 193

M-15 movement, 171, 181
Ma Hong, 26–7
madrassas, 95–7
Mamadouba, 121, 128, 130–1
Manjushuri, 75
Mao Zedong, 20, 22, 33, 44, 48, 51–3, 60, 100–3, 122, 141, 221
Maria Helena Foundation, 96
market fundamentalism, 5, 7, 10, 17, 31, 54–5, 135, 230
Marx, Karl, 3, 193, 196, 239n3
materialism, 61, 71, 74, 90, 108, 114, 139, 204
Mattel, 154–5
Mauritania, 128
media, 6–7, 11, 55, 59, 61–2, 95–6, 121–2, 124, 135, 140, 142–3, 146, 148–50, 159, 166, 173–4, 181–2, 186, 189–90, 193, 204, 207, 225–6, 2323
meditation, 32, 67, 71, 73, 78, 85, 97, 114, 117, 141
Merkel, Angela, 176, 207
Meynen, Nick, 206
micro-financing, 110–14
military spending/expansion, 8, 97, 148, 165, 197, 217
Millennium Village, 129
Miró, Juan, 177–8
moai, 169
Mongolia, 34–5, 60, 62, 133, 152, 216, 218, 237n3, 238n1
Morales, Evo, 186
Morgan Stanley, 2, 4
Mother Jones, 4
Mubarak, Hosni, 119–20, 145

Naidoo, Kumi, 154
Namibia, 131–3
Nayan, Anita, 207
neoliberalism, 5, 7, 10, 18, 26, 30–1, 39, 50, 107, 135, 173, 176, 182, 194, 201, 204, 230
Nepal, 85, 100–4, 106, 116, 122, 133, 152, 161, 189, 238n1, 240n1, 241n3

Netherlands, 160, 174, 213
New Earth Consensus, 14–15, 135–6, 170
Nicklaus, Jack, 217
Nietzsche, Friedrich, 239n3
Nixon, Richard, 52, 197
Nkrumah, Kwame, 124
No God But One God (Aslan), 98
Nobel Peace Prize, 110–11
nongovernmental organizations (NGOs), 116, 121–3, 125–7, 129, 132–4, 153, 195, 204, 206–7, 209–11, 227
North American Free Trade Agreement (NAFTA), 124
North Korea, 152
Northern Alliance for Sustainability, 206
nuclear power, 156, 200, 213
Nyima Tsering, 73–5, 81, 88, 90, 94, 108

Obama, Barack, 140, 149, 154, 184, 197–8, 207
Occupy movement
  civil disobedience and, 148
  climate change and, 147–8
  failures of, 141, 144–50
  financial architecture and, 147
  globalization and, 147
  Homeland Security and, 149
  Indignants and, 180–1, 184
  influences on, 7, 171, 180–1
  M-15 movement and, 171
  media and, 148–9, 207
  military expansion and, 148
  Occupy Green, 167–9
  overview, 137–8, 141–4
  People's Microphone, 142
  political systems and, 148
  protests, 139–41
  U.S. and, 137–41
  Zuccotti Park and, 139–44, 224
Olivella, Martí, 171–3, 175, 177–8, 181
Oliveres, Arcadia, 179–86
Olympic Games, 89
Omidyar, Pierre, 161
"One Million Climate Jobs Campaign," 155–6

"One Million Green Jobs Now," 213
O'Neill, Jim, 200–1

Pakistan, 93, 95–7, 99, 103–4, 116
Pang Jiying, 40
Parenteau, Rob, 222
Pathet Lao, 33, 36–8
Paulson, Hank, 51
PBL Netherlands Environmental
  Assessment Agency, 213
"peaceful revolution"
  see Occupy movement
Pele (goddess), 163–4
Pembala, 70, 80, 82, 85–7, 89, 240n5
Phuntsho, Thsheing, 108
Picasso, Pablo, 177
Podor, 128, 130–1
Portugal, 180, 218
positive energy bank
  Bodhisattvas and, 73–5
  compassionate capitalism, 73–5
  earning interest on what you give,
    71–3
  overview, 69–71
poverty
  Africa and, 121–2, 125, 127, 134,
    156
  China and, 10, 13, 18, 27, 42, 48
  cyclical nature of, 116
  economic empowerment and, 92,
    95, 204
  fusion economics and, 10
  globalization and, 232–3
  green economy and, 211
  IMF and, 232
  Kali Yulga and, 71
  localization and, 92
  micro-credit and, 110, 112–14
  Nepal and, 116
  Occupy movement and, 227
  political movements and, 100–3
  Rio+20 and, 209
  shock therapy and, 5
  UNILO and, 99
  violence and, 127
Power 28, 51–2
Prachanda, 100–1, 103
Prada, 6, 25
pragmatic idealism, 14, 48, 57–8, 227

productivity, 6–8, 12, 44, 79, 99,
  172–4, 183, 186, 212
public transportation, 157
Puck, Wolfgang, 11–12
Puck's Alley, 21, 151, 158–60
Putin, Vladimir, 189, 192, 194, 200

quantum economics
  see positive energy bank

Rahman, Ashfquar, 110
Raj hunters, 85–6, 223
Rajapaksa, Mahinda, 115
recycling, 174
renewable energy, 14, 135–6, 148,
  153, 156–8, 161, 163, 166–8, 174,
  185, 212–14, 217–18, 220, 222,
  227, 231, 242n4
  see also solar energy; wind power
restorations, 80, 87, 89–90, 97, 157, 191
Rijnhout, Leida, 206–7
Rinpoche, Beru Khyentse, 81
Rinpoche, Nanquin, 70–1, 78
Rio+20, 203–11, 223, 242n4, 244n5
Rio Principles, 205
Roach, Stephen, 2
Roche, 51
Rock, Joseph, 61, 161
Rogers, Henk, 160–3, 168
Rokhaya, 120–2, 129–30
Roosevelt, Franklin D., 1
Roy, Arundhati, 103–4, 107
Russia
  Bitcoin and, 166
  BRICS and, 11, 18, 198–201
  globalization and, 189–91
  grassroots movements in, 116
  neoliberalism and, 194–6
  shock therapy and, 32
  Soviet legacy, 32, 196–8
  water security and, 191–3
  WTO and, 189, 193–4

Sachs, Jeffrey, 31, 126, 196
San Bao, 62
Sankara, Thomas, 125
Sayalath, Kham Leuang, 33–4
SEB (Skandinaviska Enskilda
  Banken AB), 176

Senegal, 119–21, 123, 125, 127–8, 130, 138–9, 190, 241n1
Shambhala Serai, 70–1
Shanghai, 20, 40, 45–6, 61, 84, 237n2
Shangri-la, 61–3, 71, 74, 78, 80, 107, 161–2, 239n3
shock therapy, 5, 10–11, 26–7, 30–2, 37–41, 46, 50, 54, 126, 196, 204, 230
Sisane, Sisavath, 37
Sister Teresa, 186–7
"Sixteen Measures for Macro-Economic Control," 50, 219–20
Smith, Adam, 3–6, 31, 175, 235n3, 235n5
Snow, Edgar, 52
social entrepreneurs, 14, 58, 63, 116, 159–61, 163, 222, 227
social media, 148, 172, 179, 185
see also Facebook; Twitter
socialism, 3, 9, 17–18, 22–3, 25, 27, 30, 34, 36–7, 44–6, 50–1, 54, 101, 119, 143, 183, 195–6
solar energy, 90, 151–3, 156, 161–3, 213–14, 217, 219, 221–3, 228, 246n5
Soros, George, 63
Souvannasao, Samane, 36
Spain, 173–5, 178–83, 186–7
Special Drawing Rights (SDR), 198, 200
Sri Lanka, 114–16
stakeholder's value, 227–8
Stalin, Joseph, 191, 196
Starbucks, 6, 11, 62, 238n2
State Commission for Reform Economic Systems (SCRES), 44, 245n4
Stern, Todd, 154
Stiglitz, Joseph, 235n5
Struggling Beggars Members Program, 113
subprime lending crisis, 5, 8, 185
Sun Yiting, 212
sustainability, 4, 10, 12, 14, 59–60, 65, 73, 84, 91–2, 96–8, 107, 109, 113–14, 125–6, 132, 134, 136, 147–8, 159, 162, 166, 174, 203–10, 222, 227–8, 233

Taiwan, 24, 26–7, 101, 138
Tara temple, 69–70, 87
tech stocks, 185
Teng Jixin, 51–2
terrorism, 5, 71, 91–7, 103–4, 116, 134, 148
Thinley, Lyonpo Jigmi Y., 109, 204
ti leaves, 164
Tiananmen Square massacre, 22, 25–6, 42–3, 52, 237n2
Tibet, 60–7, 69–74, 77–90, 131, 145, 223–4
Tibet Children's Initiative, 87
tiger economies, 6
tiger skins, 84–6
Time Dollars, 175
Time for Outrage: Indignez-Vous! (Hessel), 180, 182
Tine, Alioune, 127, 133–4
top-down, 9, 12–14, 102, 111
Trace Foundation, 63
triangle debts, 47, 49–51
Triodos Bank, 174
Trump, Donald, 4, 47, 151
tsong, 105, 108
Tsongsikhang market, 82, 85
Twitter, 13, 112, 120, 154, 185

unemployment, 8, 99, 140, 147, 155–6, 173–4, 178, 186, 193, 226
United Nations Educational, Scientific, and Cultural Organization (UNESCO), 106
United Nations Framework Convention on Climate Change (UNFCCC), 153–5, 157, 167, 212, 242n1
United Nations International Labor Organization (UNILO), 99
United States Agency for International Development (USAID), 102, 129
Universal Declaration of Human Rights, 180
urbanization, 114, 116, 219

Vajrapani, 75
Venezuela, 186

Vietnam, 18, 27, 30, 33, 36, 38–43, 139, 152, 189
Vodin, Ian, 190–1, 194–5
voodoo economics
    BRICS and, 198
    fusion economics and, 41–2
    legislation and, 32–3
    monetary shuttle diplomacy, 37–9
    moveable assets and, 34–6
    overview, 4–8
    reform and, 36–7
    shock therapy and, 29–31, 39–41
    Smith, Adam and, 31

Wallenberg family, 176
Wan Li, 23
Warhol, Andy, 5, 177
water
    Africa and, 126–8, 130–4, 156–7
    Bhutan and, 113
    bottled, 51–2
    China and, 66, 89, 195, 215, 217
    climate change and, 147, 205
    compassionate capital and, 228
    conservation of, 185–6, 231
    contamination of, 89, 195, 215, 217
    drinking water, 113
    economy and, 9
    glaciers and, 66, 69, 228–9
    globalization and, 191–3
    localization and, 91–2
    security of, 14, 91–2, 126–8, 147, 152, 191–3, 205, 209, 232
    shortages of, 156–7, 162, 167, 226–7, 230
    Tibet and, 66, 69
Waxman, Henry, 2

Wealth of Nations, The (Smith), 4–5
Wen Jiabao, 214–15, 220–1, 236n2, 237n2
Williamson, John, 4
wind power, 156–7, 166, 213, 217–18, 221
World Bank, 1, 5, 7, 10, 27, 30, 32–5, 40, 101–3, 111–12, 114–15, 122, 177, 191, 193, 198–200
World Economic Forum (WEF), 7, 15, 59, 121
World Is Flat, The (Friedman), 182
World Social Forum (WSF), 120–1, 125, 127, 146, 172
World Trade Organization (WTO), 1, 7, 45, 59, 189–90, 192–4, 200
World Wildlife Fund (WWF), 212
Wu Jinglian, 26–7

Xi Jinping, 200, 214, 220–1

Yathotou, Pany, 29
Yu Xiaoyu, 44
Yunnan Province (China), 61, 162
Yunus, Muhammad, 110–14

zakat, 97–9
Zero Dark Thirty, 93
zero waste, 157
Zhao Qizheng, 46, 61–2
Zhao Ziyang, 22, 25–6
Zhu Rongji, 27, 38, 40, 45–6, 49–52, 54–5, 61, 213–16, 219–20, 238–40, 247
Zhu Yanlai, 219
Zuccotti Park, 139, 141–5, 173, 224, 227

This page intentionally left blank

GPSR Compliance

The European Union's (EU) General Product Safety Regulation (GPSR) is a set of rules that requires consumer products to be safe and our obligations to ensure this.

If you have any concerns about our products, you can contact us on

ProductSafety@springernature.com

In case Publisher is established outside the EU, the EU authorized representative is:

Springer Nature Customer Service Center GmbH
Europaplatz 3
69115 Heidelberg, Germany

www.ingramcontent.com/pod-product-compliance
Lightning Source LLC
LaVergne TN
LVHW020328260326
834688LV00037B/922